THE
MOTHER–DAUGHTER
RELATIONSHIP

THE
MOTHER–DAUGHTER
RELATIONSHIP

Echoes Through Time

Edited by
Gerd H. Fenchel, Ph.D.

JASON ARONSON INC.
Northvale, New Jersey
London

The editor gratefully acknowledges permission to reprint excerpts from the poetry of Anne Sexton: "The Death Baby," "Baby Picture," and "Grandfather, Your Wound" in *The Death Notebooks*, copyright © 1974 by Anne Sexton; "Pain for a Daughter" in *Live or Die*, copyright © 1966 by Anne Sexton; "The Wifebeater" in *The Book of Folly*, copyright © 1972 by Anne Sexton; "Red Roses," "End, Middle, Beginning," and "Divorce, Thy Name Is Woman" in *45 Mercy Street*, copyright © 1976 by Linda Gray Sexton and Loring Conant, Jr. Used by permission of Houghton Mifflin Co. and Sterling Lord Literistic, Inc. All rights reserved.

Production Editor: Elaine Lindenblatt

This book was set in 11 pt. Goudy by Alabama Book Composition of Deatsville, AL, and printed and bound by Book-mart Press, Inc. of North Bergen, NJ.

Copyright © 1998 by Jason Aronson Inc.

10 9 8 7 6 5 4 3 2 1

Library of Congress Cataloging-in-Publication Data

The mother-daughter relationship : echoes through time / edited by
Gerd H. Fenchel.
   p.   cm.
   Includes bibliographical references and index.
   ISBN 0-7657-0101-4 (alk. paper)
   1. Mothers and daughters—Psychology. 2. Developmental
psychology. 3. Life cycle, Human. I. Fenchel, Gerd H.
HQ755.85.M675   1997
306.874'3—dc21   97-14588

Printed in the United States of America on acid-free paper. For information and catalog write to Jason Aronson Inc., 230 Livingston Street, Northvale, NJ 07647-1731. Or visit our website: http://www.aronson.com

Contents

Part IV
Clinical Considerations

Part V
Aging Parents

Acknowledgments

Many people contributed to the successful Annual Scientific Conference of the Washington Square Institute, held in February 1996, which focused on the mother–daughter relationship and served as the catalyst for this book. The long-term efforts of Stewart Crane to develop the core topic with the principal speakers of the conference need acknowledgment as well as his mobilization of the professional community to become involved and contribute chapters to the evolving book. Joan Heitschel, Institute registrar, not only helped to organize publicity and registration activities at the conference but also coordinated editorial communications with those of the contributors. Rosemarie Gates, enthusiastic about the topic, found the sculptor, Mrs. Gerda Quoohs, who brought her work of art representing the mother–daughter relationship to the conference meeting.

Last but certainly not least, I would like to thank the contributors to this book, who have been in constant contact with me while developing their ideas. It has been exciting and interesting to touch base with them, exchange ideas, and then help them evolve. I trust that it was as wonderful an experience for them as it has been for me.

—*Gerd H. Fenchel, Ph.D.*

Contributors

Helen O. Adler, M.S.W.

Director of Training, Westchester (New York) Center for the Study and Training of Psychoanalysis and Psychotherapy; senior supervisor, faculty and training analyst, Psychoanalytic Institute, Postgraduate Center for Mental Health.

Anna Aragno, Ph.D.

Received analytic and supervisory training from Washington Square Institute and the Postgraduate Center, New York; author of *Symbolization* and a second volume on communication, in progress.

Diane Barth, M.S.W.

Faculty and supervisor, National Institute for the Psychotherapies; Psychoanalytic Institute, Postgraduate Center for Mental Health.

Anni Bergman, Ph.D.

Training and supervising analyst, New York Freudian Society;

faculty, Institute for Psychoanalytic Training and Research (IP-TAR) and Postdoctoral Program, New York University.

Maria V. Bergmann, Ph.D.
Training and supervising analyst, faculty emeritus of the New York Freudian Society; training and supervising analyst, International Psychoanalytic Association; member, IPTAR.

Joel S. Bernstein, Ph.D.
Co-director, New Jersey Institute for Psychoanalysis; member, National Psychological Association for Psychoanalysis (NPAP).

Molly Walsh Donovan, Ph.D.
Private practice, Washington, DC.

Maria F. Fahey
Research associate to Anni Bergman; Director of Studies, Friends Seminary, New York.

Gerd H. Fenchel, Ph.D.
Dean, Washington Square Institute, New York; fellow, Council of Psychoanalytic Psychotherapists, International Council of Psychologists, American Group Psychotherapy Association, Pennsylvania Psychological Association.

Robert M. Gordon, Ph.D.
Director, Institute for Advanced Psychological Training, Allentown, Pennsylvania; diplomate, American Board of Professional Psychology (ABPP); fellow, American Psychological Association, Pennsylvania Psychological Association.

Ronald Katz, Ph.D.
Chair of training, faculty, and supervisor, Washington Square Institute, New York.

Agnieszka Leznicka-Los, M.A.
Graduate of Warsaw University, Poland, and Washington Square Institute, New York; teaches regularly scheduled seminars on psychotherapy in Poland.

Dale Mendell, Ph.D.

Training and supervising analyst, Psychoanalytic Institute, Post-graduate Center for Mental Health; training, supervising analyst, and Director of Professional Development, Training Institute for Mental Health, New York.

Marilyn B. Meyers, Ph.D.

Faculty, Washington School of Psychiatry; past president, Washington Psychologists for the Study of Psychoanalysis.

Jill C. Morris, Ph.D.

Staff therapist, Washington Square Institute, New York; author of *The Dream Workbook, Creative Breakthroughs,* and *Transformational Dreaming.*

Arlene Kramer Richards, Ed.D.

Training and supervising analyst, New York Freudian Society, IPTAR; training analyst, International Psychoanalytic Association.

Judith B. Rosenberger, Ph.D.

Hunter College, doctoral faculty; associate professor, School of Social Work; supervisor, Psychoanalytic Institute, Postgraduate Center for Mental Health.

Roberta Ann Shechter, D.S.W.

Supervisor and faculty, Washington Square Institute, New York; Postgraduate Center for Mental Health, Psychoanalytic Institute, Associate editor, *Journal of Analytic Social Work.*

Ava L. Siegler, Ph.D.

Founding director of the Institute for Child, Adolescent and Family Studies, New York; has written extensively on child and adolescent treatment and psychoanalytic theory.

Introduction

Gerd H. Fenchel

The important topic of the mother–daughter relationship was thought about and talked about for two years at the Washington Square Institute's Continuing Education Program. This long gestation period, as viewed today, was attributed to careful planning, but also may be seen as an underlying ambivalence toward the topic. Some of the comments exchanged were doubts about who would be interested, whether men would attend, or whether only women would be interested. Was it possible to make it palatable to persons of both genders?

The issue was finally resolved with the understanding that it was possible that we could not please both men and women, and a program was developed with eminent authorities in this area. The conference was a huge success, with 270 people attending. But out of the total attendance there were only five men! While working on the program, the committee, under the chairmanship of Stewart Crane, decided to request further theoretical and clinical contributions from other professionals and to work toward the publication of a book on the mother–daughter relationship.

In retrospect we may assume that the topic created much

ambivalence and frightened men away from attending. The title suggests that we were focused on a unique and mysterious relationship that had long-lasting consequences into adult life. It is certainly different, in most cases, from the mother–son relationship, in some ways more intense and more awesome. Its unique aspects are that (1) the mother remains the identification object for the daughter but not for the son; (2) it is a relationship between two persons of the same gender—and by definition a homosexual one; (3) it is intense and ambivalent; and (4) it requires fusion as well as separation for the proper developmental sequences to occur. Difficulties that arise along the way have consequences concerning how the daughter feels about her body, self-esteem regulations, career choices, and relationship to men.

Early analysts, including Freud, believed that growing daughters needed to make libidinal connections to the father and—unlike boys—had to overcome the rivalry with the mother. Similarly, it was believed that the girl had a "bit of masculinity" in her that had to be overcome to grow into a feminine woman. For Freud, the mysteries of womanhood remained unanswered and he requested the curious to ask women themselves.

Jones (1924) observed female dominance in a variety of primitive cultures but attributed this to the wish to moderate the father's hostility and achieve a transition of the Oedipus complex. Since those early times our theories have expanded (Blum 1977); still, there are complications in female development when contrasted to male development. Kestenberg (1968) had called attention to the different focus boys and girls have toward inner and outer worlds. She observed that women were more preoccupied than men with "inner space" while boys are oriented toward the external world early on. She assumed that girls were mystified by their own anatomy and that hidden inner genitalia evoked such orientation.

Sophie Freud (1991), granddaughter of Sigmund Freud, biographically commented that a mother has a large narcissistic investment in her children, particularly her daughters. She attributed this investment to psychic space, women having a great many self-doubts and feeling overly responsible for what they are or what they produce. They transmit female narcissism through the generations. It becomes an adaptive effort because the woman's survival depends on loving and being loved, which is displayed in their relationship to their daughters.

The problems with narcissistic involvements is that they are ambivalent ones and easily evolve into sadomasochistic relationships. Such involvements may be replete with cruelty and negativity. And that is possibly the crux in the mother–daughter dyad: to be a woman, a daughter must have sufficient libidinal resources to identify with her female partner, overcoming ambivalence in order to have confidence to go out into the world and find her own man and to be loved by him as she was loved by her mother and as her mother was loved by her father.

Motherhood stresses include ambivalence toward children. Often depression found in women is related to stresses of motherhood. Symbiotic yearnings continue through life. When a woman becomes a mother she seeks to establish that unity that she had hoped for or had experienced with her own mother. If the daughter does not meet the expectations of her mother's ego ideal, or when the child has conditions that interfere with the mother's wanting to bond, then depression and rage may develop. For the mother the child is an external representation of herself, the spouse, and other family members. It is an intergenerational wish to continue the family eternally. The daughter's behaviors and accomplishments affect her mother's self-esteem regulations.

A mother's unconscious memories are stored unconsciously in her soma so that the mother does to the infant what she has kept as a memory but does not remember consciously. If a mother's frustrations take over, the relationship develops into a "good" and "bad" dichotomy from which there is no escape. Whether the mother is not attuned, or is abusive or inattentive, the child experiences strain traumas that in later life translate into the child's maladaptation to the world, where reality becomes a shock trauma.

This volume addresses a variety of developmental consequences having their origin in early mothering. We begin with a discussion of the necessary interdependence women have on each other. We observe the mother–daughter bond and muse about the quirks of homosexual bonding. Other contributions look at daydreams and fantasies and how mothering is reflected in them. We approach the important and turbulent adolescent phase and are attuned to the necessary separation from the mother with all its ups and downs and heartaches. The unavailability of mothers and fathers is discussed in another chapter, along with its consequences in adulthood. We also focus on narcissistic compensation and the inability to "fit in." The "good" and "bad" dichotomy gives rise to the fantasy of the "witch mother" who impedes oedipal resolution. Several contributors explore transference relationships. What goes on in female therapist–patient dyads? Finally, there is a sensitive chapter on ministering to the aging and dying mother—a fate we all face since we have to bury our parents. The life cycle is thus complete: from birth to death, the echoes of mothering in the mother–daughter relationship.

REFERENCES

Blum, H., ed. (1977). *Female Psychology*. New York: International Universities Press.

Freud, S. (1991). *My Three Mothers and Other Passions*. New York/London: New York University Press.

Jones, E. (1924). Mother right and sexual ignorance of the savages. In *Essays in Applied Psycho-Analysis* 2:145–173. London: Hogarth, 1951.

Kestenberg, J. (1968). Outside and inside, male and female. *Journal of the American Psychoanalytic Association* 16:457–520.

PART I

THE BASICS
OF DEVELOPMENT

We start our explorations with the developmental research of Anni Bergman and Maria Fahey. Their study, part of Margaret Mahler's (1971) comprehensive study of separation-individuation phases, describes two mother–daughter pairs. Neither are examples of pathology but represent various shadings of development leading to different adult outcomes. A number of developmental observations the authors offer enable us to speculate about psychic processes.

When we speak about the importance of the early relationship between mother and daughter and its echoes through adult life, we need to keep in mind that development is not necessarily straightforward and that it must be understood within a contextual matrix. Freud suggested that biological underpinnings represent the constitutional aspects of the personality. Chess and Thomas (1984) demonstrated that early temperament was an important aspect when cases were followed over a period of thirty years. Whether the mother was sickly, or had physical problems or experienced depression—all of these variables contribute to the mastery of developmental tasks. Quite aside from constitutional endowment, we are curious to know whether the mother enjoyed her child. Did she demonstrate empathy and encouragement? Was the mother disappointed in her child? What was the mother's experience with her own mother when growing up? Was the mother influenced by her experiences, either repeating them or wishing to compensate for them? The birth of siblings and other factors, such as early separations or physical moves from a home, contribute significantly to outcomes in development. Finally, and this is not mentioned by the contributors to this volume, we need a little bit of good fortune in our lives. From early on, we can trace influences of grandparents, peers, and teachers as either being helpful or disturbing to the developing daughter.

Ava Siegler carefully examines the two mother–daughter pairs presented by Bergman and Fahey. She informs us from the outset that she is looking for developmental events and trends that coalesce into adult character. She focuses on early attachment behavior and notices that one mother–daughter pair enjoyed it and this joy was retained as an adult. In the other pair, the daughter evidenced discomfort with being held. Both were loved and loved their mother but in a markedly different way, leading to different internalizations and a different outlook on life.

Experience or inexperience in parenting also becomes an important variable. The first couple had already parented a son and looked forward to their second child. The other parents had the daughter as their first child, followed by two younger brothers. Thus she did not have sufficient time for herself to enjoy her role. The first mother was optimistic and encouraged separation. The second mother was shy, pessimistic, and experienced her satisfaction from the precocious performance of her daughter.

The father too becomes an important person in female development. When the girl becomes ambivalent toward her mother in the service of separation, she can turn to the father as a libidinal object. It is important at this stage for the father to be a steadfast and empathic person and for the mother not to hamper her daughter's turning toward the father. In Bergman and Fahey's study, one daughter fell in love with her father and did not have to contend with younger brothers. She also retained a loving relationship with her mother. The second daughter had experienced a one-year separation from her father during a vital state of development and upon his return had to endure the birth of two younger brothers.

The different experiences of the two daughters, both in mothering and in relationship to their fathers and siblings, produced different ways of loving—anaclitic and narcissistic. Since perception, memory, thought, and symbolic representations consolidate in adult character traits, the lifestyle and temperament of the two daughters differed.

Indeed, we find that early attachment style is quite similar to Freud's (1912) definition of transference as "a style of loving" (p. 312) and we carry this disposition with us through life. The way we have been loved and loved in return is transmitted from generation to generation. Most of the style has become character, stays unconscious, and is rationalized in everyday life. Only shocks, trauma, or psychotherapy will modify it. As Charles Brenner has repeatedly stated, personality is born of conflict and compromise formation. Arlene Kramer Richards addresses a pathological character attachment style. Taking as an example the biography of Anne Sexton, she demonstrates how maternal abuse of a daughter has dire consequences in later life.

Although the importance of the mother–daughter dyad and its contributions to adult development is stressed throughout this section, other women in a daughter's life have significant influences in the shaping of her identity. Judith Rosenberger defines such influence as "meta-identification with womanhood," a developmental line in addition to biological foundations and cultural role. Connecting historically with women in the present and in the past intensifies issues of ever-evolving new forms of being a woman without damaging core relatedness to the maternal object.

REFERENCES

Chess, S., and Thomas, A. (1984). *Origins and Evolution of Behavior Disorders: From Infancy to Early Adult Life.* New York: Brunner/Mazel.

Freud, S. (1912). The dynamics of transference. *Collected Papers,* pp. 312–322. London: Hogarth, 1949.

Mahler, M. S. (1971). A study of the individuation-separation process and its possible application to borderline phenomena in the psychoanalytic situation. *Psychoanalytic Study of the Child* 26:403–424. New Haven, CT: Yale University Press.

1

Love, Admiration, and Identification: On the Intricacies of Mother–Daughter Relationships

Anni Bergman
Maria F. Fahey

INTRODUCTION

This chapter is based on the data collected from three research studies. The first was the observational study of mother–child pairs during the separation-individuation process, from 6 months to 3 years of age.[1] This work, begun in 1959 by Margaret Mahler and her associates, was based on her hypothesis of the symbiotic origins of the human infant who, she thought, developed a sense of separate identity during the period of separation-individuation. The study focused on the mother–child pair. Mothers and children met in a playground-like setting, and the development of children of the same age was always compared while each mother-child pair was studied intensively. The data were collected by a team of participant and nonparticipant

1. This research was supported by NIMH Grant MH–08238, USPHS: Margaret Mahler, Principal Investigator; John B. McDevitt, Co-Principal Investigator.

observers as well as by a senior clinician who conducted regular interviews with the mother and observed the mother–child interaction. A brief follow-up study during latency consisted of interviews with both children and mothers, psychological testing, and school visits. Thirty years after the original research, an adult follow-up study was undertaken by John McDevitt and myself, both members of the original team of observers. This study included interviews with the original subjects, psychological testing of the subjects conducted by Wendy Olesker, and thorough re-working of the original data.[2] It needs to be emphasized that the adult follow-up is quite different in scope from the original research, in which data were based on daily observations by multiple observers. The data of the follow-up study have been collected by single observers, and contact with the subjects has been much more limited, especially because most of them no longer live in New York City.

The data gathered on the adult subjects is studied in the context of the data collected on the mother-child pairs during a period that was largely preverbal. The availability of the extensive mother–child observations of the preverbal period provides an unusual window through which the influence of the earliest mother–child relationship on adult life can be viewed. We are faced, however, with a difficult question: whether direct connections can be made between early childhood and adulthood without taking into account the intervening formative experiences of later childhood and adolescence of which we have only a glimpse gained from the intermediate follow-up study. This intervening period is accessible to us mostly through the accounts of the subjects, based on the memories they wish to share. This clearly is a limitation; however, the preverbal period is usually available only through reenactments in the transference in the analytic situation. The fact that we have actual observations of mother–child interactions during the preverbal period gives us another avenue of studying the influence of these earliest interactions on adult life.

In this chapter, I discuss two mother-daughter pairs who have been participants in all aspects of the longitudinal study. I describe the

2. Follow-up studies supported by The Rock Foundation: John B. McDevitt, Principal Investigator; Anni Bergman, Co-Principal Investigator.

course of the daughter's development during separation-individuation, give a glimpse of their development during latency, and describe the life of the daughters as it has evolved in early adulthood. One of the unique aspects of the observational separation-individuation research was the emphasis on both longitudinal and cross-sectional methods: individual mother-child pairs were observed over time, and observations of mother-child pairs were continuously compared with each other. These comparisons were a natural outgrowth of the very design of the research in its playground-like setting during which mother–child pairs were always present. The comparative aspects of the original research, from which patterns in the mother-child dyad emerged, allowed for the formulation of the theory of subphases of the separation-individuation process. I have found in working with the data of the follow-up study that comparing mother-child pairs has proven to be a fruitful method of discerning patterns of ways in which the experience of the mother–child relationship can influence adult life.

It is important to remember that while the original study focused on the interaction between mother and child, the emphasis was always on the separation-individuation process in the child. In the adult follow-up the emphasis is even more strongly on the child-now-young-adult. We are studying the ways in which early patterns have been internalized and absorbed into the adult personality structure, and we are studying the continuing relationship between the child-now-young-adult and her mother. Our knowledge of the mother herself and the motivating forces that moved her to relate to her child in a particular way are not available with the same clinical richness. It should be remembered, however, that observations of mothers and children and interviews of the mothers were conducted by psychoanalysts who were concerned always with understanding the meanings of what they saw and heard.

Mary and Laurie, as adults, have been able to create satisfactory lives for themselves and have maintained good relationships with their mothers. We know that both were desired daughters, because both mothers had expressed preference for a girl child in their initial interviews at the center. While both mothers experienced great satisfaction from their girl children, the emphasis in this chapter is on the difference in how each mother derived pleasure and gratification from her daughter.

On Laurie's first birthday her mother held her close and talked about her loving feelings and how she had never experienced such feelings before. Laurie's mother was very sensitive to Laurie's attachment to her. Mrs. L talked a lot about her pleasure in Laurie and how from early on she was able to quiet her daughter when she was upset just by talking to her. At 8 months Laurie had cried for the first time when her mother left her, and mother was proud and pleased by this clear sign of Laurie's unique attachment to her. Mrs. L also described with pleasure Laurie's attachment to her father. At the center, Laurie was described as lively, vigorous, and curious. She was content and peaceful, yet active and interested in the world around her.

Mrs. M described how she was completely absorbed by her baby, Mary, during her first year. She described how she and her daughter spent all their time together and how she had always taken her daughter everywhere and that Mary had never shown any stranger anxiety. Mary was described by her mother as a very independent baby who had never liked to be held closely. Mrs. M felt that Mary had always been able to let her know what she needed. At the center, Mary was admired by the observers for her unusual competence. She walked and climbed very well and her language development was precocious. She said many words quite clearly, and her mother said she had a very good ear and had been able to imitate sounds from an early age. Mary was able to let her mother know what she wanted, and her mother was responsive.

Here, the contrast between Mrs. L and Mrs. M emerges. Mrs. L was most pleased by her little girl's attachment to her and by their mutual pleasure in closeness and the uniqueness of their relationship. Mrs. M was also pleased by her relationship with her baby, and emphasizes Mary's independence and ability to relate to others. In what follows we examine each girl's separation-individuation process to the achievement of object constancy and consider how each mother's greatest pleasure in her daughter influences storms that arise during the separation-individuation process. In particular, we look at each mother-child pair's navigation through the rapprochement subphase and the process of its resolution.

LAURIE AND HER MOTHER:
THE FIRST THREE YEARS

Two weeks after her daughter's first birthday, Mrs. L said that for the first time she had been angry with Laurie, who insisted on playing in the toilet bowl. After removing her several times, she had finally yelled, whereupon Laurie went into a corner and cried quietly. Her mother was quite shocked by this and worried that she could break her wonderful spirits. She recalled the strictness of her own upbringing and talked about her determination to be different. At this point her husband encouraged her to take off one afternoon a week from child care to go shopping.

At the age of 13½ months Laurie began to walk, but preferred to crawl and usually walked only when asked to by her mother. Perhaps Laurie experienced walking alone as too much of a separation from her mother and therefore would walk only when encouraged by her mother. Mrs. L also seemed to express some ambivalence about Laurie's growing up and out of the blissful union of babyhood. By the time Laurie was 14 months old, observers noticed some misattunement. One observer described her interaction:

> Laurie has been put down by her mother and apparently wishes to be held some more. She cries when she is put down. Mother says, "Laurie, Laurie, what's the trouble?" She does not pick her up, and Laurie continues to stand near her. Later Laurie seems to have recovered and plays by herself, crawling about. She walks to Mother and looks at her. Mother does not see her and turns away from her. She then walks a bit away from Mother, and there seems to be a kind of almost playing at falling, which happens for a while. Then Laurie walks to Mother and just as she arrives at Mother's chair, Mother gets up to get some coffee. Laurie follows, wraps herself around Mother's legs. Mother doesn't take notice and returns to her chair, and continues conversation, taking little notice. Laurie cries a bit. Mother gives Laurie juice and Laurie again wraps herself around Mother's legs and does not want the juice. Mother continuously talks to other mothers while caring for Laurie. She finally gives her pretzels but does not look at her and does not speak to her, while Laurie keeps her eyes on Mother all the time.

At the age of 14 months Laurie continued to feel vulnerable and to be easily upset, crying at small frustrations and hurts. Laurie also became more aggressive and demanding. She began to run away and had to be watched closely. She often wanted exactly what her brother had and began to imitate him. Mrs. L reported that for the first time Laurie was not happy when she woke up in the morning and was not eager to get out of bed. Mrs. L said, "My sweet little Laurie, who has always been so good and happy, was unhappy all weekend. She would lie down and cry and throw tantrums over the slightest provocation." Laurie was extremely jealous of her older brother, Bobby, and wanted everything he had. When Mrs. L left the room, Laurie was inconsolable, yet when taken to her mother, her mood did not really improve.

Thus, at just 14 months, Laurie was displaying behaviors typical of the rapprochement crisis, and Mrs. L was clearly baffled and upset by the loss of Laurie's blissful babyhood. It is interesting to note that the rapprochement crisis occurred so early for this child, in whom there had been some inhibition of the full enjoyment of the practicing subphase, perhaps because the prepracticing union was so important. When at 16 months Laurie started to sleep through the night, her mother said, "Laurie's growing up so quickly." Laurie loved food and made humming sounds while eating. Her mother wondered if her zest for life had something to do with her love for food. Mrs. L loved to cook and thought that food was such an important part of life. On a deeper level she must also have connected Laurie's love for food with Laurie's love for her.

Around the age of 17 months Laurie made a great spurt in cognitive development, which took the form of remembering and evoking events from the past. She made great strides in language. Mrs. L reported that for the first time Laurie had come over to her and given her a spontaneous hug and kiss, which touched her very deeply. Mrs. L talked about wanting another baby, but not wanting Laurie to become a middle child. At 18 months there seems to have been a resolution of the rapprochement crisis. Laurie began to imitate her mother and liked to do things with her, such as putting things in their place, for example, dirty laundry into the hamper. She also imitated her brother and did not want to wear dresses or play with dolls. As she became reconnected to her mother following the rapprochement crisis, Laurie also guarded her budding autonomy, and became sensitive to the interference of other children and aggressive toward them.

When Laurie was 2 years old her family moved to a new

apartment. Laurie cried from the time her crib was put into the moving van until it was in its new place. Once the crib was there, Laurie was all right again. It seems that the crib took on a special symbolism for her, which is interesting in light of Mrs. L's special feeling about Laurie as a baby. At this time Laurie herself began to be aggressive toward other babies. When her mother tried to stop her by telling her she was a big girl, she got very angry and said, "No, I'm a baby." Laurie spent a lot of time sitting in the big doll carriage at the center. She was very possessive and unwilling to share anything. At the center she screeched at one of the babies who had followed her around and pulled herself upon a chair. Mrs. L said, "this is the most venom she has right now. She really hates babies. My sweet little Laurie. I couldn't imagine that she would ever be like this." Here we see that both Laurie and her mother had feelings about the loss of the special union they had felt when Laurie was a baby. Even though her crib could be moved to her new house and console her about the loss of her old house, she could not be a baby again, and maybe therefore hated other babies who could have what she could no longer have.

At around 2 years, there was a further resolution of the rapprochement crisis as Laurie's language development progressed. Once again Laurie became more purposeful in her play, and she liked to listen to and tell stories. At times she could tolerate sharing the attention of an observer with another child, and her periods of aggression toward babies began to alternate with periods of tenderness. Here we see how Laurie began to identify with the mother who loved her and treated her with tenderness.

A big step in individuation was noticed first by Laurie's mother, who reported a shift in Laurie's relationship to her older brother. Until now she had imitated everything he did and wanted. For example, she had always taken ketchup on her hamburger because Bobby did, but now she decided that she wanted her hamburger without ketchup. Along with this new step in individuation, Laurie seemed to have begun identifying with her mother in a new way, namely, by internalizing her prohibitions. On the playground, when Laurie saw another child putting sand in his mouth, she said, "Mommy say, 'No, don't eat that.'" Thus the asserting of her own individuality went hand in hand with internalization of her mother's prohibitions. At the same time, she became more possessive of her father, calling him "My Daddy" and asking him rather than her mother to do things for her. Thus a new level of triangulation occurred, indicating a loosening of the exclusive mother–baby bond.

At 26 months Laurie seemed well on the way toward emotional object constancy. Observers noted how she now showed her understanding of the feelings of others. Laurie also referred to the future and the past. When she didn't like to be left by her mother she would say, "Mommy will come" or "Mommy will take me home." Laurie was very able to express her feelings to her mother. She managed well in her mother's absence, and when her mother returned, she immediately said to her, "I did not want you to go away." Then she went on playing. Once when she was at the center without her mother and an observer asked, "Where's Mommy?" Laurie answered, "Shopping." When asked when Mommy would return she looked down at her new shoes and said, "Mommy always buys me new shoes." In this way Laurie showed that she could keep the connection to the good mother in her mind and was not easily thrown by questions from a strange observer. After her mother had returned, she again went out to pick up Laurie's brother from school and asked Laurie if she wanted to go with her. Laurie said, "I want to stay here while you pick up Bobby. Then you come back and pick me up." She hugged her mother and said good-bye.

When Laurie was 31 months old, Mrs. L talked about how confident she felt about Laurie, who seemed so self-sufficient. What is notable here is that Laurie's mother, who had had some difficulties as Laurie began to show signs of growing up, especially during the practicing subphase, seems to have been able to accept Laurie's self-sufficiency at the point it was more free from conflict. However, Mrs. L's ambivalence about how much she should baby her daughter remained discernible when Mrs. L reported how Laurie had suddenly given up her pacifier. One night Laurie announced that she didn't want the pacifier anymore but woke during the night, became very upset, cuddled up with her father, and asked for the pacifier. Mrs. L gave it to her and worried whether she had done the right thing. Laurie did not ask for it again. Around the same time she became very proud of a band that she wore in her hair that she did not like to be without. We might ask the meaning of this new, strong attachment to a hair band. Was this a new way of being close to her mother, the band being a symbolic tie between them and a sign of identification with her mother, wearing her hair in a grown-up way? Laurie's mother had worried she had discouraged her from growing up by giving in to her demand for the pacifier. In fact, the opposite may well have taken place: as long as the pacifier symbolizing mother was available, she could in fact enjoy closeness to mother in a new way, wanting to be like her.

Mrs. L reported that Laurie was developing a strong preference for her father and a renewed strong identification with her brother. During one observation at the center, Laurie played that she was Bobby and wanted her mother to play the roll of Laurie. She said, "I am Bobby. Feel my muscles." Later, playing with play dough, she rolled it into a long piece and said, "Look at the big snake." She started to eat it and spit it out and said, "Bobby spits, and I am Bobby." When mother scolded her, Laurie insisted that she should telephone Daddy so she could tell him what had happened. She did not play with her dolls, and liked only the stuffed animal her father had given her. Thus, at the age of 2 years and 9 months, Laurie showed signs of an oedipal attachment to her father. At the same time she began to have much greater difficulty separating from her mother. She did not like to be left at home with the babysitter she knew very well, but demanded to go everywhere with her mother. During an interview with Mrs. L, Laurie insisted on remaining with her mother and then could not become involved in play, remaining continually aware of her mother. She called her father on the play telephone. Mrs. L reported that Laurie was jealous of a new kitten in the family, and she also reported that Laurie had asked her father to sleep with her and this new kitten in her bed.

One day, when she was 35 months old, Laurie was extremely upset, and upon arrival at the center screamed and did not want to stay. Mrs. L explained that before leaving she had been wearing dressy shoes and red boots and had then refused to wear them and had demanded her white ski boots instead. Mrs. L had complied with her wishes, but when they were out on the street Laurie wanted to go back home and change her boots again. Her mother refused. Upon arrival at the center, Laurie refused to take her coat off and sat on her mother's lap fully dressed. Mrs. L seemed very distressed and looked pleadingly at the observer. At the time oedipal conflicts emerged, posing a new threat to losing the exclusive early bond with her mother, we see the return of typical rapprochement behaviors. Mrs. L seemed very distressed and puzzled. An observer encouraged Laurie to play with a new doll, and Laurie took her mittens off. Mrs. L was then able to interest Laurie in dramatic play with dolls sitting around the table and said to Laurie: "Oh, here is a family having breakfast." The other children joined Laurie and they continued to play. In this way Mrs. L showed her sensitivity to Laurie even though she said she was feeling so helpless. In play, she took Laurie back to the breakfast table scene that had preceded the tantrum and reassured Laurie that the family would remain intact and withstand her attachment to her father and hostility to her mother. Eventually Mrs. L left the room for an interview. At first Laurie said nothing and continued to play as if she had not seen her mother leave. After a few minutes she asked where her mother was and then threw the mommy doll on the floor and screamed, "Mommy is on the floor. I threw her on the floor." Laurie became increasingly reluctant to go to the center, which she associated with being left by her mother. Mrs. L was able to convince Laurie to go to the center by reassuring her that she would not leave her.

Summarizing Laurie's third year, we saw at first a calm period during which she was able to tolerate separations from her mother and in many other ways showed she had indeed overcome the rapprochement crisis and reached a degree of object constancy. With the advent of the oedipal conflict, as indicated by her strong turning toward her father, we saw an increase of hostility toward the mother and a resurgence of separation reactions—tempter tantrums and refusal to be left by her mother. The wish to be mother's baby remained present throughout, but may also have been replaced in part by being father's baby or having a baby with father, as illustrated by accepting only the stuffed animals that her father had given her and expressing a wish to sleep in bed with father and the new kitten. During the time of beginning oedipal conflict, expectable regression to typical rapprochement behaviors occurred. Mrs. L was able to respond reassuringly.

LAURIE: FURTHER DEVELOPMENT

Laurie made the transition to nursery school fairly easily. At the time her competition with her brother Bobby was still very much in the foreground, and she was conflicted about her own gender identity. She fought with her mother about clothes: she liked to wear very feminine clothes but was very particular about them and would not wear clothes if she perceived the slightest thing to be wrong with them, possibly a displacement of a fear that something could be wrong with her own body. An observer described her as being very tomboyish and at the same time very feminine.

It was characteristic of Laurie throughout her latency years and beyond that she kept both the male identification with her brother and father and the female identification with her mother very much alive. During a home visit, Laurie proudly showed the observer the large collection of stuffed animals on her bed. She liked all kinds of physical activities, from dancing and gymnastics to ball playing and skiing, and at one point became very involved in going to circus school. At the same time Laurie recalled that during her latency years she liked to be with her mother a lot.

LAURIE AS AN ADULT

In looking at Laurie as an adult, our focus here is on the way the mother has continued to take pleasure and satisfaction in Laurie's development even if that development was very different from anything she might have envisioned. It seems that Laurie's mother is able to respect and enjoy Laurie's separateness and difference and that this has not alienated mother and daughter from each other, but has instead provided the opportunity for new bonds to be formed because of the mother's efforts to share in Laurie's present lifestyle.

At one point during the follow-up interviews, Laurie was given the opportunity to look at a videotape from the original study of herself as a baby with her mother. Laurie was very moved and spoke about how she had always known that her mother loved her, but actually seeing how tender and loving she was with her as a baby almost brought tears to her eyes.

Laurie recalled her close relationship with her brother during childhood and her desire to be included in everything he did. Laurie has maintained a close relationship with her brother and his family, has become a close friend of her sister-in-law, and also continues to enjoy skiing and hiking alone with her brother. Laurie expressed appreciation for her father, who had always included her in the games he played with Bobby, and as an adult Laurie continues to share interest in team sports with her father.

The themes that had been so important at the time of Laurie's rapprochement resolution, that is, closeness and identification with her brother and identification with her mother, especially by way of cooking and eating, were still very strongly present. In one of her adult interviews she recalled her favorite toy—a little toy oven in which she had baked little cakes. Food and cooking were a very important part of Laurie's adult life, and she involved not only her brother and his family but also her parents in her health-oriented eating. In an interview when Laurie and her mother talked about early memories, Laurie remembered a game in which she would come from her bedroom downstairs into the living room to visit mother with her baby doll, and Mrs. L would make tea for them.

In a joint interview Mrs. L and Laurie remembered that when Laurie was around 8 years old, going shopping together was always a disappointment. Laurie would want certain shoes her friends had that her mother found too expensive or not suitable. Eventually the shopping trip would end in disappointment, and they would go home sitting at opposite ends of the bus. Laurie said:

> I can remember we always liked different things. I'd say, "I like this," and you'd say, "No, that's not right." And then you'd say, "Why not get this?" and I can remember sometimes saying, "Well, O.K., it's not that bad." But I would never wear it because I didn't like it. And I can definitely remember that I would get very sulky and sullen and angry that I couldn't have what I wanted. I hated that.

Laurie and her mother's recollections about shopping are interesting in light of the observation thirty years before in which Mrs. L had left Laurie at the center, and when asked, "Where's Mommy?" Laurie had said, "She's shopping. She always buys me new shoes." Shopping had been Mrs. L's way of taking time off from Laurie, yet she maintained a connection to her daughter by shopping for her. It is interesting that both Laurie and her mother recall joint shopping trips in later life as disappointing.

Later in the interview, Laurie's mother remembered her wishes to see her little girl in dresses. Laurie in turn remembers not wanting to wear frilly dresses and wanting the same clothes as her brother. Laurie said, "I felt a little bit trapped in this image, like I couldn't wear a skirt or a dress even if I wanted to." Then Laurie remembered her mother crocheting a little miniskirt for her, which she liked. Laurie had chosen the colors, and Mrs. L remembers buying leotards to match. Laurie said that she loves shopping now and that even though she and her mother have different taste they like the *idea* of going shopping together, and they like to look at each other's clothes. Laurie said: "We have fun together." And her mother agreed: "We are good pals, I would say, really I think so. I would say to this day I couldn't ask for a better daughter." Laurie said, "I feel the same way. I love my mother."

Having described Laurie and her mother in some detail, we turn now to another mother–daughter pair, describing in somewhat skeletal form Mary and her mother's journey through the separation-individuation process.

MARY AND HER MOTHER: THE FIRST THREE YEARS

When Mary and her mother began to attend the research center, observers found Mary to be captivating, in contrast to her mother who faded into the background. Mary and her mother attended regularly and usually came early. Because they arrived before the other mothers and children, they were assured special attention. Mrs. M may have found in our center a place comfortable for her where she and her daughter were supplied with mirroring attention, perhaps attention for which the mother unconsciously longed. This is different from Mrs. L who basked in the attention given to her by her little girl. For Mrs. L, it was the loving attention from her daughter that made her feel good as a mother, whereas Mrs. M felt good as a mother when her child was admired for her precocity and attractiveness.

Though Mrs. M had remarked that Mary was an easy baby, she reported that they arrived early because she found it difficult to be home alone with Mary who, she said, had difficulty occupying herself. This contradiction illustrates the mother's tendency toward denial of the ways in which Mary might not have been the perfect baby she needed her to be. It also illustrates the gratification Mrs. M derived from being watched as the mother of her little girl. Mary's mother seemed to see Mary as an idealized version of her own self. Mary always came to our group in very pretty little-girl clothes that Mrs. M made for her. This was in contrast to the way Mrs. M dressed herself, always playing down her looks. Thus she may have put all her wishes to be admired into Mary. One observer noted the pride this mother took in her child. It seemed to him that the child filled the mother's life and that the mother–child pair gave the impression of amazing self-sufficiency. One observer described watching her.

> I had first seen Mary when she had just turned 13 months. Her effect on me was almost immediate and very profound. I realized after some time I had surrendered a certain observational distance. Instead, I felt myself captivated and in a state of great pleasure, sympathy, and almost complete admiration for this phenomenal little creature. The energy and vigor of the pretty little child's activity was indeed a joy to watch. What a contrast there was between this child and her mother, who sat almost immobile, and one could almost immediately sense her painful and self-conscious shyness.

Mary was at the height of her practicing subphase, enjoying her explorations and precocious locomotor capacities. This period ended abruptly when she was 15 months old, probably catalyzed by the sudden absence of her father, whose work took him abroad. Mary developed a sleep disturbance: she woke up several times each night, her mother unable to comfort her for quite a long time. At the center a marked change in the child was noticed. Mary started to play bye-bye games and became very alert to the comings and goings of everyone. During the same period she became listless and fatigued, which contrasted strongly to her former boundless energy. She fell more frequently and was generally irritable; she cried a lot and ran to her mother for comforting. She demanded food, such as cookies, pretzels, and juice. The former confident expectation and the aware-ness of her ability to command a response from others seemed to be replaced by an almost desperate appeal for attention. The feeling of pleasure and joy in her performance was no longer there. Mrs. M did not connect these marked changes in Mary to the absence of her father. It would appear that Mrs. M's life was so filled by her daughter that she could not see how her daughter's life was affected by anyone other than her, even the father.

Mary began to fight for unique possession of her mother and eventually of other adults at the center. The period of Mary's upset, apparently triggered by the father's absence, became more acute when she was 17 months old, around the age of the expectable rapproche-ment crisis. During this time Mary became almost phobic about her mother's efforts to pick her up or comfort her, efforts that simply resulted in more anger toward her mother. Mary was frustrated easily and broke into tears. She consumed great quantities of juice, asking for it from all the adults who came into the room. Mary was happiest when she was at the center alone with her mother and the observers. Mrs. M became very depressed and distraught and was not very attentive to Mary. She complained that Mary was impossible at home with crying, temper tantrums, and what seemed like incomprehensible behavior. At the center Mary became very aggressive toward the other children. She was unable to share her mother or any other adult. Even on better days she remained extremely sensitive to any deprivation, such as her mother talking on the telephone or any toy being taken from her. Mary's mother looked harassed and worn and worried about what was wrong with her daughter. Perhaps Mrs. M was especially hard hit by her child's rapprochement crisis because it was such an abrupt ending to the period during which Mary could be the ideal baby and she could be the ideal mother.

As Mary came to some resolution of her rapprochement crisis she began to internalize her mother's prohibitions by saying, for example, that she should not pull other children's hair. She also began to play with dolls, acting toward the dolls the way her mother acted toward her. Identification with the mother emerged as playing mother who both prohibits aggression and takes care of the child. (In his analysis of another subject from this follow-up study, John McDevitt [1994] has shown how identification is used to resolve rapprochement conflicts. Manuel Furer [1967] and Jacob Arlow [1982] have recognized the development of the preoedipal superego.) At this time Mary's mother became sensitive to Mary's turning to observers. She easily felt rejected and jokingly remarked that Mary would someday prefer her teacher to her.

Throughout Mary's further development, Mrs. M continued to express her concerns about the loss of the exclusive relationship between her and her daughter. For example, when Mary was 2 years old her father returned from abroad. When Mary greeted him as if she had always remembered him, Mrs. M was surprised and seemed to experience Mary's remembering and welcoming her father as a sign of the loss of their exclusive relationship.

Another event that further threatened the exclusive relationship was Mrs. M's pregnancy, which she first spoke about when Mary was 29½ months old and she was in her fifth month. Mrs. M was very worried about Mary and said: "This will be the end of Mary. She will be 3, it will be just around her birthday. Mary won't like a new baby for a birthday present." She talked about the wonderful, special baby that Mary had been, already very interesting when she was only 5 months old. Mrs. M's worry that Mary would not be able to tolerate a sibling was heightened by her own worry that her cherished relationship with her daughter would be forever changed. In fact, Mary became increasingly demanding of exclusive attention. At the center, for example, she wanted to play ring-around-the-rosy with an observer and was furious when other children were included. At story time she pushed the other children away and insisted on sitting on the observer's lap. She showed marked jealousy and aggression toward all babies. It was almost as if Mary began to enact her mother's fear about the dissolution of the perfect and exclusive mother–baby union in which Mary was the center of her mother's and the observer's attention.

When Mary was 31 months old, her mother reported that she noticed for the first time Mary accepting a disappointment without crying, which made her mother very sad because it further signified her daughter's growing up. Mrs. M was reluctant to tell her daughter about her pregnancy or the new baby coming and was shocked when it turned out that Mary already knew because she had been told by another mother who was also expecting a new baby. Mother was disturbed that other people could talk to the child and tell her important things. After Mary's mother finally spoke to Mary about the baby, she reported that Mary was looking forward to it. Observers noted that in her play Mary was the devoted mother to her teddy bears. Thus, despite her mother's concerns, at this point Mary was able to use the idea of a new baby in the family to identify with her mother.

MARY: FURTHER DEVELOPMENT

When Mary first came to the center, all eyes had been focused on this precocious, beautiful, verbal little girl. When Mary left the center to go to nursery school, it was a difficult transition for her and her mother, who had just given birth to a baby boy who required a lot of attention. Mary demanded exclusive attention from her nursery school teachers, reacting to the other children as rivals. Mother was concerned that Mary was not treated well enough by her teachers. Thus this first contact with the outside world of school turned out to be difficult for both mother and child. These difficulties continued to some extent throughout her school years and became especially exacerbated during her early adolescence when the family moved and Mary had to adjust to a new school and community. Mary was extremely shy and had difficulty making friends. Many of her teachers reported that she did not live up to her academic potential. Once again, mother was disappointed and anxious and took Mary's difficulties as a sign of her failure.

MARY AS AN ADULT

In looking at Mary as an adult, we focus here on how the nature of her early relationship with her mother was ongoing in her adult life. During separation-individuation—and maybe beyond—the ending of the exclusive relationship had been painful to both. It seems that in adult development, the relationship was preserved by way of Mary's identification with her mother. Mary worried about her mother, perhaps comparable to how her mother had been worried about her. She felt that her mother was not realizing her own potentials and was instead continuing to serve the needs of others, especially her brothers and father. It was important to Mary to have her mother come and stay with her so the two of them could enjoy things together and her mother could be free of some of the burdens of remaining caught in the confines of the immediate family.

Mary did well in college and in her profession, which she described as having fallen into rather than having sought actively. In this way she was similar to her mother, who always stressed her lack of academic ambition even though she had gone to a top college. In her interviews Mary underplayed the importance of her professional choice, but in fact she had become very successful in her field. Her style of appearing casual about important decisions is congruent with her mother's style and contrasts sharply with the child Mary who did not easily accept that she was not the only child and the star. It is almost as if, having fallen from stardom at a very early age, she had given it up forever and could not retain even the wish or fantasy of being special. On the other hand, she rose to the top of her field, though she did not regard this as a big success. We see both a defensive resignation like that of her mother and, though more hidden, an expectation to be outstanding in her surroundings. Mary was not entirely happy in her current professional activities and hoped to continue her studies.

Mary married a man she met at work who had lost his parents early in life and had little family of his own. In this way she may have fulfilled her childhood longing for an exclusive relationship with her mother. She described her husband as someone with whom she got along very well, although he was moody. She was able to tolerate and handle his moods, and said: "His moods are unpredictable. When he gets moody, I just sort of let him." Thus Mary may unconsciously have played the role of mother to the moody child she herself had been. Mary gave the impression of being stable in her own moods and not easily upset. One might wonder if she allowed her husband to express the moody side of her, thereby remaining closer to being the perfect child her mother had seen her to be.

Mary described her pleasure in her garden and how her mother sometimes came to help with gardening. She enjoyed these visits and described how well her mother got along with her husband. She felt it was good for her mother to get away from her father and brothers who constantly demanded that she take care of them. Mary felt close to her mother, but less close to her younger brothers, who, she said disapprovingly, had lived at home for a long time, allowing her mother to continue to serve them. By gardening with her mother, Mary seemed to be able to refind the early mother for whom she was the perfect little girl. She took her mother away from her father and two brothers, the rivals to the exclusive relationship.

DISCUSSION

It is interesting to compare two mother–daughter pairs who are similar and yet very different. Both members had wished for a daughter and both were very happy with their girl babies. While both mothers derived great pleasure from their girl babies, there is a crucial difference.

In the case of Laurie, the greatest pleasure seemed to come from the mother's realization of her baby's love for her, which triggered the mother's loving and tender response. She reacted to the inevitable difficulties in the relationship beginning in the second year of life with ambivalence and insecurity about how much to allow Laurie to remain a baby as she grew up so fast. This ambivalence may have been mirrored by Laurie's ambivalence about growing up, especially during the practicing subphase during which she was able to walk but would do so at first only with her mother's encouragement.

Notwithstanding these ambivalences and conflicts, Laurie's mother seemed to remain quite secure in her love for her little girl and her little girl's love for her. The continuity of her child's primary attachment to her was not threatened by her awareness of Laurie's attachments to others—especially her love for her father and her identification with her brother. It is important to note that the father was present as the important other for both members and daughter.

Mary's mother, on the other hand, seemed to derive her greatest joy in admiring Mary and her ability to elicit the admiration of those around her. The mother's pleasure and need for attention from her daughter were expressed indirectly, as if the mother had to defend against her need for direct expressions of love from her daughter. This may enlighten the observation that the mother did not seem to enjoy close physical contact with her daughter, but took great pleasure in her daughter's practicing subphase, which distances mother and baby in space while preserving the power of the mother's watchful presence.

While Mrs. M took pleasure in the admiration of the observers, she could not easily accept the importance of others in Mary's life, including the child's father.

When Laurie was difficult, her mother frankly showed her disappointment, but was able to recuperate from the disappointment fairly easily, perhaps in part because of her close relationship to her husband, with whose help she could be more attentive to her own needs. Mary's mother tended to interpret Mary's difficulties as a personal reflection on herself, and it was harder for her to recuperate from the disappointments. She tended to deny her own needs and did not have the presence of a supportive husband, nor did she seem to seek other close, supportive relationships. Laurie's father provided support for both mother and daughter as well as offered himself for closeness and identification. Mary's father, on the other hand, was absent during an important period in the life of both mother and child, but the child seemed to fill the mother's life so much that she did not need him and therefore could not identify with her daughter's need for him.

In adulthood Laurie's interests and lifestyle were different from her mother's, and these differences inspired Laurie's mother to learn from and share in Laurie's new life. Mrs. L accepted that Laurie was different from her and wanted to bridge that difference by becoming involved with Laurie's interests. Laurie's choosing a lifestyle different from that of her family may reflect her identification with her mother, who had left her country of origin at a young age and met her husband while traveling. It also may reflect her identification with a mother who had expressed a desire for a mothering style different from the one she had been raised with. Laurie seems to have identified with her mother's joy in homemaking: her love for food, cooking, and home-making remain important elements in her life, though she has given them a coloring very much her own. Laurie's father and brother, who had been important objects of identification in her early life, remain present as important others in her adult life as well. It would seem that Laurie's ability to enjoy life has its source in an identification with her mother's joy in her as a baby.

As an adult, Mary has moved away from home and has a profession, but her basic lifestyle is not very different from that of her mother. Like Mrs. L, Mrs. M likes to share in her daughter's life and does so by visiting Mary and helping her with gardening, an activity they both enjoy. These visits are pleasurable for Mary not only because of what they provide for her, but also for what she feels they provide for her mother, namely, a break from obligations to the men in the family. Mary seems to have identified with her mother's needs for exclusivity by forming a relationship with a man in whose life she could be the exclusive love object. As a baby, Mary did not have the opportunity to identify with her father or older siblings—her relationship with her mother was, in fact, exclusive. In adulthood, Mary seemed less free than Laurie to pursue her individual desires, perhaps because she had identified with her mother, who had not pursued her own intellectual interests. Nevertheless, Mary had created an independent and constructive life for herself, though she had the tendency to underplay her achievements.

By comparing Laurie and Mary during separation-individuation and then again in young adulthood, we hope to show the subtlety and complexity in which the earliest, preverbal period of development— and in particular the earliest relationship with mother—may be recognizable in the character structure and emotional life of the adult. In the light of present knowledge about the mother–infant relationship, it is interesting that Freud thought about identification as a form of attachment. In his lecture on "The Dissection of the Psychical Personality" (1919) he says that identification "is a very important form of attachment to someone else, probably the very first" (p. 63). Through the cases of Mary and Laurie, we see how the outcome of the process of identification reflects the nature of the mother's attachment to the baby. The child's first identification with mother is influenced by the ways in which the mother experiences her child's attachment to her.

Laurie's mother reacted with joy to the love she felt from her baby daughter. This basic joy may have given Laurie the freedom to pursue her life without being inhibited by how well she performed. The things she shared with mother as a little girl, she later incorporated into her own lifestyle.

Mary's mother reacted with joy and pride to Mary's abilities and to the admiration Mary inspired in others. As Mary grew up, she could not always continue to evoke admiration from others, which upset her mother, who wondered who was at fault—herself, nonadmiring others (such as her teachers), or Mary. Because Mary may have identified with her mother's wish for admiration and an exclusive relationship, she did not have as much freedom to identify with people other than mother. Mary's inability to freely pursue other identifications may have limited her own development.

Both Laurie and Mary achieved a healthy resolution of the earliest mother–daughter conflicts, which enabled them to have separate lives and yet remain connected to their mothers. Still, we can see important differences that we attempt to explain by a detailed analysis of the nature of the earliest mother–baby relationship. In these two cases we can see the influence of early identifications on the unfolding of the daughter's personality and the ongoing adult mother–daughter relationship.

REFERENCES

Arlow, J. (1982). Problems of the superego concept. *Psychoanalytic Study of the Child* 37:229–244. New Haven, CT: Yale University Press.

Freud, S. (1919). The dissection of the psychical personality. *Standard Edition* 22:57–80.

Furer, M. (1967). Some developmental aspects of the superego. *International Journal of Psycho-Analysis* 48:277–280.

McDevitt, J. (1994). *The continuity of conflict and compromise formation from infancy to adulthood: a 25-year follow-up study.* Unpublished manuscript.

2

Some Thoughts on the Creation of Character

Ava L. Siegler

Margaret Mahler's (Mahler et al. 1975) theoretical contributions have focused our attention on the ways in which infants and toddlers negotiate the psychic hazards of separation from the mother, modulate aggressive impulses, and develop an individual sense of self. Her insistence on the enduring significance of the earliest ties to the mother have enabled us to approach preoedipal phases of development with a scrutiny and a specificity that has greatly added to our understanding of the human condition.

Bergman and Fahey's thoughtful tracing of the lives of two daughters and two mothers who were intensely studied during early childhood and then subsequently revisited thirty years later demonstrates once again how powerful and persuasive these theories are. We cannot help but be convinced by the authors that "the earlier, preverbal period of development—and in particular the earliest with mother—may be recognizable in the character structure and emotional life of the adult" (Bergman and Fahey, this volume).

It is inevitable, of course, that longitudinal studies like this, which offer us such exceptional information, inevitably raise more questions than they can answer, because the complexity of the information they reveal is bound to be greater than our ability to devise or to demonstrate particular hypotheses. Luckily, we have a century of psychological understanding to draw upon, and this understanding has provided us with an increasingly specific map of the mind.

Through our theories we have developed both a way of seeing (which informs what we look for) and a way of understanding (which lets us know what we have seen). In my discussion of Bergman's rich data, I would first like to take the liberty of elaborating some general propositions that I believe are inherent in our current understanding of psychoanalytic developmental theory, and then, turning to the lives of Laurie and Mary, demonstrate the particular usefulness of these propositions.

PROPOSITION 1

Separation and individuation from the mother, like all developmental phases, is a lifelong struggle, differently experienced by boys and girls, but never wholly resolved.

From the time a baby is born and she leaves the safety of the womb, the struggle to separate from the mother is already taking place. This first separation is initiated by the cutting of the umbilical cord, but then, quickly, more separations follow: the baby moves out of the mother's arms as she begins to walk; she moves out of the mother's orbit as she begins to go to school; she moves out of the mother's protection as she begins to act on her own initiative. These ongoing separations are—all along—helping to prepare the mother and the child for the biggest separation of all—the eventual ability to lead an independent life, no longer wholly dependent on a parent's care. That's why being a parent is such a peculiar job. You spend twenty years preparing a child to be able to live without you.

But because the mother is a woman, there are differences in the ways in which boys and girls move out into the world. While both boys and girls need to establish a sense of separateness from their mothers and both need to internalize aspects of the mother as parts of themselves, the boy child's sense is based on a more fixed "me/not me" distinction. Separateness and difference are heightened in boys. By contrast, the girl child's sense of self is always less separate because it involves a less fixed "me/not me" distinction. This probably predisposes her to more *affiliative* and less *autonomous* ties. On the other hand, core gender identity for a girl is seldom as problematic as it can be for boys because it is built upon, and does not contradict, the girl's primary sense of continuity and similarity with her mother. The little girl's connection to her mother then not only serves as the source of love, nurturance, and support that is so necessary to healthy development, but also as the inner representation of her femaleness.

PROPOSITION 2

Our understanding of the ties to the mother applies not only to the daughter's actual relationship to her mother, but to the symbolic representation of the mother as well.

That is, as the child changes physically and psychologically, she is also changing the way she thinks and feels about her mother. Her *idea* of mother undergoes an inevitable alteration as she moves through preoedipal, oedipal, latency, and adolescent phases of development—moving from the nurturant, protective figure of infancy (the mother of symbiosis), the powerful but ambivalent figure of toddlerhood (the mother of separation), the erotic and envied mother of the oedipal phase (the mother of desire and identification), to what often seems to us to be the hardest to bear, the repudiated mother of adolescence.

The young girl is always simultaneously involved in and engaged by the ongoing relationship she has with her *real* and *imagined* mother, and this dual relationship forms the basis of her identification. But what is *identification?*

PROPOSITION 3

In psychoanalysis, identification is a special case of the broader concept of internalization—the process by which aspects of the outer world and our interactions with it are taken in by us, and represented within the internal structures of mind—id, ego, and superego. It is a process that enables all of our learning, and it takes place on both unconscious and conscious levels.

Freud, Hartmann, and, later, Loewald described internalization as the means by which aspects of need-gratifying relationships and functions provided for one individual by another are preserved by making them part of the self. This understanding inextricably links drive and object and provides the basis for Freudian object relations theories. In other words, we feed the baby so that she will one day feed herself, dress her so that she will one day dress herself, speak to her so that she will one day speak herself, soothe her so that she will one day soothe herself, and love her so that she will one day love herself and others. The daughter must take over the functions that were originally fulfilled for her by the mother.

Interestingly, internalization occurs particularly throughout the life cycle whenever relations with a significant other are disrupted or lost. Freud noted this in his famous paper, "Mourning and Melancholia" (1917). In this respect, forms of internalization can support the purposes of both separation and attachment. We see evidence of this in the lives of Laurie and Mary. The failure to internalize is, in this regard, the failure to develop. We can note how these failures are represented in the pathological behaviors that we treat in our consulting rooms: the oppositional disorders of childhood, for instance, which represent the child's failure to internalize self-control and her continued reliance on her mother for behavioral intervention; or the eating disorders of adolescence, in which the teenager is unable to internalize rational eating habits, and continually engages her mother's external care; or the exaggerated anxieties of panic disorders, in which the adult is unable to soothe the self, because this crucial maternal regulatory function is lacking.

In analytic theory, internalizations are found to occur at progressively higher and more complex developmental levels—*incorporation*, *introjection*, and finally *identification*. *Incorporation* is a relatively primitive process, and occurs early in infancy at an undifferentiated level, where the basic distinction between self and object has been achieved only in the most global form. Implied in this term is a fantasy of swallowing, and/or the destruction of the object, which appears in all our fairy tales where mothers or children are gobbled up—*Little Red Riding Hood*, for instance, or *The Three Billy Goats Gruff*.

Introjection, a somewhat higher-level preoedipal process, lacks this quality of destruction through ingestion. This more mature (but still infantile) process permits the person to appropriate properties and functions of the object, but these properties are not fully integrated into a cohesive and effective sense of the self. These introjected components become part of the self-representation, as expressed through the ego, superego, or ego ideal in childhood. For example, the regulating, forbidding, and rewarding aspects of the superego are originally formed by the introjection of parental directions, admonitions, and praise, and only later during oedipal phase development do they become further transformed into identifications.

Identification is usually reserved for the process that takes place under conditions of object–subject differentiation, that is, after object constancy has been established in the oedipal phase. In this process, various attitudes, functions, and values of the other are integrated into a cohesive effective identity and become fully functional parts of the self, compatible with other parts. Identification in this sense differs from the other modes of internalization in terms of the degree to which it becomes central to the individual's basic identity, sense of self, or core ego. These transformed self-representations are stable, and enable the individual to establish an increasing sense of continuity, power, mastery, and intentionality. They become part of what Erikson (1956) called the achievement of "continuity of personal character" (p. 102).

Perception, memory, thought, mental representation, and symbolic function are all called into play by the individual to serve the purposes of these three levels of internalization, so that the development of interests and ideals, as well as the adaptive and defensive reaction patterns that become a part of our personalities, can be consolidated into our characteristic functioning.

The process of identification then provides us with the psychological strategy for building psychic structures. But what is the fate of these structures?

PROPOSITION 4

All psychic structures are formed *and* transformed *throughout the course of life.*

Development is not achieved once and for all, as analysts of the past generation believed; neither does it move upwards and onwards. Rather, it is better described by the process Levi-Strauss (1969) has called *bricolage*, the accruing and layering of experiences one upon the other. We continue to develop throughout our lives, with certain phases characterized by the emergence of characteristic conflicts and issues. But since, in real life, we never fully resolve the issues that are presented at any time in our lives, we carry over the residue of these unresolved issues from one phase to the next, influencing the outcome of each successive stage from infancy to childhood through adolescence, young adulthood, mature adulthood, and old age.

For each developmental task, then, there can be only more or less success resolution. *More or less*—that is the very basis of a Freudian idea of normality and pathology. The abnormal is always seen as a variant of the normal, and the normal can be expressed through widely differing choices. In Chapter 1 we glimpsed two such differing choices in the lives of Mary and Laurie. But to capture the nature of their resolutions more fully, I offer a fifth proposition.

PROPOSITION 5

Only an exploration of the intersection of biology, psychology, and destiny can provide us with a full reflection on the creation of character.

Using this last proposition, I turn now to Laurie's life. What do we know of her *biology*, that is, the genetic predisposition that helped define the kind of baby Laurie was? Bergman and Fahey describe her as a content and peaceful child, yet active and interested in the world around her. From this language we get the impression of a temperamentally sturdy child, endowed right from the beginning with good and stable ego strengths.

What are the psychological influences in Laurie's life? First and foremost, of course, is the influence of her mother. As I have noted, the child internalizes her sense of reality through her mother, that is, it is the mother who initially defines the meaning of the child's early experiences.

Bergman and Fahey emphasize that Laurie's mother appears particularly focused on the pleasures of attachment. She talks of her special loving feelings for Laurie, is happy about Laurie's delight in her father, seems willing to share Laurie's love, is empathic toward her feelings, and generally appears to use parenthood as a developmental phase for herself, emphasizing the ways in which she wishes to give Laurie more freedom than she herself was permitted as a child so that she can preserve "Laurie's spirit." From this phrase alone, we can see that Laurie will be permitted, and indeed encouraged by her mother, to develop an independent sense of self.

Laurie's mother also appears to display a great deal of maternal confidence. She seems to derive satisfaction from her maternal role and enjoys other aspects of domesticity as well, like cooking and feeding her family. So in Laurie's case we start with a sturdy baby and an apparently sturdy mother, secure in her own identity and determined to raise a spirited child. In addition, Laurie seems blessed with an empathic and supportive father. Both psychologically and physically present, he appears generous-spirited and secure in his dynamic role.

Laurie's early development is relatively smooth and unremarkable. While both she and her mother seem to be experiencing some ambivalence about leaving what Bergman and Fahey call "the blissful union of babyhood," their emotional storms are manageable, and mitigated by the presence of the father who supports both mother and daughter. When Laurie turns away from her mother, she is always able to turn toward her father. And her libidinal attachment to him is deep and steady. We could speculate about whether this attachment precipitated Laurie's turning away from her mother, or conversely, her mother's turning away from Laurie. But clearly father plays an important role for mother and for Laurie.

At 17 months Laurie is described as making a great spurt in cognitive development, including language development. It is at this point, as Laurie moves out of infancy, that Mrs. L describes relinquishing her wish for another baby because she doesn't want Laurie to become a middle child. Again, this decision underscores this mother's profound empathic connection with her little daughter—*her* ability to identify with Laurie, an important parental capacity, and one that permits the mother to separate her own needs from the needs of the child.

By the time Laurie is 1½ years old, she begins to display signs of her internalization. Interestingly, she internalizes aspects of both her mother and her brother. Along with these new internalizations there is an upsurge in assertion and aggression toward other children, signaling Laurie's emerging individuation. Psychologically, Laurie seems to stand on firm ground.

But what of Laurie's *destiny*? Here, too, Laurie has been fortunate. Her mother and father are not anxious new parents. They have already successfully raised one child through his infancy. Laurie is both the baby of the family (a gratifying role in and of itself) and the only girl. And few untoward events impinge upon what Winnicott (1988) would call Laurie's "continuity of existence" (p. 127).

Laurie appears to have been a healthy baby, easy to *have* and easy to *hold*. The only bodily insult reported was a fungal infection when she was 14 months. Interestingly, this infection is accompanied by an upsurge in aggression and a rise in envy of her older brother. The heightening of sensitivities in the genital region may have forced Laurie's attention on the anatomical distinctions between herself and her brother and increased her yearnings for what appeared to be his more intact equipment. It may also have precipitated an early rapprochement crisis, as infantile pain and discomfort diminish the mother's omnipotence and, interestingly, frequently spur growth, since the ego is struggling to master the painful experience.

The only other disruptive event in Laurie's early years appears to have been a move when she was 2 years old to a new apartment. Her reactions to this move demonstrate how the toddler mobilizes both aggression and regression to cope with loss and disruption. Laurie makes it clear that she wants to stay a baby (the regressive piece), and becomes intensely rivalrous and reactive to other babies (the aggressive piece). Soon calmed down and reintegrated into her new home, Laurie again begins to modulate her aggression and relinquish her regression through internalization of her mother's love and tenderness. At the same time, she begins to give voice to externalized prohibitions ("Mommy say, 'No, don't eat that'"), the first evidence of superego internalizations, and to demonstrate a new level of triangulation with her father as she begins to move from the preoedipal dyad (Mommy and me, Daddy and me) to the oedipal triad (Mommy, Daddy, and me).

By the age of 2, Laurie is described as being well on the way to emotional object constancy, and her capacity for empathy (an internalization of her mother's primary maternal attitude) is well developed. By 2 years and 9 months, her oedipal development was far enough along to demonstrate her clear preference for her father. Her greater difficulty, separating from her mother at this time, probably reflected her fears about the effects on her mother of her rivalrous and competitive feelings. (Children at this age often need to keep their mothers in sight to protect them from their hostile wishes.) Under these new oedipal pressures, Laurie regresses for a bit, displaying more typical rapprochement behaviors as her heightened ambivalence toward her mother is expressed in her alternately clinging and demanding behaviors. However, throughout these storms, Laurie's mother and father remain capable of responding to their daughter in supportive ways, and Laurie herself is capable of transforming both her actual relationship to her mother (reflected in her interpersonal relationship to her) and her symbolic relationship to her (reflected in the clear signs of progressive resolution of later phase-specific tasks).

We notice something right away about Laurie: her later sense of self seems remarkably continuous with her earliest presentation. As an adult she could still be described as a "lively, vigorous, and curious" young woman. She has chosen a field that bears on issues of health and nutrition, remains a friendly, attached member of her family, seems to have resolved late-adolescent choices in work and love, and has even retained her sense of herself as a tomboy through her continued physicality and her sports skills. While sufficiently separating and individuating as an adult, Laurie has become a woman who greatly resembles the baby she had once been. A strong biological disposition, supportive and nurturant psychological family dynamics, and a lucky destiny. The fates have been kind to Laurie in every way.

The intersection of biology, psychology, and destiny in Mary's life is an altogether more precarious affair. First, biology: we find two things of interest about Mary right from the beginning. Her mother reports that she "had never liked to be held closely," an indication that attachment and separation struggles may become more of an issue between Mary and her mother than they were between Laurie and her mother, who both felt comfortable with their close ties. Does Mary's reluctance to be held reflect a temperamental sensitivity to stimulation? Was Mrs. M already subtly encouraging a premature autonomy in Mary? How did Mary's mother absorb her baby's wish to hold herself apart? Did she experience Mary's sensitivities as a rejection? As a narcissistic insult? Was Mary's ego easily overwhelmed?

The second biological factor that attracts our interest is Mary's early precocity (which was so striking and enchanting to all observers). This must have increased what Freud called the *narcissistic* shading of the loving relationship between mother and child, just as Laurie's mother's joy in attachment appears to have increased the *anaclitic* shading of their loving relationship. From the beginning of Mary's infancy, her precocity plays an important role in the nature of her relatedness to mother and others. Her precocious skills increased her responsivity to the admiration of others, and of course the continued admiration of others undoubtedly increased her wishes to display her precocious skills.

And what of the *psychological* factors in Mary's life? Her relationship to her mother is certainly good enough. Mary's mother takes pride in her baby and is nurturant and encouraging of Mary's growth. But the aspect of maternal confidence that we saw in the mother–Laurie pair seems conspicuously lacking in the mother–Mary pair. Mary's mom seems anxious and insecure, and it is only through Mary's *achievements* that her mother is capable of feeling self-esteem, again underscoring Mrs. M's narcissistic investment in her little girl rather than the empathic investment we saw with Mrs. L.

Mary's mother is described as a drab woman who faded into the background, her personality and even her clothes in contrast to the description of her daughter as a "phenomenal little creature." Mary's energy and vigor are seen by everyone to be in sharp contrast to her immobile, self-conscious, and painfully shy mother. By the time both must negotiate the rapprochement crisis, Mrs. M seems worried and worn-out, while Mary's light is rapidly dimming.

The mother's insecurity, anxiety, and pessimism are reflected in her fears about her second pregnancy ("This will be the end of Mary"). And indeed, something is ended for Mary—she is no longer able to shine for her mother, enabling her to bask in Mary's reflected glory. Mary goes on to become a classic underachiever who is unable to generate the industry or productivity necessary to a successful latency, or the social competence necessary to a successful adolescence. Yet in early adulthood she is able to rally. She does well in her college years, and is able to choose both a profession and a husband.

And what of Mary's *destiny*? Here this mother–daughter pair do not fare well at all. Certainly the most profound event is the father's unusually long separation from the family. He leaves home to go abroad when Mary is only 15 months, and does not return until almost a year later, when she is 24 months. While we have no data about this separation, his departure constitutes a significant disruption in both Mary *and* her mother's "going-on-being." Mary reacts with clear signs of childhood depression. She displays listlessness, fatigue, a propensity to have accidents, irritability, and alterations in appetite. Not only must mother and daughter deal with the *symbolic* losses of the separation-individuation phase, now they must deal with an *actual* loss as well.

Mrs. M too is described during this period as depressed, distraught, and even inattentive to Mary. It is important to note that when children are dependent on caregiving adults who themselves are psychologically compromised, they become more vulnerable to pathologies in development, particularly in relation to phase-specific tasks like those presented by the rapprochement crisis. The father's absence constitutes a significant loss.

Abelin (1971) reminds us that the most conspicuous turning toward the father occurs at the beginning of the practicing subphase, when he becomes "the other," the different parent. He serves as a new, interesting object for the child in this phase whereas the mother is taken for granted as a home base and used for periodic refueling. It is exactly at this phase that Mary abruptly loses her father and her mother becomes depressed, rendering her an emotional orphan.

In the rapprochement phase, while the relationship with the mother tends to become normally fraught with ambivalence, the father remains the more uncontaminated parent love object. In fact, Abelin (1971) suggests that the father's internalized mental representation during this phase may be a necessary condition for the satisfactory resolution of the ambivalent rapprochement position.

Little Mary's psychic ability to achieve individuation through the process of intrapsychic separation from her depressed mother may have been severely undermined as neither she nor her mother had access to the uncontaminated, reality-based father. The loss of the father at this crucial stage may have precipitated a hypercathexis of the lost object (both the absent father and the depressed mother) and resulted in the split representations of the parents that appear to continue into Mary's adult life—the idealized mother and the deidealized father.

Abelin's (1971) research into the role of the father during the phases of separation and individuation suggests that the father's presence also serves to help the child explore a more elated, exuberant reality. It is the father's absence at this crucial subphase that echoes in Mary's noticeable lack of adult exuberance. Mary's unresolved pre-oedipal dilemma seems to have constrained her entry into the oedipal phase. It is necessary to have access to an early internalization of a positive father in order to precede and prepare the way for the Oedipus complex. Since this internalization seems missing in Mary's life, a great deal of negative oedipal resonance remains in her protective, loving ties to her mother and her hostile, rivalrous feelings toward the men in her family.

But it is not only the *departure* of her father that Mary must deal with, his *return* also deals her a painful blow. Her sense of loss and exclusion are heightened as her parents are reunited, and, to confirm her worst fears, her mother soon becomes pregnant. By the time Mary is 3, she must cope with the birth of a baby brother as well as her own entry into nursery school. It is hardly surprising that she has difficulty adapting and becoming a member of a group. Desperate for attention, Mary presses for more and more adult recognition. She had previously received enormous positive rewards from adults; however, now, she is exposed to negative and painful criticism of her efforts to remain special.

Finally, on the verge of adolescence, Mary is again disrupted and displaced. By now she has *two* younger brothers and a family decision to move compels her to cope with a new home, a new school, and a new community. From the point of view of development, this is probably one of the worst times in one's life to absorb such a momentous change. Just when Mary needs to turn to the company of her peers to help her separate from her family and to seek love outside her family circle, she is separated from everything she knows and thrust back into dependence on her family. Her identification with her mother has now almost obliterated all evidence of her early sparkle.

She appears to have sacrificed her phallic-narcissistic needs in order to preserve her tie to her mother through identification with her mother's more depressive, masochistic stance. Shy, self-diminishing, and self-sacrificing, Mary appears almost wholly identified with her lost infantile object. Her cognitive skills remain in place and carry her into her professional life, but they lack the libidinalization that would have infused them with passion, power, and pleasure. Her mother continues to stand at the center of her emotional life, but Mary has *disidentified* with both her father and her brothers, whom she sees as the aggressors. She places her mother in the role of their victim (perhaps her way of preserving the good preoedipal mother by splitting off the anger toward males).

Mary's yearning to be reunited with her earliest relationship to mother and her subsequent use of identification in the service of attachment have shaped Mary's adult character. Does her concern about her mom shield her from her rage at her mother? Is her worry an identification with her perenially worried mother? Can her anxieties about her mom represent a way of always keeping her mother in mind? Does she feel guilty about outshining her mother, and has she therefore relinquished her sparkle in order to keep her mother's love? As the new, parentified, child-turned-adult, Mary seems to have sacrificed a portion of herself to protect her ties with her mother.

Mary's life, in contrast to Laurie's, provides us with many interesting instances of discontinuity. Her earlier "enchanting" presentation of herself seems diminished in the transition from preoedipal to oedipal development. Unable to maintain herself as the sparkle in her mother's eyes, displaced from centrality in her mother's emotional life with the reappearance of her father at the age of 3, and faced with a no-win situation in which she must choose between retaining her mother's love or risking all for her father's love, the continuity of Mary's self is disrupted. She has become a woman whose adult sense of self no longer resembles the baby she had once been.

SUMMARY

From an analytic vantage, then, the separation-individuation phase and every subsequent phase of development is threaded with necessary losses as well as important gains. As the child moves toward independence and identity, she must relinquish her symbiotic bliss, her infantile omnipotence, her erotic desires, and the sanctuary of her parents' comfort. Compensation for this is found in burgeoning ego capacities, autonomous functioning, a realistic self-concept, and deeper object relations.

I have tried in this chapter (without access, of course, to the crucial phase of adolescence, which makes such a significant contribution to the consolidation of the girls' character) to expand our understanding of the lives of Laurie and Mary by drawing upon some more current developmental propositions that I believe are central to our understanding of the ways in which character is consolidated throughout the course of life. To summarize:

1. Development is a lifelong, continuous process, and no phase-specific task is ever wholly resolved.
2. Internalization is the process by which self and object representations are created.
3. Development always takes place in two simultaneous realms of experience: what Erikson (1964) calls "historical actuality" and "psychic reality" (p. 201), or for our purposes, the *interpersonal relationship* between mother and child and the *intrapsychic representation* of that relationship.
4. Psychic structures continue to be formed and transformed throughout the course of life.
5. Only an analysis of the intersection of biology, psychology, and destiny provides us with the fullest reflection on development.

While both Mary and Laurie have been more or less able to resolve universal developmental issues, while both have built lives that function within normal boundaries and are not suffering from significant pathology, and while both have ultimately achieved what Freud considered the two most important goals of life—"*lieben und arbeiten*" (to love and to work)—the differing outcome of the bricolage of preoedipal, oedipal, latency, and adolescent issues has created a particular resolution for each that differentiates one from the other and defines the consolidation of their character.

Both Laurie and Mary were loved and remain loving daughters, and both of them have gone on to develop a unified self-representation. But the individual nature of their earliest love *for* and *from* their mothers, as Bergman and Fahey have emphasized, continues to echo in their adult lives.

REFERENCES

Abelin, E. L. (1971). The role of the father in the separation-individuation process. In *Separation-Individuation: Essays in Honor of Margaret S. Mahler*, ed. J. B. McDevitt and C. F. Seattlage, pp. 229–253. New York: International Universities Press.

Erikson, E. (1956). The problem of ego identity. *Journal of the American Psychoanalytic Association* 4:56–121.

———— (1964). *Insight and Responsibility*. New York: Norton.

Freud, S. (1917). Mourning and melancholia. *Standard Edition* 14:239–258.

Levi-Strauss, C. (1969). *The Raw and the Cooked*. New York: Harper & Row.

Mahler, M. S., Pine, F., and Bergman, A. (1975). *The Psychological Birth of the Human Infant*. New York: Basic Books.

Winnicott, D. W. (1988). *Human Nature*. New York: Schocken.

3

Anne Sexton and Child Abuse

Arlene Kramer Richards

One of the most important poets of the twentieth century, Anne Sexton, won the Pulitzer Prize for poetry in 1967, the same year she won the Shelley Memorial Prize of the American Poetry Society. Sexton was what many critics call a confessional poet and what Helen Vendler has called a post-Freudian lyric poet. Sexton lived in her native Massachusetts in a middle-class suburban setting from 1928 until 1974. The mother of two daughters, born in 1953 and 1955, she was hospitalized with suicidal depression after each of the births. Her work as a poet began in 1957 as a way out of her second deep depression. According to her best friend and fellow poet, Maxine Kumin, Sexton's poetry kept her alive for the eighteen years she was writing. Her suicide occurred when her daughters were 16 and 18 years old. She made twelve suicide attempts during the intervening years. Whatever else we know about her as a parent, she certainly did not protect her children from the horrors of her depression.

Being a confessional poet, she filled her poems with her guilt, her shame, and her misery. In some few of her works she dealt directly with her feelings for her daughters. Reading them, we can try to educe the delicate web of feelings and behavior that constitute one artist's relations with her own children. I would like the reader to keep in mind the following questions:

1. To what extent was writing about her children itself an abusive act?
2. What can we learn about the feelings of an abused child?
3. What can we learn about the motivations of an abusive parent?

WRITING ABOUT CHILDREN

Pain for a Daughter

Blind with love, my daughter
has cried nightly for horses, those long-necked marchers and
    churners
that she has mastered, any and all,
reining them in like a circus hand—
the excitable muscles and the ripe neck;
tending, this summer, a pony and a foal.
She who is too squeamish to pull
a thorn from the dog's paw,
watched her pony blossom with distemper,
the underside of the jaw swelling
like an enormous grape.
Gritting her teeth with love,
she drained the boil and scoured it
with hydrogen peroxide until pus
ran like milk on the barn floor.

Blind with loss all winter,
in dungarees, a ski jacket, and a hard hat,
she visits the neighbor's stable,
our acreage not zoned for barns;
they who own the flaming horses

and the swan-whipped thoroughbred
that she tugs at and cajoles,
thinking it will burn like a furnace
under her small-hipped English seat.

Blind with pain she limps home.
The thoroughbred has stood on her foot.
He rested there like a building.
He grew into her foot like they were one.
The marks of the horseshoe printed
into her flesh, the tips of her toes
ripped off like pieces of leather,
three toenails swirled like shells
and left to float in blood in her riding boot.

Blind with fear, she sits on the toilet,
her foot balanced over the washbasin,
her father, hydrogen peroxide in hand,
performing the rites of the cleansing.
She bites on a towel, sucked in breath,
sucked in and arched against the pain,
her eyes glancing off me where
I stand at the door, eyes locked
on the ceiling, eyes of a stranger,
and then she cries . . .
Oh, my God, help me!
Where a child would have cried *Mama!*
Where a child would have believed *Mama!*
she bit the towel and called on God
and I saw her life stretched out . . .
I saw her torn in childbirth,
and I saw her, at that moment,
in her own death and I knew that she
knew.

[Sexton 1981, p. 72]

In this poem, written in November 1965 (the other poems I discuss follow sequentially), Sexton describes both her daughter's pain and Sexton's own experience of it. The poem takes place in the bathroom, a place for nakedness and intensely felt bodily sensation.

She documents the way the young girl is hurt by the very being she loves best, the horse—a thoroughbred horse, high spirited, exciting, and dangerous. Having been hurt, she comes home to be tended lovingly—but the loving care is provided by her father. Her mother watches—"I stand at the door"—detached and alert. At the end, the daughter calls out to God, not to her mother; the mother notes it, and, realizing that her daughter does not expect comfort from her, turns on her in rage. In the last four lines of the poem, in 23 Anglo-Saxon words without a single image or metaphor, Sexton describes the ultimate horror. The mother, giver of life—"I saw her torn in childbirth"—has become the giver of death—"and I saw her, at that moment, in her own death. . . ." In another twist, she sees that her daughter understands her mother's death wish for her—"and I knew that she knew."

Sexton's niece told Diane Middlebrook (1991), her biographer: "When she was presenting the material, it was marvelous to listen to—dramatic and daring. But for those who suffered at the expense of her success, the impact can never be measured" (p. 329). Her daughter Linda resisted her mother's intrusions into her physical and emotional development. Linda's guilt and ambivalence about keeping anything from her mother became obvious when she did not tell her mother about losing her virginity, but did leave her journal in her drawer where her mother could find and read it. According to Middlebrook, Linda tried to protect herself from her mother's invasiveness as Anne wrote about it in "Mother and Daughter." While the whole family had accepted Anne's "Little Girl, My Stringbean, My Lovely Woman" when Linda was 12, concern for the daughter prompted both Linda's psychiatrist and Anne's to object to the invasion when Linda was 18.

SUFFERING ABUSE

How did things come to this pass? How did the mother turn into the death wisher? The next poem is written, not in the bathroom, but in a study. It deals with the feelings of a husband, seen from the point of view of the wife who is anticipating becoming his victim. Here the wife is also a mother, but a mother who does not protect her daughter, but shares her fate.

The Wifebeater

There will be mud on the carpet tonight
and blood in the gravy as well.
The wifebeater is out,
The childbeater is out
eating soil and drinking bullets from a cup.
He strides back and forth
in front of my study window
chewing little red pieces of my heart.
His eyes flash like a birthday cake
and he makes bread out of a rock.

Yesterday he was walking
like a man in the world.
He was upright and conservative
but somehow evasive, somehow contagious.
Yesterday he built me a country
and laid out a shadow where I could sleep
but today a coffin for the Madonna and child,
today two women in baby clothes will be hamburg.

With a tongue like a razor he will kiss,
the mother, the child,
and we three will color the stars black
in memory of his mother
who kept him chained to the food tree
or turned him on and off like a water faucet
and made women through all these hazy years
the enemy with a heart of lies.

Tonight all the red dogs lie down in fear
and the wife and the daughter knit into each other
until they are killed.
[Sexton 1981, pp. 307–308]

The mother and the daughter in this poem are equally victims of
the husband who is a wifebeater and the father who is a childbeater.
A fearful man, he brings mud into the house, blood into the food,

makes bread out of stones, and kisses with "a tongue like a razor." Father, mother, and child are the unholy trinity, ready to "color the stars black." And why are they going to celebrate this anti-mass, this anti-sacrament? "In memory of his mother/ who kept him chained to the food tree/ or turned him on and off like a water faucet." His mother is the one who by her binding and inconsistent behavior "made women through all these hazy years/ the enemy with the heart of lies." But knowing does not help. Even though she is aware, even though she sees that "he strides back and forth/ in front of my study window" and thus sees him from a distance, still he will kill her. Still, mother and daughter will have to die at his hand. By contrast with the previous poem, this one speaks with a much less persuasive voice. Rather than the immediacy of the feelings flashing back and forth between mother and daughter, this poem relies on a speculation about her husband's feelings and motivations; the first poem was written in the poet's bathroom. It was all affect. This one is written in the poet's study. This one is all intellect.

Turning away from trying to figure out the man's anger intellectually, Sexton looks at her own feelings. She is searching in herself for the origin of her compulsion to die.

The Death Baby

1. Dreams

I was an ice baby.
I turned to sky blue.
My tears became two glass beads.
My mouth stiffened into a dumb howl.
They say it was a dream
but I remember that hardening.

My sister at six
dreamt nightly of my death:
"The baby turned to ice.
Someone put her in the refrigerator
and she turned hard as a Popsicle."
I remember the stink of the liverwurst.
How I was put on a platter and laid

between the mayonnaise and the bacon.
The rhythm of the refrigerator
had been disturbed.
The milk bottle hissed like a snake.
The tomatoes vomited up their stomachs.
The caviar turned to lava.
The pimentos kissed like cupids.
I moved like a lobster,
slower and slower.
The air was tiny.
The air would not do.

[Sexton 1981, p. 354]

The image of death is here at capitulation to her sister's wish, a wish that almost every small child has at the birth of a younger sibling. Why would this wish be so important to Anne that she would take over her sister's dream as her own? Why would she long for the refrigerator of death rather than feel rage at her sister for that wish? She hints at an answer in a later comment in that same poem: "you have seen my father whip me./ You have seen me stroke my father's whip" (p. 358).

The bringer of death, the enemy, is not only *his* mother, but *hers* also.

Baby Picture

It's in the heart of the grape
where that smile lies.
It's in the good-bye-bow in the hair
where that smile lies.
It's in the clerical collar of the dress
where that smile lies.
What smile?
The smile of my seventh year,
caught here in the painted photograph.

It's peeling now, age has got it,

a kind of cancer of the background
and also in the assorted features.
It's like a rotten flag
or a vegetable from the refrigerator,
pocked with mold.
I am aging without sound,
into darkness, darkness.

Anne, who were you?
I open the vein
and my blood rings like roller skates.
I open the mouth
and my teeth are like an angry army.
I open the dress
and I see a child bent on a toilet seat.
I crouch there, sitting dumbly
pushing the enemas out like ice-cream,
letting the whole brown world
turn into sweets.

Anne,
who were you?

Merely a kid keeping alive.
[Sexton 1981, p. 362]

This poem starts in the study or the living room, a place where the poet sees an old picture of herself dressed in a prudish, high-collared dress and a "good-bye-bow." The picture has been artificially colored, painted over to look nicer just as the child has been dressed up to look nicer. Both are lies, as we hear in the thrice-repeated line "where that smile lies." The line repeats as if to give it the full weight of each of its meanings. One meaning is that the smile is in the heart of the baby, the grape. Another meaning is that the smile is added like the bow and the collar to make the little girl appear proper. The third meaning is that the smile is itself a lie.

The lie turns rotten, moldy and dark, the rot hidden in the darkness of a refrigerator. And when she opens herself up, we see agony in the bathroom again. Now she is the 7-year-old "bent on a toilet seat," an image of absolute honesty and implied pain. She transforms the pain in a grotesque parody of the painted picture. The shit is ice cream. The lie is total. Why did she do it? Now she sees it, lying was the strategy she adopted for keeping alive. The meaning of this self-understanding for her lie is frightening. If keeping alive is pretending that shit is ice cream, where can truth be but in letting go of life, in death?

The context of a statement adds to its meaning. Sexton published this poem in the second section of her 1972 *Book of Folly*, a section called "The Jesus Papers." It follows a poem called "Grandfather, Your Wound." That poem ends with the lines:

> Now it comes bright again—
> my God, Grandfather,
> you are here,
> you are laughing,
> you hold me and rock me
> and we watch the lighthouse come on,
> blinking its dry wings over us all,
> over my wound, and yours.
> [Sexton 1981, p. 362]

The transition is to her wound so that "Baby Picture" is the picture of her wound. Furthermore, the "Baby Picture" is followed by a cycle of fifteen poems collectively entitled "The Furies." Sexton's response to "Baby Pictures" is rage. Her rage spills out everywhere—in death images, bones, skulls, skeletons, killing lover, father, mother, the earth, the whole world. She is transforming shit into ice cream, remaking pain into poetry, discovering her rage in her writing. The ultimate invasion of her body is the enema, the pain inflicted by loving parents who wanted her to be cleaned out, as prim and proper on the inside as they made her on the outside with their collars and bows.

There are many meanings of child abuse in Sexton's poetry. Invading the child with enemas, telling her of the hostility with which her sibling greeted her birth, giving her dress-up clothes that constrict her and make her feel like a lie, and whipping her and making her caress the whip. Middlebrook (1991) makes a convincing case that

Sexton has been sexually abused by her drunken father and that she recorded the experience in the seduction scene of her autobiographical play *Mercy Street*. In the play the father forces whiskey on his daughter, praises her breasts, and caresses her between her legs. At the same time, the maiden aunt is seen "pacing, twisting her hands in an obsessive private ritual, chanting and raving, cracking a small riding whip" (p. 323). This combination of incest with the father and a perverse sadomasochistic relationship with the aunt who was her primary caregiver was what Anne called "the remembrance scene" (p. 322).

PASSING IT ON

The most explicit statement of what child abuse means to Sexton is embodied in her posthumously published poem.

Red Roses

Tommy is three and when he's bad
his mother dances with him.
She puts on the record,
"Red Roses for a Blue Lady"
and throws him across the room.
Mind you,
she never laid a hand on him,
only the wall laid a hand on him.
He gets red roses in different places,
the head, that time he was sleepy as a river,
the back, that time he was a broken scarecrow,
the arm like a diamond had bitten it,
the leg, twisted like a licorice stick,
all the dance they did together,
Blue Lady and Tommy.
You fell, she said, just remember you fell.
I fell, is all he told the doctors
in the big hospital. A nice lady came
and asked him questions but because

he didn't want to be sent away he said, I fell.
He never said anything else although he could talk fine.
He never told about the music
or how she'd sing and shout
holding him up and throwing him.

He pretends he is her ball.
He tries to fold up and bounce
but he squashes like fruit.
For he loves the Blue Lady and the spots
of red roses he gives her.

[Sexton 1981, pp. 492–493]

Here again we have the secret images of Anne, the fruit, like the grape and the vegetable squashes and blemishes. The sweets, like the ice cream transformed from shit, like the baby frozen into a Popsicle, like the liar in the colored photograph. Tommy is Anne. Yet Anne is also the mother who fails to protect, the victim of the bloody wifebeater and childbeater, the inadequate, intellectualizing, cold, and hateful mother who sees and wishes her child dead for not needing her. Anne is Tommy's mother. The abusing mother is the depressed mother. The mother who does not protect is the mother who destroys.

A very late poem, also published posthumously, is clearly autobiographical and an attempt to understand her pain by tracing the roots of it.

End, Middle, Beginning

There was an unwanted child.
Aborted by three modern methods
she hung on to the womb,
hooked onto it
building her house into it
and it was to no avail,
to block her out.

At her birth
she did not cry,
spanked indeed, but did not yell—
instead snow fell out of her mouth.

As she grew, year by year,
her hair turned like a rose in a vase,
and bled down her face.
Rocks were placed on her to keep
the growing silent,
and though they bruised,
they did not kill,
though kill was tangled into her beginning.

They locked her in a football
but she merely curled up
and pretended it was a warm doll's house.
They pushed insects in to bite her off
and she let them crawl into her eyes
pretending they were a puppet show.

Later, later,
grown fully, as they say,
they gave her a ring,
and she wore it like a root
and said to herself,
"To be not loved is the human condition,"
and lay like a statue in her bed.

Then once, by terrible chance,
love took her in his big boat
and she shoveled the ocean
in a scalding joy.

Then,
slowly,
love seeped away,
the boat turned into paper
and she knew her fate,
at last.
Turn where you belong,
into a deaf mute
that metal house,
let him drill you into no one.

[Sexton 1981, pp. 534–535]

From her biography we know that Sexton was ashamed of her relationship with her daughters. She was a stranger to them in their earliest years. When she became psychotically depressed after each of their births, the babies were sent to her mother-in-law to raise. Barely able to tolerate them as little children, she was unable to feel pleasure in loving or nurturing them. Later, when they were adolescents, she was preoccupied with love affairs, poetry, her failing marriage, her own quest for parental nurturance, the deaths of her parents and her loving maiden aunt. From her poetry we can see that she was consumed with horrific images of her own childhood and her own victimization. In a poem she had written early in her career and not published she makes it explicit:

> Later,
> when blood and eggs and breast
> dropped onto me,
> Daddy and his whiskey breath
> made a long midnight visit
> in a dream that is not a dream
> and then called his lawyer quickly.
> Daddy divorcing me.
>
> I have been divorcing him ever since,
> going into court with my mother as my witness
> and both long dead or not
> I am still divorcing him,
> adding up the crimes
> of how he came to me,
> and how he left me.
>
> [Sexton 1981, p. 545]

The visit required a divorce, implying that it must have been a marital visit, an instance of sexual abuse of an adolescent daughter by her drunken father, with her prudish cold mother as the not-witnessing witness. This poem links sexual abuse to the other forms of abuse suffered, perpetrated, or imagined by Anne Sexton. In the 1970s, when she was writing, the idea of sexual abuse was not the central and controversial one it is today. Analysts did not deal with it in the open and direct fashion with which we have been forced to deal with it since people like Alice Miller, Jeffrey Masson, and others wrote about it. What seems reasonable to me is to see the abuse as a form of interaction that gives rise to certain fantasies that in turn guide the person's behavior. For Sexton to have suffered abuse and passed it on by abusing her own child seems to fit the pattern of what we know about abuse and how it works. For her to have written about how this process of internalization occurs as she did in "Red Roses" allows us a valuable window into troubled souls of the sort we can get only from great artists.

What is unique to the record of child abuse in Anne Sexton's case is not only that she was an artist, but also that she was the mother of a daughter who became an artist as well. Her daughter, Linda Gray Sexton, wrote a description of being Sexton's daughter that corroborates the inferences from Anne Sexton's poetry. The daughter describes sitting on her father's bed in the afternoon, watching television with her mother. Her mother is suddenly naked from the waist down, masturbating. The daughter says:

> Naked from the waist down, she is making noises and her fingers curl through her crisp black pubic hair. She pushes her long clitoris back and forth against the dark lips of her vagina. I drop my eyes, ashamed. She does not stop even though I am in the room. Her eyes don't seem to see me or know I am here. I am scared. Maybe she is having some kind of a fit? Maybe they will take her away to the hospital again?
>   I close my eyes on this scene and try hard not to see it, though it happens again other times, once in the bathtub, more times on the bed. [L. Sexton 1994, p. 41]

The daughter experiences the pain of being beaten, the hunger of neglect, the fear of watching her parents drunkenly punching each other. Clearly, the sexual abuse and the violence that scarred Anne Sexton's childhood are repeated in that of her daughters. A mother so damaged, so scarred, turns her hurt against her daughters and creates another generation of mothers who, unless they are helped and supported, go on to abuse their children also.

DISCUSSION

Among the feelings for a child experienced by a parent is the urge to protect. From the child's point of view nurturance is important, but protection vital. In the most important sense, child abuse may be defined as the failure to protect. In *Mother, Madonna, Whore*, Ann Welldon (1988) describes the dangers of mothering in terms of her clinical experience with women with sexual disorders, perversions, and criminal involvements. Welldon not only shows how women use their power as mothers to inflict sexual and aggressive harm on their children, but also describes in detail the intergenerational propagation of pathology through what she shows to be perverse mothering. In Welldon's view, the mother is caught in a world where she is powerless except for her power over her child. Isolated, neglected, and denigrated by being denied the power to earn money, the single mother may be unable to resist the pull to use her child to meet her own sexual needs and satisfy her own aggressive impulses.

Aware that the political climate makes it unacceptable to use the word *perversion* because it is a term of opprobrium, yet not willing to use *deviation*, with its connotation of a merely statistical difference, Welldon carefully defines perversion to include the phenomenon she is describing. Perversion, she reminds the reader, is a syndrome in which the sufferer feels compelled to substitute some aggressive action for genital satisfaction. In this sense, the frustrated mother beating her child is the epitome of perversion. Welldon enables us to understand that the mother who sees her child as part of herself also maltreats her child as an expression of her own self-hatred. When she beats her child, it is a masochistic self-injury just as much as it is a sadistic attack. In view of the paucity of analytic data on child abuse from the abuser's side, Welldon's case vignettes and clinical conclusions are extremely valuable. Most important, I believe, is the formulation of child abuse as a perversion.

The essential aspect of perversion is the aggressive dehumanization of the object. The object is made to serve the pervert as a piece of equipment, equivalently valued or even less important than the whips and chains and dildos of the obligatory scenario. This is so much the case that when the object does not go along with this one aspect of the scenario, the whole thing becomes too unsatisfying and the perverse scenario is over. Welldon (1988) gives a vignette as an example: "Suddenly she stopped these beatings altogether when she realized that her baby had a triumphant look and, according to her, 'he was even enjoying' her ill treatment of him" (p. 74).

She describes a similar outcome in Shengold's (1979) case of mother–son incest. The mother stopped the abuse when the son ejaculated for the first time. Both Shengold and Welldon attribute this to the mother's fear of becoming pregnant by her son. But it seems to me worth following up a hypothesis that the mother stopped for the same reason Welldon's patient stopped her beatings of her 2-year-old. When the "victim" enjoys the experience, the perversion no longer serves as an aggressive discharge.

The perverse scenario fits Anne Sexton's pattern of first eroticizing and then reproducing the abusive behavior all too well. Publicizing her symptom is also characteristic of the person with a perversion. It fits the perverse way of understanding sexuality that values defiance and aggression above intimacy and harmonious interaction. By understanding her abusive pattern as a perversion, I think we have the answers to all three of our original questions. Writing about the children was an important aspect of the abuse. Their feelings mirror the feelings of their abuser when she herself was a child. And the abuser's feelings are an erotic form of the misery she suffered as an abused child herself.

Is this kind of child abuse characteristic of artists? I believe that it is just as abusive for a mother to tell her child's secrets to her friends and family in casual telephone conversations, just as abusive for a father to make jokes about his developing son's sexual characteristics to his son's friends, just as abusive for a nonartist to expose her children to her own sexual needs and compulsions, just as abusive for any parent to do to a child whatever was done to him or her as a child that caused pain and suffering. The point of this chapter is not that parents who are artists are any less protective of their children than parents who are not artists. The point is that parents who are artists can show us the ways in which nonartist parents are motivated to abuse. Parents who are artists can articulate what we need to know about what our nonartist patients are suffering.

REFERENCES

Middlebrook, D. (1991). *Anne Sexton: A Biography*. Boston: Houghton Mifflin.

Sexton, A. (1981). *The Complete Poems*. New York: Houghton Mifflin.

Sexton, L. (1994). *Searching for Mercy Street*. Boston: Little, Brown.

Shengold, L. (1979). Child abuse and deprivation: soul murder. *Journal of the American Psychoanalytic Association* 27:533–559.

Welldon, E. (1988). *Mother, Madonna, Whore*. New York: Guilford.

4

Female Kin: Functions of the Meta-Identification of Womanhood

Judith B. Rosenberger

A woman's sense of a cohesive self hinges on the congruence of a core gender identity as female (Gould 1994, personal communication, Stoller 1968) with the myriad forms in which she expresses that identity in her social context. Discontinuity between the way a woman experiences her female self and the ways she is constructed by important objects and responded to as a woman in her interpersonal world creates conscious and unconscious conflicts both in her self-representation and in her relations to the world of objects through her representations of self-with-other. Discontinuities that can be contained within a meta-representation of womanhood that includes wide variation in the forms of being woman allow the gendered self-representation to remain more cohesive. Conversely, the gendered self, which is a core self-dimension, is painfully disrupted when its expressed forms are interpreted as nonwoman. This is most evident in the ordeal of transsexuals who would sacrifice body integrity through surgery to achieve social congruence: to feel trapped in the "wrong" gender body for one's gendered self-representation is unbearable.

Less dramatic if no less painful are the struggles of females who cannot achieve congruence with the only available prescribed forms of expressed womanhood. The affective tone of these identifications, even including negative valuations or devaluations, plays a secondary role in self-integration to issues of core gendered self-congruence. This is clearly documented in the predominant absorption by females of "second sex" status as synonymous with being woman (de Beauvoir 1952, Gilligan 1982, Lang 1984).

Progression from the formula for womanhood received in early development (mother's intended paradigm and enacted model) to a diversified framework that includes contextual adaptations is mediated by the flexibility of the original representation of being woman. Transmitted from mother to daughter, the boundaries defining woman and nonwoman will be relatively open or closed. Transmission of open boundaries, accompanied by positive affective tone, permits alteration based on individual qualities and social context, and facilitates a meta-identification of womanhood that can be sustaining in a complex and changing world.

WOMANHOOD AS A LINE OF DEVELOPMENT

As with all lines of development, the development of a woman's gendered sense of self proceeds from primary object relationships to the wider realm of relationships. The impact of discontinuity, or continuity, between self-experience as nascent woman in the maternal bond and self-experience as woman in the wider social context depends on mother's own relationship to an internal paradigm of womanhood. More than oedipal object-ties are involved. The pull beyond the maternal matrix (Stiver 1991) to wider expressions of self may be aided by father (Benjamin 1988), but its self-strengthening outcome rests on building bridges between the early female identifications and ongoing relations as equal women, that is, as female kin. A powerful factor in the degree of conflict the girl will experience as she encounters discontinuities in her childhood gendered self-experience is the degree of rigidity in the maternal object's experience of continuity with variations in expressed female identity in her own life. Where mother's intrapsychic representation of her daughter is as beloved female kin in a network of wide variability, daughter's journey through different forms of being woman will be relatively free of the threat of self-fragmentation along this developmental line. Conversely, where deviation from mother's own formula for living out femaleness is rigid and resistant to changing social context, deviation is perilous both intrapsychically and interpersonally.

The literature on the separation-individuation process of all individuals (Ainsworth et al. 1978, Bowlby 1969, 1973, Mahler et al. 1975) provides a general developmental model for the issue of elaborating the self in the present while retaining relational ties to the objects of the past. Features of psychosexual development unique to female identification also have been explored, from Freud (1905, 1931) to the contemporary feminists (Chodorow 1978a,b, Miller 1991, Surrey 1991). The issue is always how the daughter can obtain a secure and valued sense of self within her female core identity, remaining connected in this way to mother, while creating her own expression of female identity in a new context.

This new context contains objects and configurations of relationship and modes of self-expression that both assert her individuation per se and confirm her capacity to function in the here and now of her particular world. It is in this here-and-now arena that the self of primary relationship with mother meets the social imperatives that propel as well as confound the often treacherous separation-individuation process. A broad sense of connection to women, who interpret and live out their biological femaleness and their socially determined role constraints in an infinite variety of negotiations, is a meta-identification as part of womanhood; this meta-identification mediates between the internalized life history of mother and the emerging life history of daughter in a way that allows incorporation of shifting social context.

WOMANHOOD IN A PATRIFOCAL CONTEXT

Mothers and daughters share in their gendered self-representation not only as biologically female, but also as socially constrained by patrifocal culture. These themes are inextricably intertwined, as women are worshiped and feared for their sexual/reproductive powers.

Efforts at social control over expressions of womanhood follow (Cixous and Clement 1986, Irigaray 1993).

This fact complicates the daughter's navigation between the safe port of primary maternal attachment through the rough waters of conflicting social signals (be strong but not tough, be productive as well as reproductive, be your own woman but with a man, etc.). Today's young woman faces more hazards along with more choices, and mother may have no experience interpreting the gendered meanings of choices that go beyond her own decoding of the social ambiguities for women.

The self-in-relation theorists of the Stone Center (Surrey 1991) have addressed the ambiguity of separation-attachment for women by valuing continued attachment among women as the manifestation of empowerment through mutuality. They challenge idealization of separation, independence, and dominance as self-justifying solutions to male anxiety about merger with the powerful maternal object.

Feminist writers have attributed boys' disidentification with mother to their perception of her lower social status and access to power (Chodorow 1978b). Thus the imperative of differentiation from the maternal object for the consolidation of self is an artifact of male gender-identity development based on "matrophobia" (Rich 1976). Gender "prestige overrides libido" (Ortner and Whitehead 1981, p. 24). Meta-identification with womanhood in such contexts spells self-devaluation. Mother–daughter attachment means identification with the oppressed, and a further threat to the only route to power, namely, attachment to a man. Freud's (1905) evaluation of women as possessing weaker superego development reflected the prevailing social context of womanhood, in which power by manipulation of men was women's only recourse. This paradigm is little changed today and little varied across cultures.

FEMALE KIN: A SOURCE OF CONFLICT AND COHESION

Cultural anthropology documents the splintering of women as a social group when their routes to self-preservation and influence are limited to association with powerful males (Lamphere 1974). Conversely, political history has shown the relationship of unification of women, or any group, for mutual aid and benefit, as flowing together with self-valuing. Social action of this kind manifests a positive meta-identification with womanhood overthrowing the eroticization of gender hierarchy (Ortner and Whitehead 1981). Sisterhood as collective membership to extend female influence and self-determination reintegrates mother and daughter (Chodorow 1974, Rich 1976). Lack of positive female kinship ties betrays anxiety about preserving safety through attachment to patriarchy. Therefore, uninterrupted positive affinity of mother and daughter as female kin provides a source of security through many changes in individual expression of womanhood. Mother and daughter partake individually, as well as in their own bond, in their experience of female kinship as a valued meta-identification with womanhood.

Mother's own internal paradigms of female kin influence the girl's acquisitions of her gendered self-representation in two ways. One dimension of mother's internal paradigms is diagrammatic: she illustrates her internal schema of male and female relatedness. Another dimension of mother's internal paradigm is affective: she expresses and thereby inculcates feeling states attached to these male and female configurations of relationship. The collective impact of these diagrammatic/affective transmissions, as they are pulled to one gender pole or the other, builds an internal model of the meanings and workings of womanhood. The meta-identification of womanhood then includes self as female and self in relation to other women. Mother is the source of the girl's core experience of herself as part of the female gender, of the girl's understanding and capacity in her interactions with multiple others of both genders, and of the sum of these variations in an affectively toned paradigm of herself as part of the history, social present, and future of women.

Where this metaidentification is positive in affective tone and strong in interactional possibility, the girl's experience of self is reinforced across myriad contradictory encounters in the here and now. Conversely, when the meta-identification as part of womanhood is negatively toned and interactionally devalued, the girl's experience of self is chronically threatened along gender lines. Both individual power and value, and power and value in relation to social context, are transmitted from mother to daughter by "psychic osmosis" (Rich 1976;

quoting Sylvia Plath, p. 189). Also transmitted are conflicts between self and self-in-relation with other women. When identification with available female kin threatens prestige, because of their social devaluation, self-value may be won only at the cost of devaluing membership in the collective of womanhood.

SHIFTING CONTEXTS FOR WOMEN

Each mother carries a vision for her daughter that is limited by the parameters of her own experience, and literature is replete with stories of mother–daughter struggles between new and old ways. The issues are clearest when daughters cross over boundaries of culture or class; however desirable the adopted social context, mother and daughter still face anxiety and conflict about retaining connection (Alvarez 1991, Dangarembga 1996 to name only two recent examples of these stories). The potential for intrapsychic dislocation accompanying social change is greater for women than men due to the lifelong relational pull in women's development.

Future shock permeates adaptation in the developed world. Each woman embodies womanhood as part of sociocultural history, not just her personal interrelational history and her present sociocultural conditions. The wider the sociocultural context of a woman's experience, the more complex, at least potentially, is her internal paradigm of herself as a woman. For contemporary Western women in advanced societies, especially women with access to higher education, the social context is not only wide but also enormously diverse. The developing woman's mother, raised in a very different context, may engender conflict if her own womanhood identification is threatened by social change. Resistance to the inexorable nature of social change in herself can stifle her daughter's capacity to elaborate her self-representation as a woman who can change and encompass new variations without loss of core connection to the primary relationship. Disidentification with mother as the price of congruence with the prevailing social context leaves a residue of conflict within the gendered self. Conversely, disidentification with a social context that presents new and multiple models of womanhood as the price of retaining connection stifles adaptation to new demands. This quandary is reduced when mother herself can embrace a meta-identification with womanhood as a diverse form in itself. Whatever her personal limits, a mother who can form a positively toned attachment to many variations of womanhood allows her daughter to widen her own scope: attachment by association, rather than replication, makes a bridge.

NEGATIVE IDENTIFICATIONS VERSUS IDENTIFICATION, INCLUDING NEGATIVES

Negative identifications with individual women, especially with the mother and associated maternal objects, signals conflict within the gendered self. Even when maternal or associated objects contain abhorrent or destructive features—abuse, rejection, abandonment, and so on—female kinship needs to remain intact. In one startling example, women of a Brazilian slum have created a positive, mutually supported representation as good mothers and good women that includes detaching from their less robust children, allowing them to perish, while they share the crumbs of their existence only with those children who can bring them comfort (Scheper-Hughes 1990): at their below-subsistence level of survival, female kinship includes the Darwinian principle as a shared rationale. Rather than seeing their nonmothering as abrogating their roles as women, these mothers have adopted an altered vision that preserves self and maintains mutual aid and regard.

Equivalent to the depressive position as a developmental gain over the paranoid-schizoid position (Klein 1964), relinquishing fusion as a progression toward kinship is a condition of reality-based adaptation. Mother and associated primary objects, and thereby womanhood as a whole, acquire more reliable value as a part of the self when failings and misalignments are tolerated within bonds of attachment. Real sisterhood transcends hatred and envy and disappointment about some sisters' qualities. Defensive not-me/not-us solutions weaken the gendered self-representation. Womanhood as a positive meta-identification disowns none of its own, allowing its organizing value to be ruthlessly used (Winnicott 1980) for personal support and affiliation.

CLINICAL SIGNIFICANCE IN COPING

A capacity to form positive, supportive functional ties to diverse women is growth-in-connection put into action. It is what I call the meta-identification with womanhood. The clinical significance of a positive meta-identification with womanhood can be seen in adaptability of functioning as well as in subjective measures of intrapsychic well-being. Regardless of the degree of social change in women's diversity of roles and options for individual self-determination, the contemporary social context requires substantial interdependence in daily life. Interdependence serves crucial social purposes as women fulfill caregiving roles as well as occupational ones. Industrialization, the age of technology, and advances in occupational parity have not altered the fusion of femaleness with domestic responsibility. Women working outside the home have only transferred their interdependence skills, or lack thereof, to the workplace. Moving between these realms, and moving within them, requires cooperation that is not hierarchical. Attempting self-sufficiency is a depleting and isolating business.

It is intrapsychically and socially conflictual for women entering male-identified work roles to attempt to enact them in a male-socialized way. Both self-experience and role fulfillment can be fragmented by attempting to adopt a gender-incongruent manner of functioning. Efforts to find common ground with other women, in support or parallel positions, can baffle women whose representation of womanhood defines mutuality and achievement as antithetical. Women at all tiers of the occupational ladder may have trouble with female configurations that are different from the socially defined paradigms of women's and men's relations that their mothers portrayed. Even if overtly at odds with the new roles a daughter takes on in the workplace, a mother *can* perceive such innovative forms as continuous with her own gendered identity. In such a case, the internal connection retains affirmation and strength for the daughter who is forging a new path. Overt disagreements can be part of the fabric of connection in this way. The doting grandmother who pitches in while complaining that daughter is doing too much may be voicing disagreement but supporting change. A mother also can perceive a daughter's innovative forms of living as adversarial or at least alien to her core gendered self. Disapproval and disidentification, more than disagreement, shape the psychological impact. In such a case, daughter must surmount mighty obstacles to integrating her life choices with her primary experience of self-cohesion. She cannot be a nonwoman without terrible cost to her psychological wholeness, yet she cannot adapt to her social context that requires disparate roles for herself and that presents disparate roles among the women around her.

Conscious commitments to self-determination may be foiled by unconscious conflicts with functional expressions that do not yet fit into the meta-identification of womanhood. Receiving or providing service between women, for instance, may run counter to expectations of nonhierarchical relationships with each other. This is particularly true when women are employing or managing other women who are fulfilling roles traditionally allotted to them as supporters and helpers of men (secretaries, nannies, assistants, etc.). Sharing child care outside the family, including with men, may challenge internalized boundaries and promote confusion and dysfunction. Mother's internal prohibitions based on gender influence daughter's adaptation.

Polarization of roles along gender lines surely is the message of the social-political-economic sector. Choices are forced and exaggerated by resistance to accommodating multiple or innovative roles for women. Conflict even within the literature of feminist advocacy reveals individual women's struggles with whether feminism means attempting to loosen constrictions without breaking from traditional roles (the "mommy track" for female lawyers in firms, for example) or whether such ties to domestic primacy should remain intact, with more male-identified endeavors added on. The issue can be framed as what constitutes irredeemable requirements for a core representation as part of womanhood.

CLINICAL IMPLICATIONS FOR INDIVIDUAL PSYCHOANALYSIS: A CASE EXAMPLE

A constellation of clinical indicators reveals the health-promoting functions of a positive metaidentification with womanhood. A social indicator is a woman patient's participation in a network of women kin that supports her individual endeavors. This network expresses and supports self-cohesion around female gender identity and role flexibility in love and work with men as well as women. Conversely, negative affects and defensive disidentifications reinforce discontinuities in the gendered self and in social roles. Some frequent forms of the conflict include masculinization of the self in performing nontraditional women's roles, alienation from women who are performing traditional roles, and suffusing sexuality with power struggles. Certainly all these painful patterns have many sources, yet strong among them are often themes of a self that is fragmented around issues of being female, being woman, and being part of the sociocultural context of women. Mother–daughter conflicts often remain active, both internally and interpersonally, when such fragmentation abounds. Not just a vehicle for expressing other unresolved conflicts, exclusive and rigid interpretations of womanhood can promote such conflicts.

The case of Elaine is a modern parable about the perils of inadequate meta-identification with womanhood as an affirming self-experience. Elaine had expected praise and star status in her family when she won admission to a prestigious graduate program that propelled her in a career direction similar to her father's, an atypical career path for a woman of her generation. While in school she received general support and approval from her parents. She was able to share interests with her father, or so she thought, and her mother saw her enrollment as a feather in the family social-status cap. Upon graduation and the acquisition of a high-paying job in her field, the difference between approval as advancing the family's interests, and rejection as seeking individual achievement, became all too clear. Being a good student was an appropriate female achievement; being a player in a typically male field was threatening to the men (father and three brothers) and distasteful to the women (mother and one sister). When Elaine told her father of her starting salary—at least equal to his own, it is surmised—he said, "They must be crazy to pay you that." He continued to dote on Elaine's sister, who was nonachieving, frivolous, and happy to wheedle him for money. He had bland camaraderie with her brothers, who were in different types of work. He would not engage with Elaine when she tried to have conversations about their mutual field. Mother took much the same position, expressing empty, generalized approval when confronted ("Of course I'm proud of you"). Bitter and frightened, Elaine blamed her sister's manipulativeness and engaged in futile efforts to disclose her shortcomings and the deviousness of her character, indirectly endorsing the skills of derivative power seeking as superior to independent achievement for women. On the job, Elaine began a continuing pattern of trying to best the male employees and win approval from their superiors (always male), becoming enraged when she was kept out of their circle and not recognized as their better. She lost out on many job promotions, over which she fought many sex discrimination battles. She made no women friends at her level. Instead, she would hire women and then inappropriately attempt to tie them to her with bonds of female loyalty while being their boss, which created conflict and disappointment as these women became confused or attempted to assert their own trajectories of development. She expected blind loyalty from the women based on gender and fellowship from the men based on job sameness, and got neither.

When her parents divorced, Elaine sought her mother's support and approval by taking over her financial support. She expected an alliance against the selfish man, but found hostile dependence instead. Mother much preferred emotional alliance with the dependent daughter, who remained at home, occupied with boyfriends. Coming to treatment at this time, Elaine displayed extreme oscillation between experience of herself as powerful and self-sufficient, but also as helpless and abandoned in relation to her bids for maternal affirmation. This fragmentation of self-representation disrupted her work life, her relation to her family of origin, and her brief and catastrophic marriage to a successful, philandering man. She craved sex and romance, but inevitably transformed nascent relationships with new men into familiar power struggles. When her sister had a baby out of wedlock, her mother supported her enthusiastically. Elaine hastily adopted a child from another country, which gained only grudging support.

My dynamic formulation of this case included careful attention to the fragmentation of Elaine's sense of self as a woman. She was heterosexual as a female, enjoying sex and taking pride in a voluptuous body. She did not eschew women's traditional roles, finding great pleasure in mothering her infant son. Her relations with nannies and sitters, however, upon whom she depended to be able to work, were tumultuous; she found their having their own ways of doing things to be enraging and was critical and arrogant. She continued to work in her field, although here as in her parenting and sexual endeavors she ended up repeatedly in lonely adversity, with a growing string of failed attempts to find a place in a supportive relationship with other adults. Highlighting the issue of womanhood, I saw Elaine struggling in vain to retain intrapsychic connectedness to mother, and other women by extension, due to mother's antipathy to those aspects of Elaine's self that mother herself experienced as male and thereby, in her definition, alien and adversarial.

Through a series of projective identifications, the two daughters of this mother had become embroiled in a struggle between a self-representation as dependent, devalued, passive-aggressive, and accruing power through reproduction on the one hand and as independent, capable, and openly aggressive toward men and things male as the sources of "real" power on the other. Mother expressed her conflict by displaying helpless dependence on Elaine for money and management, while resentfully discrediting the value of her support. Elaine reciprocated by seeking ongoing connection with mother through her contributions, while experiencing despair and rage at the impenetrable disconnection from mother as emotional ally. Just as these gender-polarized definitions of role and self were not reconciled in mother, so too Elaine could not unify her self-experience as a woman both capable and connected.

Many threads and themes of female development appear in this case story, and there are many dynamic explanations. The concept of a meta-identification of womanhood offered an orientation to the dynamic picture that had clinical as well as theoretical potential. How would Elaine configure our relationship? With what parts of her self-representation would she align me? And how would that reveal conflicts with other parts of her self-representation and representation of me?

In the transference, Elaine constructed me as in alliance with her opposition to mother's internal representation of womanhood as debased and dependent. I was clearly seen as a different kind of woman from mother, and our alliance was predicated on this difference. It was only in the second year of treatment that Elaine noticed that I was wearing, as always, a wedding band. She concluded I had never worn it before, had recently acquired it, and when I challenged this as "fact" and asked what her interpretation might mean, she was skeptical and angry. Her shock and dismay enabled us to reveal that this "fact" was at odds with her idealizing transference, which was constructed around one pole of her conflict with womanhood. How could I be aligned with a man and still be a good enough object? Similarly, how could I really be supporting her career strivings while also confronting her alienating power struggles on the job? Did this make me the paternal object who sounded encouraging and then dismissed her? What internal schema of womanhood enabled me to move ahead professionally while she floundered? Was this the price of my attachment, in the same way mother required renunciation of Elaine's personal power and success as the price of her interest and affection?

In working from this overarching perspective, the multiple facets of her fragmented self-experience as a woman came into view. I saw their resolution as lying not only in releasing from repression the component instincts fixating drives at the oedipal and preoedipal levels, nor only in repairing empathic failures with her emerging self-experiences and thereby reestablishing object-relatedness within her present self-experience. Seeing her suffering and dysfunction as generated by her defensive solutions to struggles with biologically driven and relationally driven imperatives provided a valid formulation. I felt, however, that a central role in the creation of this pattern was the representation of her place, and her mother's place, in the sociocultural evolution of womanhood. Both women were attempting to mediate between their individual histories and their current place in the history of women. Mother's inability to advance from her own sociocultural beginnings and daughter's inability to expand from her own sociocultural present were enmiring them in a battle over reality interpretations. They shared their adamancy about their interpretations; I saw this as a potential bridge rather than an uncrossable divide.

My role, as consolidator of the disparate self-fragments of my patient, which included her internal representations of mother, was to synthesize without destruction. I found, and find, the meta-construct of womanhood helpful in this work. My retention of a sense of kinship with both mother and daughter, and with the sister enacting her role in the stable dysfunctional triangle of conflicted female roles, was my internal work against the divisive force of split identifications. My interpretation of Elaine's struggles as expressions of a drama in which she played an equally authentic woman's role supported her ability to value her self-representation as a woman who was joined with a contradicting representation in her mother; contradiction meant conflict, but need not mean destruction if she could expand her own internal representations of female kin. Attaining cohesion meant reconciling within a larger construct their ongoing disparities as well as integrating discontinuities within a self-representation.

SUMMARY

A meta-identification as part of womanhood, flowing through time and across boundaries, describes a space wide and deep enough to include mother–daughter divergence within secure connection, including divergence based on changing sociocultural context. Moreover, the inclusion of difference within the safety of shared womanhood, by recognition of varied contexts, permits functional flexibility as well as intrapsychic elasticity. Women of many circumstances can, and do, form a network of interdependence and mutual affirmation that can be experienced as an extension of their individual identifications as biological females and sociocultural women. The capacities for empathy and caregiving of valuing self-in-relation, established in the primary female relationship dyad, can expand to new and changeable forms. Even identifications as part of the group as a whole, which includes negatively experienced variations of womanhood, rather than disidentification by repudiation as "nonwoman" of such forms, enlarges the potential for self-cohesion across changing women's context and roles.

Women have always enacted many configurations of interdependence and responsiveness across the life span within their families and sociocultural groups. However, historical variations on this theme may not be adequate to contemporary demands as the rate of change and variability accelerates. Therefore, the issues involved in expanding the internal paradigm of womanhood come increasingly to attention in clinical work.

REFERENCES

Ainsworth, M. D. S., Blehar, M., Walters, E., and Wall, S. (1978). *Patterns of Attachment*. Hillsdale, NJ: Erlbaum.

Alvarez, J. (1991). *How the Garcia Girls Lost Their Accents*. New York: Penguin.

Beauvoir, S. de (1952). *The Second Sex*. New York: Knopf.

Benjamin, J. (1988). *The Bonds of Love: Psychoanalysis, Feminism, and the Problem of Domination*. New York: Pantheon.

Bowlby, J. (1969). *Attachment and Loss. Vol. 1: Attachment*. New York: Basic Books.

———— (1973). *Attachment and Loss. Vol. 2: Separation*. New York: Basic Books.

Chodorow, N. (1974). Family structure and feminine personality. In *Woman, Culture and Society*, ed. M. Z. Rosaldo and L. Lamphere, pp. 43–66. Stanford, CA: Stanford University Press.

———— (1978a). Mothering, object-relations, and the female oedipal configuration. *Feminist Studies* 4(1):137–158.

———— (1978b). *The Reproduction of Mothering: Psychoanalysis and the Sociology of Gender*. Los Angeles: University of California Press.

Cixous, H., and Clement, C. (1986). *The Newly Born Woman*. Minneapolis: University of Minnesota Press.

Dangarembga, T. (1996). *Nervous Conditions*. New York: Seal.

Freud, S. (1905). Three essays on the theory of sexuality. *Standard Edition* 7:149–221.

———— (1931). Female sexuality. *Standard Edition* 21:223–246.

Gilligan, C. (1982). *In A Different Voice: Psychological Theory and Women's Development*. Cambridge, MA: Harvard University Press.

Gould, E. (1994). Personal communication.

Irigaray, L. (1993). *An Ethics of Sexual Difference*. Ithaca, NY: Cornell University Press.

Klein, M. (1964). *Love, Hate, and Reparation*. New York: Norton.

Lamphere, L. (1974). Strategies, cooperation and conflict among women in domestic groups. In *Woman, Culture and Society*, ed. M. Z. Rosaldo and L. Lamphere, pp. 97–112. Stanford, CA: University of Stanford Press.

Lang, J. (1984). Notes toward a psychology of the feminine self. In *Kohut's Legacy: Contributions to Self Psychology*, ed. P. Stepansky and A. Goldberg, pp. 51–70. Hillsdale, NJ: Analytic Press.

Mahler, M., Pine, F., and Bergman, A. (1975). *The Psychological Birth of the Human Infant*. New York: Basic Books.

Miller, J. B. (1991). The development of women's sense of self. In *Women's Growth in Connection*, ed. J. V. Jordan et al., pp. 11–26. New York: Guilford.

Ortner, S. B., and Whitehead, H., eds. (1981). *Sexual Meanings: The Cultural Construction of Gender and Sexuality*. London: Cambridge University Press.

Rich, A. (1976). *Of Woman Born: Motherhood as Experience and Institution*. New York: Norton.

Scheper-Hughes, N. (1990). Mother love and child death in Northeast Brazil. In *Cultural Psychology: Essays on Comparative Human Development*, ed. J. W. Stigler et al., pp. 555–565. New York: Cambridge University Press.

Stiver, I. P. (1991). Beyond the Oedipus complex: mothers and daughters. In *Women's Growth in Connection*, ed. J. V. Jordan et al., pp. 97–121. New York: Guilford.

Stoller, R. (1968). *Sex and Gender*. New York: Jason Aronson.

Surrey, J. L. (1991). The "self-in-relation": a theory of women's development. In *Women's Growth in Connection*, ed. J. V. Jordan et al., pp. 51–66. New York: Guilford.

Winnicott, D. W. (1980). *Playing and Reality*. New York: Penguin.

PART II

ADOLESCENCE

Adolescence is best viewed as a way station in development, which proceeds from moving away from primary narcissism toward object relatedness. Classic theory holds that emancipation from the mother occurs at the phallic phase (Loewald 1980) as a prelude to moving through the Oedipus complex. Others, like Bergler (1992), believe that every neurosis is built upon unintegrated sadomasochistic attachments to the preoedipal mother and that the importance given to the oedipal mother is in the service of defense to ward off the monstrous and threatening aspects of the first mother.

According to Freud (1905), puberty sees the overcoming of incestuous fantasies that loosen the attachment to parental authority. While, constitutionally, girls have bisexual potentials, they turn to a heterosexual love object once optimal distance from the mother of infancy has been attained. There are, however, those girls who have never gotten over their parents' authority and have withdrawn their affections only incompletely. They behave like latency girls and retain their childish love far beyond puberty, providing their husbands with devotion but asexual or infantile sexual love.

Anna Freud (1966) saw in puberty the important convergence of physical and mental processes. According to her, adolescence provides the root of sexual life, the capacity for love and character as a whole. Puberty is the first recapitulation of the infantile sexual period. The second takes place with menopause. At each of the phases a relatively strong id confronts a relatively weak ego. It is during adolescence that oral and anal interests come to the surface again and aggressive impulses are intensified to the point of unruliness. In the psychic sphere genitality acquires a dominant position. But the heightening of genital cathexis does not preclude interference from pregenital fixations. The nature and efficiency of defense mechanisms at the ego's command will determine the outcome of the adolescent crisis. Anna Aragno provides an extensive overview of the literature in addition to discussing the period as "a rite of passage." Mary Walsh Donovan describes what happens in the mother–daughter dyad when ambivalence intrudes in the separation-individuation process.

Psychological changes during adolescence have to be understood in relation to bodily changes that lead to an intensification of sexual and aggressive impulses. Upheaval during this period leads to deepening of the girl's later personality (Ritvo 1977). The restructuring of psychic organization is accompanied by a firmer establishment of the ego and the adult ego ideal. First and foremost during adolescence is the girl's perception and attitude toward body changes such as the menarche and breast development. They can be either a source of pride and pleasure or a phenomenon that evokes shame and fear and needs to be concealed. The attitude of the mother is decisive here. How the puberty girl feels and behaves is determined by the ego's response to the original pregenital and phallic strivings and to the quality of object relations to the parents. This aspect is exceptionally illustrated in Aragno's chapter.

The choosing of a heterosexual love object is very complicated. Mastery of the "change of object" depends on the vicissitudes of mother–daughter relations, the quality of the parental marriage, the father's attitude toward women, and the opportunities and roles society at large provides for women. Psychic crises that occur depend on ego organization to allow a regressive revival of the Oedipus complex that includes all aspects of the incomplete mastery of earlier developmental phases.

According to Ticho (1977), preoedipal envy and the resulting aggression toward the mother make a change of object very difficult. The resulting guilt feelings inhibit libidinal investment and identification with her. Consequently, the relationship with the father will also show disturbances. Superego identifications laden with guilt can lead to work inhibitions and/or sexual disturbances. Ticho believes that our "liberated" society with its greater freedom wreaks havoc with female development. With greater freedom, she asserts, there is more fear of male hostility, which is based, in part, on women's competition with men. The flaunting of sexual freedom, including lesbianism, creates more conflicts than the ordinary turbulent adolescent crisis period. Even in liberal homes, girls get a double message. They are to be discreet in their sexual activities but active, curious, and adventurous in all other areas.

REFERENCES

Bergler, E. (1952). The life blood of neurosis-psychic masochism. In *The Superego*, pp. 47–89. New York: Grune & Stratton.

Freud, A. (1966). Adolescence as a developmental disturbance. In *The Writings of Anna Freud, VII*, pp. 39–47. New York: International Universities Press, 1971.

Freud, S. (1905). Three essays on sexuality. *Standard Edition* 7:125–245.

Loewald, H. (1980). On internalization. In *Hans Loewald: Papers on Psycho-Analysis*, pp. 69–86. New Haven, CT: Yale University Press.

Ritvo, S. (1977). Adolescent to woman. In *Female Psychology*, ed. H. Blum, pp. 127–137. New York: International Universities Press.

Ticho, G. (1977). Female autonomy and young adult women. In *Female Psychology*, ed. H. Blum, pp. 139–155. New York: International Universities Press.

5

"Die So That I May Live!" A Psychoanalytic Essay on the Adolescent Girl's Struggle To Delimit Her Identity*

Anna Aragno

Any affect or emotion which, in its raw and unaltered form, is too intense to be controlled by will alone may need its ritual. Without ritual, such energies may inundate the ego and force it into acting out or into obsessive behavior. Ritual brings about containment and acceptance, control of intensity and "dosage." . . . Ritual offers us an alternative to repression for dealing with potentially overpowering affect.

E. C. WHITMONT (1982)
Return of the Goddess

No matter how informed, how knowledgeable, psychologically sophisticated, mature, or ready a mother may believe herself to be regarding her daughter's coming adolescence, *nothing* adequately prepares for the tumultuous rifts and wrenching shifts to occur in this most cherished, most enduring, and uniquely passionate of human bonds. No matter how separate, how individuated and different, how distanced or removed from her mother a daughter may believe herself to have become, throughout a woman's life, at the periphery of female consciousness and at the core of her psyche, there continues to loom the long shadow of mother's influence. At all the great female psychobiological turning points—menarche, parturition, menopause—there lingers an awareness of her having passed by here before us; we contemplate her ways, her manner, her voice. . . . At times of intense stress, it is her face we see in the mirror.

Without the gripping cords of this relationship, from which, with gossamer threads, is woven the fabric of an early self, female identity cannot adequately be forged, since only from such vital kindred coils of attachment spring buoyant psychic muscles from which to bound into autonomous flight. In fact, so life giving is this sap, this indelible succor of maternal introjections and internalizations for the little girl, that without their trenchant stamp—good or bad—there seems to be virtually nothing but a void. "My mother died at the moment I was born, and so, for my whole life, there was nothing standing between myself and eternity; at my back was always a black wind . . ." (1996, p. 1) are the stark words with which Jamaica Kincaid begins her *Autobiography of My Mother*, a work defined by the narrator Xuela's scarred, sad, barren inner life. Unconstrained, with too much freedom, unsustained by an internal maternal image impinging on the inner eye, this woman's existence is propelled only by her own aimless uncontoured dark nihilism. Yet within the confines of this bond, nurtured by all its benefits, lifelong there nags a remnant longing to revive or replicate the symbiotic residues of an unparalleled blissful union, a longing tempered only by the polarized draw of dominant dimensions pulling for differentiation, independence, separateness, fulfillment. "The more I grow away from her and define myself, the more I see this other person she was before she became Nancy Friday's mother," writes Friday (1977, p. 413), at the close of a book transparent in its efforts to help free its author from the grips of an entrenched ambivalence. "That is the magic," she concludes, "not that we can ever re-create that Nirvana of love that may or may not have existed between us as mother-and-child, but that once we have separated, we can give each other life, extra life, each out of the abundance of her own" (p. 413). Thus disentangled, the distant strains, still echoing from splits or polarized regressive and progressive tensions, can finally come to a harmonic resolution. Dropping the illusory shackles that maintain mother as omnipotent or as the sole impediment to the fulfillment of a personal identity in a mutually exclusive battle—my mother *or* myself—opens the door to the possibility of establishing a mutually enriching and sustaining relationship between two women: the woman who is our mother and the woman who is her daughter.

This chapter explores the often tortuous pathway trod by mothers and daughters today, one filled with hurdles, unforeseen obstacles, and sudden bursts of storm that may or may not lead to such a place. I will speak from the voice of personal experience, my own and that of other mothers, as well as through the ideas of seminal psychoanalytic thinkers and anthropological studies of rites of passage in order to contrast two very different solutions to this necessary life crisis—that of ritual versus that of rebellion. I am interested in understanding the phenomenology of the daughter's struggle to delimit her identity as this relates to women in general by observing how this struggle is played out in the dialectic of specific mother–daughter pairs, in a particular time and place, with reference to the particulars of their situation and the culture in which they live. And I am interested in examining the dynamics and features of female initiations and rites of passage in the belief that the nature and function of their externalized symbolism has much to tell us of the timeless psychological elements constituting this transitional, normative crisis that, in this culture, must be endured in the private crucible of the home.

One cannot speak of "identity" without considering the impact of psychosocial factors on individual psyches, just as one cannot understand psychomorphic transformation without examining the dynamics of crisis and transition in and of itself. Thus, "identity," and its closely allied concept of "self," is formed in adolescence through the resolution of conjoint biological, psychological, and social forces, fused at the interstice between simultaneously finding one's place and role within a social group and separating and individuating from the relationships and attitudes of childhood.

*   *   *

I am a daughter and a mother of daughters, bridging two generations, two continents, two eras. The gap between my daughters' world view and my own is wider, deeper than it might have been had we shared the continuity of upbringing and education that comes from common cultural values. Yet change between one generation and the next, particularly for women, has been so rapid and so widespread during this century that our daughters have before them a panoply of possibilities and alternatives that were unthinkable for our mothers and grandmothers, options and life choices that have, in great part, been won for them through the thrust of our generation and the efforts of our foremothers.

From my vantage point along a multigenerational matriline, like a mirror with two faces, I can look backward at my mother, my grandmothers, and great-grandmothers, noting how the circumstance and style of each of these women impacted on the outcome of their daughter's characters and compromises. And I can look forward to my own daughters' futures with a dawning awareness of how my own psychological inheritance, our family circumstance, and the culture and time in which we live will have influenced their development, their characters and choices. Transgenerational transmissions of patterns of anxiety, communication, regulation of self-esteem, attitudes toward femininity, sexuality, education, marriage, motherhood, men, and so on seem to seep through unconsciously from mother to daughter. The residues of expectations, disappointments, assigned roles, habits, and unquestioned beliefs, colored by historical events, descend from one generation to the next, seemingly by osmosis, through stories and histories that transform and are transformed as they are transmitted. Our heritage is in us as are the narratives of our mothers' memories. Like the Russian *matrioshka* dolls, carved to fit snugly one inside the other, unconscious representations interpenetrate through the generations, seeping silently into a psyche that is at first porous, accommodating, undifferentiated.

Despite our best intentions, when our daughters' adolescence pushes, we snap, finding ourselves trapped once more in the painful terrain to which we had determined never to return, struggling not to, yet inevitably repeating our own mother's patterns of response. Pressured by her persistent cries and outcries, her deeds of defiance and taunting opposition, up springs our mother's voice from within, ardently preserving *our* values, *our* expectations, *our* integrity, *our* ideals. Having sworn we would never thwart as we were thwarted, we find ourselves this time on the other side, forced somehow to be the ones to impose interdiction, to endure insult, to restrain, threaten, set limits. Uncannily, our daughters find our weakest spot: when hair was dyed or kinked into a reckless mop and clothes draped to disclose more than they covered, I tried to look the other way. But when my daughters fell into the mesmerizing claws of the media and embraced the laws of an avid consumerism, when rudeness became violent and acrid disdain, my hair stood up on end.

Unwittingly and unwillingly we are dragged along to participate in a scenario and perform a role we vigorously resist, to serve a function for our daughters' development from which we recoil with all our might. The function is that of a trampoline—that from which to rebound. Separation, after all, entails separating from something. As one daughter put it, "Mother is the biggest part of what you say 'no' to." Yet mother must also never be too far away. For those women obliged to raise their girls alone, the pain of their daughters' devaluing provocations and smoldering disdain often appears unbearable. One is rejected by virtue of being mother, but one is also rejected for being perceived as *having been* rejected. Without a father to buffer the sudden rise of unmanageable new tensions, emotions, and behaviors, the entire force of the storm is funneled onto mother who, often without familial or societal support, must weather it alone. For some mother–daughter pairs, the damaging rift created as the aftermath of this tempestuous time leaves wounds that continue to fester, or that end up shaping a lifetime of acrimonious discord and frustrating attempts at reconciliation. For others, endurance and acceptance finally triumph. The outcome seems to be very much determined by degrees of personal awareness and the pliancy or fluidity of personality structure, but even more by the essential quality of the mother–daughter fit in a bond the nature of which was established in mutual interactions from the very beginning.

In my interviews with a diverse group of mothers living in the New York City area, again and again I was impressed by the richness, variability, and complexity of their experiences of this phase and by the diverse patterns of factors contributing to the nature of its resolution. More and more it became clear to me that the mother–daughter dance, particularly in this phase, is a duet embedded in a broader familial, community, and societal context in which the culture exerts an indomitable influence, pulling toward standardizing adolescent trends and behaviors. A culture that subtly exploits the accretion of chaotic aggressive and sexual drive typical of this age group, catering to exhibitionism and impulsive tendencies by serving up a seemingly endless supply of provocative images for them to feed on, is actively undermining values that parents struggle to uphold, virtually manufacturing adolescent "problems" that are then thrown back on the parent to resolve. The pull away from early object ties parallels a corollary pull toward peer groups and the outside world at large. In infancy, mother was the environment; for the toddler and latency child, an expanding social horizon encompasses family, school, and friends. But for the adolescent, the culture *is* the environment; the tasks of early adulthood, finding one's place by choosing a profession and a mate, loom ahead in the distance as the youngster turns away from home and toward society. A genuinely personal identity, unfettered by premature foreclosure or defensive identificatory solutions, can begin to crystallize only through activities of discrimination, experimentation, and elimination, developmental processes of trial and error engaging biological, psychological, cognitive, and psychosocial aspects, all operating in dynamic interaction. For the girl these are expressed through a persistent and often harrowing turning away from mother and mother's ways. Childhood ended, the symbiotic spell between mother and daughter is broken.

Virtually every mother I spoke with recalled nostalgically, and with deep joy, a lengthy period of harmonic bliss with her little girl, a sort of prolonged psychical union that seems to characterize the more than "good enough" early mother–daughter tie. My daughter was "enchanting," "blessed," "affectionate," "easy-going" . . . these mothers chimed in chorus; she had such "grace," "ease," "charm," "everything seemed to go smoothly with us"; she was "funny," "sweet," "affectionate," "easy to get along with"; "we had such fun together" echo their reports. Where they differ markedly, however, is in their willingness or unwillingness to recognize or even acknowledge the occurrence of a fundamental shift in the relationship during puberty and adolescence. Their individual accounts—ranging from complete denial to intense distress—say much about their daughters' ensuing solutions.

I too have only glowing memories of my enchanting daughters in whose childhoods I thoroughly delighted. Both, in very different ways, were filled with an abundance of grace and charm and intelligence and spunky individuality, their dispositions warmly drawn to others, and their natural differences in temperament and taste so clearly marked from the outset as to compel consideration of their differential rates of development and personality style. Perhaps because we epitomized an ever more familiar family genre—the single parent in urban-isolation-household—we formed a tightly knit, loving unit, my children talking freely with me about everything, trusting me implicitly and counting on me to be their rock, their lighthouse, and extended family all wrapped up in one, all the time! Peripherally, I was aware of the difficulties some parents were having with their "impossible" adolescents, but I was sure that whatever was happening "out there" would never happen to us. We talked things through; I made an effort to understand my daughters, we were emotionally connected, difficulties were resolved supporting differences and encouraging empathy. Nothing, it seemed, could go *that* wrong.

With two years separating them, when my first slid silently into puberty and drastically distanced herself from me, I felt I had lost a daughter. When my second, a far quieter and stuck-to-mommy child, approached the same age, however, I was not prepared for what was in store. *"Die so that I may live!"* she screamed at me, flinging herself on the floor of our hallway. And with this resounding battle cry she announced her entrance into a long, drawn-out struggle to disengage from me while never straying too far, a struggle from which it was impossible that I emerge unscathed.

While my first daughter's natural sociability, drives, and talents provided easy avenues for self-expression and energy expenditure, and appropriate vehicles to assist her separation from me, the second, in order to avoid overt competition yet needing to distinguish herself, resorted to aggression and rebellion to define her distance. Even at the height of her adolescence, language continued to be an accessible bridge for communication between me and my firstborn. The second adopted language as a weapon. All attempts to complete verbal exchanges were abruptly and sometimes violently truncated. Rudeness, disobedience, a provocative arrogance, and—most trying—an out-and-out debunking of the cherished cultural and aesthetic values she was raised with became the outward manifestations of an intense inner struggle to differentiate and disidentify herself from her sister and me while warding off a powerful pull backward against a less compelling call to go forward. Throughout her childhood we had been exceptionally close. In contrast to her sister's gregarious spunkiness and outward interests, she was unequivocal in her preference for her mother's company and the comforts of home. When, seemingly overnight, she transformed me into a mortal enemy, I attempted to continue to reach her in the old ways: understanding, reasoning, interest, empathy, dialogue. This, of course, proved to be not only futile, but possibly even exacerbating. The girl's behavior is *designed* to accomplish psychic differentiation, to distance and loosen early object ties. The *last* thing she wants is for mother to understand her! Interpsychic separation is an interactive dance, choreographed individually to satisfy the subtlest of sensibilities. For some, even an affectionate glance is enough to evoke an irate disengagement. The more the mother reaches to reconnect, whether consciously or unconsciously, the more decisively is the daughter compelled to sever this connection.

For the mother, it is the force and suddenness of the shift that is most disarming: "My daughter was a wonderful, upbeat, happy child. One day I came home to a completely different person," recounts a colleague, who described living with her 15 ½-year-old as "the hardest, most painful" time of her life. For her, the worst has been the relentlessness of the intensity and the degree of her daughter's verbal and, at times, even physical aggression. She describes a total loss of impulse control, abrupt shifts in ego states, and the repeated enactment of two sides of a conflict, simultaneously pulling and pushing her mother away: "Mommy feed me/I hope you burn in hell" . . . with the ominous declaration "One of us has to die!" (an echo of my own daughter's words) embodying the terrific struggle to overcome an infantile self while concomitantly decathecting the mother of childhood. Blaming the culture, this mother bemoans the lack of familial or societal support: "There is no one to help control or deflect the intensity," she says, adding, "I have no model. . . . My mother was strict with me into my twenties. . . . Such behavior was unthinkable." Yet, as she speaks, the premature death of her own father and the absence of her daughter's father appear important and influential factors.

A mother whose daughter's entrance into puberty coincided with her separation from a terminally ill husband recalls, "This was an extremely turbulent time in which a number of problems converged." For her, the crucial absence of a father is quite conscious: "There was no father for her, no husband for me." Yet the rancor runs deeper, and the difficulties leading to a subsequent rift are foreshadowed in the following:

> My daughter is very different from me. She has more of his traits. He might have been more patient with her, but he was too ill. Initially, puberty seemed innocuous, but then she pulled away. She stopped sharing, became rude and angry. It was so unpleasant, I would try to get away. We each had our separate existence. I remembered my own mother—she's so much in me. I tried so hard not to do it like her.

In this mother's estimation her daughter's therapy had a negative effect, further confusing and complicating their relationship, "and then," she recalls, "there was the sibling problem. Her younger brother and I always got along so well." When her daughter returned from college, for a time they tried again, but, she comments, "The more I gave, the more she wanted," their essential misattunement leading eventually to an irreparable rift.

Another mother of two daughters, whose marriage similarly was disintegrating during her older daughter's puberty, describes years of intense family upset. At a conscious level, she speaks about her daughter's inappropriate attire, her premature sexual acting out, her provocative and aggressive behavior: "We had tumultuous arguments at the time," she recalls. "I was the one who had to discipline her and set limits." Less conscious in the recounting of the following event is its prefiguring of what was to become a tragic and permanent schism, splitting the family in two. "One Christmas Day, her behavior toward myself and her sister was so outrageous, I had to tell her that by her attitude she was making a choice to leave my house for good." Her daughter left, taking up residency with her father and subsequently moving in with a college professor, severing all contact with her sister and mother. After a bitter divorce and an acrimonious parallel court battle in which the daughter, backed by her father, brought charges against her mother, the rift had become irreparable. "At one point it was devastating," recounts this mother. "I would look at her in court, totally alienated. . . . It was hard to believe this was my daughter. Now I don't know if I could ever let her come back into my life."

The above are extreme cases, in two of which the disruption of divorce coincided with the daughter's early adolescence, conflicting with the developmental needs, particularly in this age group, for family and parental stability. They illustrate how deleterious it is when a youngster's inner psychological struggles are played out in the context of a family backdrop of real schism and discord in which neither parent can function in their required roles, a scenario that precipitates the externalization and acting out—rather than resolution—of their splitting, disengagement from parental authority, loosening of early object ties, and oedipal revival. The daughter's often extraordinary attunement to her mother's emotional states and unconscious messages further complicates these issues. When the father does not buffer and the excessively strained mother is not available or able to absorb her daughter's ambivalence and separation needs, the daughter's development will inevitably suffer.

Given the dramatic psychobiological disequilibrium brought about by the hormonal and bodily changes that mark the arrival of puberty and entrance into the adolescent passage, and given the formidable psychophysical adjustments now required for maturation and an autonomous personality structure, it is all the more striking when this phase goes unnoticed. In fact, several of the mothers denied its very existence! Negation ranged from incisive denial—"I feel this is a myth. I don't buy it!"—to total obliteration of difference—"I have no particular recollection of her adolescence . . . things just unfolded . . . she slid easily from one phase into the next . . . the same wonderful creature as when she was tiny. . . ." Yet these mothers' attitudes toward their daughters' transition into sexual maturity and adulthood adumbrate the degree and nature of their daughters' necessary compensation vis-à-vis their mothers, foretelling their ensuing solutions in career choice and love relations. The former, battling a weight problem, resorted to early marriage and virtually no professional direction; the latter opted to enter her mother's field but in a capacity that would always be complementary to that of her mother rather than competitive. For the first mother, adolescence was merely a continuation of the "problem solving," which raising her daughter was very much about. The "problem" of adolescence, in her view, occurred only to parents who were "seriously remiss" in dealing with issues as they came up along the way, and when there was not "a strong connection" maintained between them. The essential need for a blissful continuation of the second mother (who nursed her daughter until well into her third year) was met by the compliance of a daughter who could tolerate such lack of separation and would subordinate her own individuation for the sake of meeting her mother's needs. The rewards of this continued union, however, are transparent in her mother's gratification and her glowing remarks. "My daughter was a blessed child, and I a very blessed parent. I always trusted her . . . she is the same poised, sensible, very centered person she always was."

Another mother was motivated to submerge or minimize the difficulties of this phase with her three daughters due to her own history and experiences at this age as a survivor and refugee in World War II: "Does it have to be so very difficult?" she queried, remembering mostly her own separation anxiety at a time when their behavior was relatively "contained." Theirs was an intact, highly religious household in which both parents shared traditional family values. While recounting the distressing story of the premature marriage of one of her daughters to a man outside their faith, however, this mother was unaware of the rebellious and defiant nature of this object choice.

Yet no matter how much a mother may want or try to smooth out the wrinkles of this phase, the fact remains that puberty and adolescence represent stages of organismic crisis, a second individuation, in which a major upheaval of the entire personality and sense of self, with correlate psychical restructuralization, must occur before an individuated, more autonomous organization can reconstitute at a maturational level appropriate for the demands of young adulthood. "In general terms," writes Blos (1962), "it can be said that a *quantitative* increase in drive characterizes preadolescence . . ." leading to the end of the latency period: "the child becomes more difficult to reach, to teach and to control. Whatever education has accomplished over the previous years in terms of instinct control and social conformity seems now doomed to disintegration" (p. 58).

By its very nature, adolescence is a fluid, liminal, transitional period of internal disequilibrium and external disharmony during which mother and daughter are propelled along by the forceful momentum of development into a complete reorganization of the conscious and unconscious threads that constitute their bond and relationship to each other, a process occurring within ongoing inter-actions, the quality and nature of which, in great part, determine its character and outcome. Separation is a difficult, slow, and painful process, often highlighting unconscious points of reciprocal projective and introjective contact between mother and daughter carried over from earlier stages that may now threaten to pull excessively toward regressive fixations or re-present themselves with renewed force, pushing for a progressive resolution. This is, as A. Freud (1958) aptly put it, a "normative interruption of peaceful growth; . . . the uphold-ing of a steady equilibrium during the adolescent process is in itself abnormal" (p. 275). Every step in the course of development requires of both parent and youngster that they be able to renounce former positions and gains in favor of relational readjustments promoting growth and maturation (A. Freud 1969). The mother is now put in the impossible position of having somehow to affirm, or at least contain, her daughter's relentless antagonism, to preserve their primal threads through a relational gale. Or, to turn to a metaphor, to safeguard the foundations of the house while the entire structure—walls and interior—undergo complete remodeling.

In the face of feeling betrayed, discarded, devalued, and provoked to boot, the mother must be able to tolerate an increasing sense of loss while standing still witnessing her daughter's petulant disengagement, realizing that this is the only way for her to establish an identity that is truly distinct and uniquely hers. Yet the energic rupture of their affiliation and mutually gratifying unconscious interdependency may deal a severe blow to a mother's narcissistic investments in her daughter, investments imbued with idealized conscious and uncon-scious wishful projections that now, in the harsh light of the reality of their differences, must be given up. From the daughter's side, in order to become a separate individual she has to "come to terms, consciously and unconsciously, with her mother's conscious and unconscious expectations," writes Bergman (1987): "There is an interweaving in the girl's identity formation of her own actual and increasingly intrapsychic experiences with the expectations and wishes of the mother that are communicated in myriad subtle ways" (pp. 388–389). These silent strings, like secure moorings, are a strong inducement backward to the fused identifications and rapturous merger of child-hood. Their reciprocal relinquishment is part and parcel of the embattled struggle, as well as the cause of the depressive aura of mourning accompanying this phase. Yet this intense inner involve-ment with mother's image and voice persists, although less conflict-ually, throughout a woman's life. Schafer (1974) finds that the girl and later the woman continues to be internally involved in a "profoundly influential, continuously intense and active relationship, not only with her real mother, but with the idea and imaged presence of her mother, and with her identification with this mother . . ." (p. 476).

The unparalleled complexity and tenacious hold of this primal mother–daughter bond cannot be overestimated. Daughters are in the difficult and paradoxical position of having emerged from, internalized and identified with, the very same person from whom they must now in part disidentify and psychologically separate (Bergman 1987, Friedman 1980). Unlike boys, whose differential essence is anatomi-cally built in, the birth of a little girl's self stems from sameness. Her psychic differentiation will be complicated by the added necessity of teasing apart the strands of a union that must selectively leave partial gender and role identifications intact, while vigorously severing those threads that bind her psychically to her mother's needs and will. It is, of course, at this developmental juncture that many daughters trip, fall, stumble, or become stuck. Her awakening to the call for separation throws her into conflicts and tensions for which her ego is unprepared, producing the characteristic ambitendency Mahler (1981) stressed as being "built into the task of the ontogenetic achievement of separation-individuation" (p. 628). Ambivalence, moodiness, dejection are the hallmarks of transitional crisis points, when the self is neither what it was nor what it is yet to become. Perhaps the endogenous strength of aggression and the degree to which it has been allowed to be employed for development and growth will now once again be of decisive importance. Normally, the robust distancing and disengaging interactions of this phase, expressed in countless acts of opposition, rudeness, abject withdrawals, and explosive tantrums—which wear the mother down—are designed to create a rift, to define difference. They are the manifest counterpart to the lengthy and painstaking labor of psychic disentanglement.

The daughter's separation process unfolds through acts of demarcation, delineation, experimentation, elimination, gradually carving out a path of autonomous choices that leaves distinct boundaries in its wake. She is exquisitely sensitive to any form of maternal intrusion into this process and wards it off with a vengeance. The little girl, whose learning had proceeded by mimicry, imitation, and internalization, often delighting in being "just like" her mommy, is now seemingly consumed by the need to reject and eject her mother, insofar as she still represents and calls up the interchanges and representations of an infantile self—one cannot be like that from which one is differentiating.

A most painful aspect of this reciprocal demand from the mother's side is to "facilitate that separation process—to stand back and permit it to happen—in fact, to encourage it," writes Friedman (1980), while never herself precipitating disjunctions, for it is precisely in the "context of emerging differences that the need for the continuation of a primary, core bond most clearly arises" (p. 92). Friedman advocates a continuing, supportive connectedness, noting that young women struggling for autonomy are also striving to maintain "a link, a stabilizing connection with their past" (p. 92).

Paradoxically, one has to have experienced a deep union and been solidly attached in order to initiate detachment and individuation. In fact, the absence of this powerful bond, as A. Freud (1958) remarked, "far from making adolescence easier, constitutes a real danger to the whole inner coherence of the personality during that period. In these cases, adolescence is preceded frequently by a frantic search for a mother image; the internal possession and cathexis of such an image seems to be essential for the ensuing normal process of detaching libido from it for transfer to new objects, i.e., to sexual partners" (p. 266).

From the classical perspective, preadolescent drive organization in normal female development is dominated by defenses against the regressive pull toward the preoedipal mother and attending self-representations of early childhood. "The struggle," writes Blos (1962) from this orientation, "is reflected in the many conflicts which arise between mother and daughter during this period" (p. 68). Yet this is a dialectic, an interpsychic pas de deux, stimulating reciprocal responses to which both mother and daughter continuously contribute in a bond described as "a two-way relationship based on a common identity and deeply felt association" (Friedman 1980, p. 92). It is impossible to loosen or modify the nature of this relationship unilaterally (Levy 1969). The mother has to accommodate to the daughter's development with behavioral and psychological adjustments that yield to change—the more she resists, the more the daughter will push, flashing the characteristic fierceness of this age group. "The primary momentum of growth," writes Mahler (1981), "the aggressive impetus, is such that it is bound to push through obstacles in its way; thus, it gives rise to phenomena that, from the observer's point of view, have accretions of violence from the beginning of life" (p. 626).

For her part the young girl, like the toddler, is again "haunted by the blissful sensory (not cognitive) memory of symbiosis" (Mahler 1981, p. 632), a yearning for the status quo, combined with an inexorable propulsion toward change. Forever torn between the safety of sameness and empathy, and the disquieting pull toward dissension and differentiation, at the epicenter of the female psyche there remains a longing to return to an "ideal state of self" (Mahler 1981, p. 632). Thus, writes Blos (1962), "The force with which the girl turns away from infantile fantasy and sexuality is proportionate to the strength of the regressive pull in the direction of the primal love object, the mother. Should she surrender, act out the regression by displacement, or return to the early preoedipal fixation point, a deviate adolescent development will follow" (p. 71).

Such were the outcomes in several of the interviewed cases, which, while certainly not an exhaustive sampling, nevertheless provide sufficient variability to illustrate each of the above posited deviations in development suggested by Blos. In two of the cases the daughters surrendered their individuality to stronger, more dominant or needy mothers. One of the daughters acted out a regression via displacement onto a therapist, but then, torn between the two, abruptly abandoned both therapist and mother, remaining stuck in ambivalence at a preoedipal fixation point that allowed for no resolution. Another acted out her intense splitting through an oedipal victory and displacement, also remaining fixated at this juncture and permanently alienated from her mother. I have observed several daughters who have apparently failed to make partial or selective identifications and seem rather to have taken on their mother's style and manner wholesale in a global identification that renders them, even in attire and appearance, virtual facsimiles of their mothers. Other daughters—particularly those whose fathers were conspicuously absent during this time—eventually found their way, although only after long, drawn-out years with their mothers punctuated by intermittent displacements onto boyfriends. So complex are the vicissitudes of the separation process, there is no telling how, or in what way, the daughter's identity will be affected by the nature and degree of her identifications with her mother.

Mahler (1981) commented on the crucial importance of the mechanism of selective or partial identifications for the successful achievement of the separation-individuation process, a task enormously facilitated by the muting and modeling functions of the father, whose presence can dilute and attenuate the intensity of cathectic focus on the mother. "Differentiation—particularly in terms of boundary formation—is from the mother, not from the father," writes Mahler (p. 631). This is true in early development as well as at this developmental recapitulation. Although peripherally a participant in the early symbiotic sphere, father was never truly part of the tight mother–daughter orbit; therefore, his representations and the real relationship with him are less wrought with regressive elements (Mahler 1981). Now, in the face of her budding sexuality and urgent need to turn away from mother, relating to her father offers the daughter a secure, less contaminated interactive playing field in which to toy with revived oedipal feelings while trying her wings at increasingly separate and autonomous functioning. Father's absence and/or disinterest at this crucial time in the crystallization of his daughter's personality immeasurably increases the difficulties she will have in negotiating the regressive pull inherent in her relationship with her mother, as well as impairing her new and necessary narcissistic investment in her awakening femininity. Moreover, the unavailability of alternate, less conflictual relationships to deflect from mother imposes an enormous burden on the mother, further straining their relationship. The exclusivity and forced proximity of the single-parent household—particularly when there are no siblings or relatives nearby—aggravates the daughter's disengagement process, leading to explosive, even violent, outbursts that express her desperate need to gain distance from an all too absorbing closeness. Aggression then becomes the only available means by which to create and titrate distance. As in infancy, when aggression was used "in the service" of disengagement in a primary separation-individuation process, now it serves to implement and maintain individual identity (Mahler 1981, p. 625). It is important in this context to emphasize that "action" in early adolescence is the vehicle and necessary precursor—the outer form—to what will subsequently become internalized as psychic boundary and structure.

"It was about finding out what was me . . . the things I liked, the people I liked, what made me comfortable . . . ," recalls a 26-year-old daughter; ". . . about creating my own circle, my own order, my own atmosphere . . ." she continues. "I wanted to divorce myself from my mother . . . to stand outside of my family . . . not too far away, but enough to look at them and feel separate from them. I was defining myself by a process of elimination and finding . . . it is still happening. . . . Elimination and finding, the two are one and the same. . . ." Succinctly, and highly attuned to her own development, she concludes, "I was beginning to find my way in the world. College was about finding my way in the group, now I'm finding my way in any group, anywhere, any time." Another 24-year-old daughter recalls a lengthy period in which she sought separateness, yet closeness, by befriending surrogate families with whom she could experience the relational medley and traditional, large-family atmosphere lacking in her own one-dimensional home. For both, their physical activities during this period were direct expressions of their personal individuating and experimentation needs: "Doing, it's about doing— all these things." For the first, her vocation and early professional choice—"who I was"—proved to be the most outstanding vehicle for organizing and expressing her identity; for the second, the surrogate families were a way station to finding her own peer group in which she felt she belonged and which, in turn, provided a springboard for the ensuing exploration of intellectual and vocational pursuits. For the first, a professional self guided the course of her individuation; for the second, relationships and affiliation were the launching pad for finding her individuality.

Another 25-year-old daughter just emerging from a prolonged and difficult adolescence feels that the struggle "to get my mother to understand me" was too embittering. She is finding herself by default, essentially by turning into her mother's opposite and remaining apart. Two other daughters in their late twenties have reconciled with their mothers, but only partially. "I know there are certain things she will never approve of or understand about me," says one; ". . . I am resigned to the fact that we are just too different from each other," says the other.

Antagonism, disobedience, rebellion, defiance, like the strident "No!" of the toddler, are the unpleasant behavioral referents of a slow process of psychic differentiation, a developmental impetus toward separateness and individuation fueled by the difficult and painful necessity of disengaging from childhood object ties, dislodging early internalizations, and disempowering parental authority (the superego of childhood) — "a process that alone makes possible the opposition, which is so important for the progress of civilization between the new generation and the old" (Freud 1905, p. 93).

Several threads emerge in the above; they constitute interactive processes, requisite cathectic and relational shifts negotiated at this time, which have been documented and accounted for by various psychoanalytic theorists and theories. In fact, the psychoanalytic exploration of the adolescent passage began with Freud's (1905) discussion of puberty in "Three Essays on the Theory of Sexuality," the "conceptual scaffolding" (p. 83) of which was based on his theory of libido development, and has progressed to the present through major contributors such as Aichorn (1925), Bernfield (1938), Blos (1941, 1962), Erikson (1946, 1980), A. Freud (1936, 1958), Jones (1922), and Spiegel (1951, 1958), to name the earlier and most outstanding. This notwithstanding, and despite the persistent glaring relevance in clinical work of the pivotal importance of this maturational juncture, and the urgent need for an expanded psychoanalytic understanding of life-span transitions and development, adolescence continues to be underemphasized clinically and only partially understood, a distant cousin, if no longer the "stepchild in psychoanalytic theory" (A. Freud 1958, p. 259).

In the most general terms, psychoanalysis views the chaotic crisislike nature of the adolescent personality as reflective of a transient fluidity underlying the normative disequilibrium of phases of psychic transformation. The theory holds that the dynamic balance of internal structural equilibrium is weakened at times when an abrupt upsurge of instinctual drive pressure exceeds the current ego's integrative and functional capacities, thereby precipitating a temporary personality upheaval. The apparent structural disintegration, however, precedes reintegration and reorganization at a new maturational level with corresponding reapportioning of id, superego, and ego ideal, and a newly strengthened ego at the helm. The synthetic and integrative functions of the ego, together with changing defensive patterns, have to catch up with both the quantitative increases in drive activity and the qualitative maturational changes this demands, particularly at puberty, so that "the so-called adolescent upheavals are no more than the external indications that such internal adjustments are in progress" (A. Freud 1958, p. 264). The great organismic perturbation encumbent upon the hormonal and somatic changes precipitated by menarche, requiring integration and the achievement of mature genital sexuality, are interpreted psychoanalytically in terms of the overturning of the previous libidinal economic stability in a structural imbalance wherein "a relatively strong id confronts a relatively weak ego" (A. Freud 1936, p. 140). According to libido theory, sexual life has two starting points and it is at the earliest of these, the preoedipal stage of infantile development in the first year of life, and *not* at puberty, that "the crucial steps in development are taken" (A. Freud 1936, p. 139). Puberty represents the first nodal point in psychosexual development that recapitulates the precursor infantile period, of which the second will be the climacteric (A. Freud 1936). Both A. Freud (1936) and Jones (1922) emphasize the epigenetic nature of the psychosexual stages, each a "renewal and resuscitation" (A. Freud 1936, p. 189) of what came before, Jones (1922) going so far as to ascribe this recapitulative quality to a "general law" of development, so that "these stages are passed through on different planes at the two periods of infancy and adolescence, but in very similar ways in the same individual" (A. Freud 1958, p. 256). Blos (1962) also makes mention of the fact that there are always residuals carried over from previous stages, or "partial retardations" (p. 130), which, it is hoped, will become adaptively woven into "stable expressions through work, love and ideology" (p. 130) in the consolidation of personality at the close of adolescence.

Spiegel's (1951) exhaustive "Review of Contributions to the Psychoanalytic Theory of Adolescence" best summarizes these early formulations of the principal developmental tasks of this passage according to the psychosexual and structural schemas as essentially "the establishment of the primacy of the genitals and . . . the capacity to find a non-incestuous object" (p. 298). In the following, Spiegel paints an evocative picture of this phase depicted through structural metaphors:

> One gets the impression that in adolescence the personality is melted down, becomes molten and fluid, and ultimately hardens again in what is to remain as the characterological core. Before that hardening, it appears that the ego's habitual relations to superego, id and external reality are frequently overthrown. If this process does not take place to some extent, if the ego remains rigid in the face of the new demands of the id, a premature setting of the personality mold with subsequent impoverishment of the emotional life will result. [1951, p. 376]

Both Spiegel and A. Freud, however, draw attention, respectively, to the inadequacy of psychosexual and structural concepts in accounting for the clinical phenomenology and specific etiology of adolescent developmental disorders. A. Freud (1958) emphasizes the need for amplification of structural concepts to accommodate the unique quality of those modifications occurring in inner and outer object relations that appear to be exclusive for this period, pointing out that "the danger is felt to be located not only in id impulses and fantasies, but *in the very existence* of the love objects of the individual's oedipal and pre-oedipal past" (my italics), while Spiegel (1958), in pinpointing the establishment of a relatively stable identity as a central task of adolescence, concludes therefore, "It is impossible to orient oneself in some of the clinical phenomenology of adolescence without introducing the concept of the self" (p. 299).

Building heavily on Freud, the early studies of the forties and fifties cumulatively contributed considerably to the psychoanalytic understanding of the psychological shifts of adolescence while simultaneously highlighting the theoretical shortcomings of limiting those observations to existing developmental schemas. It is not, however, until the seminal work of Blos (1962) on the subject that the complex network of libidinal, psychosexual, adaptive, structural, and objective relational threads, heretofore disparately presented and unevenly comprehended, is subsumed and gathered into a mature, comprehensive psychoanalytic interpretation of adolescence, woven into a beautifully crafted and richly hewn complete theoretical tapestry. Blos carefully traces the progressive course of adolescence, dividing it into well-delineated phases, each with its clearly defined tasks and resolutions, providing an exhaustive and in-depth account of the complex network of shifts and transformations occurring in normal and deviate development. Expertly welding the descriptive with the theoretical, and with frequent illustrative forays into literature, he is able to portray and convey the inner life and experience that simmers beneath an often bewildering and incomprehensible adolescent behavioral facade through consummate psychoanalytic understanding of the dynamic significance and developmental functions of these turbulent transmutations. Like the poets he frequently turns to, Blos renders a vital portrait of the outer and inner face of this phase, charged as it is with integration of some of the most profound and emotionally stirring experiences known. As a psychoanalyst who regards adolescence as a maturational period beckoning toward new psychic formations, his study abstracts from highly variable psychic qualities and contents what psychological processes may be considered specific to the various stages and to the overall continuity of such restructuring, clarifing the way ". . . each individual has to work through the exigencies of his total life experiences in order to arrive at a stable ego and drive organization" (Blos 1962, p. 9).

It is in this sense that psychoanalysis views adolescence as a "second edition" of childhood: not only a time when the emotional patterns and conflictual constellations of childhood must be recapitulated for new and qualitatively different drive and ego solutions to be found, but also an opportunity for spontaneous recovery through reworking and rectifying of those early experiences that threaten progressive development (Blos 1962). Blos comments, "The ego at adolescence has the task of counteracting the disruptive influence of infantile trauma by pathological solutions; this is achieved by the employment of stabilizing mechanisms, and finally, by processes of differentiation, stratification and integration, which are the psychological hallmarks of a cohesive personality" (p. 190).

Through a study of the transformations in ego functions occurring during the stages of this phase, Blos (1962) identifies, and is able to describe, major cathectic shifts and changes in object relations; modifications in ego boundaries, in defensive maneuvers and in the nature of those defenses; oscillations in the relationship to and testing of reality; increasing ascendance over the superego of a personalized, less punitive ego ideal as primary regulator of self-esteem; dramatic adjustments in the self-representation, now encompassing gender-specific body contours and sensations that contribute, in the girl, to a personal articulation of her femininity; the expansion and deepening of cognitive faculties now given to hypothetical and abstract dimensions, with a resultant new interest in reflective and intellectual contemplation of the nature of ideas and ideologies; a shift in the relationship to time and space, and the scope of opportunities and choices; and finally, the pulling together and consolidating into a cohesive self-representation of all these changes, through the ego's synthesizing capacity, into a stable, enduring, referential core, commonly referred to as "the self." "Character" or "personality structure" will emerge only out of the final phase-specific consolidating efforts of this developmental passage, and therefore, as Blos (1962) put it, "The heir of adolescence is the self" (p. 136).

Puberty is a biological event announcing the physiological beginning of sexual maturation: adolescence refers to the subsequent adaptive phase in which psychological processes activated by puberty complete the developmental steps required to meet the general demands and social responsibilities of early adulthood. Adolescence is thus an integration of the biological crisis of pubescence, and its particular nature, therefore, will reflect fundamental gender-determined differences between the sexes. In a general sense, psychological development tends to lag behind biological change, requiring a highly individualized and culture-bound time span for a more differentiated and complex personality structure to evolve and to crystallize (Blos 1962). This is all the more true in modern pluralistic societies where the plethora of diverse cultural and ethnic models, and multiplicity of possible selves, complicates developmental closure.

Yet identity formation need not be articulated in quite so personalized or individualistic a manner, nor its consolidation become fashioned over so prolonged a period of time. The recursive interchanges between individual and environment, and ego and self, resulting during this phase in a "solid identity," can and have been negotiated in a very circumscribed time span, allotted specifically for this purpose through ritual and symbolic action processes designed to accomplish these very transitional tasks. The term *adolescence* designates a breadth of reference encompassing an array of diverse ways in which the "psychomorphic" transformation it accompanies and accomplishes can be successfully achieved. This is not to say that ego integration and identity cannot be and are not formed with greater or lesser degrees of differentiation and individuation. Yet, while it may be true that a programmed ritual or the institutionalized assimilation of the adolescent's entrance into the adult community may induce a conventionalization or "primitivization" (Blos 1962, p. 53) of the personality precluding the personal elaboration of a more idiosyncratic and fully developed individuation, it nevertheless yields identificatory structures solid enough to ensure a cohesive sense of self—an "identity," perhaps of a different kind.

The progressive elimination of ritual and rites of passage in western culture has led to the spontaneous eruption of phase-typical attitudes and behaviors—normal and deviant—that, like restitutional phenomena, seem to cry out for containment by communal markers, both recognizing the temporary dissolution and liminality of the child-growing-into-adult condition and affirming and confirming the culmination of this status change through clearly defined closure. There is no indication that we are in any less need today of the benefits of formal ritual processes to ease life crisis points than we ever were. In fact, there is reason to believe that much mental anguish is precipitated by individuals having to accomplish these transitions in isolation (Kimball 1960). Today's youth resorts to the prolongation of this phase and to peer-group "culture" in an attempt to externalize and express what are "idiomatic" adolescent needs, writes Blos (1962), having been forced into a "self-chosen and self-made way of life" (p. 10). Yet, as Blos continues, "All these efforts of youth are attempts to transform a biological event into a psychosocial experience" (p. 10).

The universal tasks of adolescence—separation from the family of origin, selecting a partner, and assuming adult responsibilities of work and procreation—are the same worldwide. Yet the alterations in aims and interests triggered by the dramatic changes in bodily sensations and appearance, the qualitative shifts in cognition and the reevaluation of the self in light of this new countenance, have to be negotiated and elaborated according to the particular stamp given them by the environment. Consequently, while the psychological steps expressing the maturational necessities of this stage reflect cross-cultural similarities that can be abstracted into universal tasks, the means by which these steps are externalized and articulated, and the final form of their outcome, vary widely from culture to culture.

The central problems of early adolescence and adolescence proper, from a psychoanalytic perspective, concern affective predicaments over object relinquishment and object finding in a decisive turn away from incestuous ties and toward heterosexuality (Blos 1962, p. 72). The resolution of major childhood polarities—especially those involving passive and active aims, of which, typically, there has been a major recrudescence during adolescence—is marked by a conclusive shift of both the interactional field and locus of control, from infantile dominance and dependence to an active struggle toward mastery of the environment. "Character" in this program does not reveal its final form until the many phase-specific ego modifications rippling throughout the personality have acquired their conclusive configurations and reconstituted a self consonant with societal expectations and a personal ego ideal that, it should not be forgotten, is given primarily by cultural models. It is therefore at the close of adolescence, when the principal task has become that of identity consolidation, that the distinguishing features of culture and the full impact of social factors come to the forefront. Identity or self-definition (in both their conscious and unconscious aspects), which are by now marked by sharp gender distinctions and role identifications, are the surest manifestations of the compromise fusion of self and environment through which culture receives its individualized expressions. This is what Blos (1962) was referring to when he stated that processes of consolidation in late adolescence relate to "psychic structure and content, the former establishing unification of the ego and the latter preserving continuity within it; the former shaping character, the latter providing the wherewithal . . ." (p. 129).

Given the inherent dissimilarity in the male and female experience with primary object relations and the biological differences in the nature of pubertal changes, it seems obvious that the phenomenology of female adolescence, and particularly of female identity formation, cannot become intelligibly formulated without due consideration given to the dominant cultural and prevailing familial attitudes toward female biology, sexuality, femininity, and what it means to be a woman of *that* culture in *that* society. From a psychoanalytic perspective this fact accounts for the importance and enduring relevance of Erikson's introduction of the "psychosocial" orientation. His contributions to the study of identity incorporate fundamental social elements accounting for both the universal and the unique features of core conflicts to be negotiated at this nodal point of development. Identity consolidation for Erikson (1980) is but one concept within a broader envisagement of the human life cycle, expressed in his "epigenetic" principle, which conceptualizes development from childhood on as the "gradual unfolding of the personality through phase-specific psychosocial crises" (p. 129).

Echoing earlier (1946) formulations that understood personal identity as emerging out of a sense of one's constancy and continuity over time with the simultaneous recognition of one's enduring value and meaning to important others (p. 363), Erikson (1980) essentially viewed identity as a composite of ego subsystems, the ego ideal and self, that first coalesce at the close of adolescence, but that will continue to undergo reworking, largely unconsciously, throughout the life span. From a genetic perspective

> *identity formation* begins where the usefulness of multiple identification ends. It arises from the selective repudiation and mutual assimilation of childhood identifications and their absorption in a new configuration, which, in turn, is dependent on the process by which a *society* . . . *identifies* the young *individual*. [Erikson 1980, p. 122]

Identity results from the dialectic of self with other; significantly, it faces both inward and outward, forming a cohesive self-image originating in the mutual recognitions of the earliest encounter, which is fed by socially *and* endogenously determined tributaries. "Identity formation thus can be said to have a self-aspect, and an ego-aspect"

(Erikson 1980, p. 161). Its ego component reflects acculturation and the internalization of experiences in the actual social environment; its self-aspect expresses the contribution of the unique attributes and qualities of the organism. For this reason, "identity" is significantly influenced by bodily conditions and the body image, which in the earliest stages is the core of both the nascent ego and primary representations, and for the same reason neither begins nor ends in adolescence but is periodically updated and revised in accordance with the biological curve throughout life. In general, comments Greenacre (1958), a sense of identity necessarily involves interactions with others and a degree of observation, contrast, and comparison with another person, fusing with derivatives of identifications and ideals out of which the sense of a personal identity is built.

Erikson's (1980) definition of the term *identity* suggests "a social function of the ego which results, in adolescence, in a relative psychosocial equilibrium essential to the tasks of young adulthood" (p. 161). He is careful to specify that his term *psychosocial* is designed to serve as an "emergency bridge between the so-called 'biological' formulations of psychoanalysis and newer ones, which take the cultural environment into more systematic consideration" (p. 161), a concept introduced to disencumber psychoanalysis from juxtaposing inside and outside, and ego and environment, on the assumption that "an individual ego could exist against or without a specifically human 'environment,' i.e., social organization, is senseless" (p. 162). This calls for the conceptualization of not one basic environment but a whole chain of successively broader and more encompassing environments, from caregivers, family, peers, community, and nation to wider and deeper kin, gender, and even species affiliations, *all* contributing to identity at various levels of the personality. It is the ego's task to negotiate psychosexual and psychosocial facets at any given point in development while simultaneously integrating any new identity elements with preexisting representations, making the process of identity formation an *"evolving configuration"* (Erikson 1980, p. 125) that adaptively subsumes biological, psychological, and social factors.

Armed with an awareness of this three-pronged input to identity formation, it is surprising that psychoanalysis (with the exception of Kestenberg [1975]) has not taken more seriously the biological realities with which young girls are abruptly faced, with the inevitability of having to "change their relationship to their body from that of pre-pubertal child to that of a sexual adult woman" (Laufer 1986, p. 162). And while today anatomy is not destiny in quite so constraining a way as it was in Freud's time, anatomy is certainly still critical in the formation of identity.

To understand the true nature of this impact, we have to turn to more recent advances in the study of the development of female gender identity. These point to very early precursors originating in the fusion of proprioception with archaic undifferentiated primary intro-jections, and internalizations with later identifications and ideals, findings that suggest that the structuralization of identity (both ego and self aspects) occurs along somewhat different lines from those conceptualized by Freud.

The most important revision of Freud's ideas on female identity development, writes Bergman (1987), is that the sense of one's femininity or femaleness—that is, gender definition—begins as early as during the first five years of life, and is therefore already heavily influenced by mother's conscious and unconscious attitudes toward her girl child. Bergman traces the development of primary femininity (Stoller 1976) through three progressive phases, roughly corresponding to certain key developmental transitions: the first, a core gender awareness estab-lished between birth and nine months; the second paralleling the psychological steps of the first separation-individuation process from nine months to roughly three years; and the third an increasingly complex organization of femininity resulting from experiences accrued during the oedipal stage.

Focusing on a "limited but crucial area in the beginning of the sense of identity," namely, its early physical determinants, Greenacre (1958, p. 625) drew attention to the relevance of the face and genitals in their contribution to the primary body image as they relate to later, more comprehensive self-representations that play so significant a role in the consolidation of identity in adolescence. "Both face and genitals are highly differentiated body areas," writes Greenacre, "distinguished by uniquely personal features and configurations," and are therefore "obviously of basic importance in the sense of identity" (p. 616). They are the body parts that most clearly define individuality and gender distinctions, and those most significant when comparing and contrasting in establishing individual recognition of the body-self (Greenacre 1958). They are also those parts that undergo major transformations in appearance and function during puberty. To summarize, Greenacre indicates that even in the earliest stages of development there are present in the coalescing rudiments of the awareness of a body-self inner and outer aspects: the inner emerging from "intrinsic body-organizational structure" and the outer influenced by "awareness of outer surface and form" (p. 625). Thus, while a core identity depends on structural organization, the *sense* of identity is particularly affected by an awareness of external attributes and, I would add, by how these are reflected back and in what ways they are perceived consciously and unconsciously by important others. Greenacre concludes that although identity is derived from a "stable core in body and psychic structure and functioning," it is "nonetheless subject to various changes at nodal points of development, roughly following stages of body and maturational achievement" (p. 626), and consequently cannot reach full consolidation until well after the adolescent process has been assimilated.

Given the recursivity and composite nature of identity-forming processes—our sense of self is given in part by what we see in the mirror and in part by how others perceive us—we can only infer the degree to which the little girl is psychically enmeshed with her mother in the early years and, consequently, how deeply entrenched are her mother's contributions to early introjections and identifications. Psychoanalytic understanding of her subsequent energetic rebuttal and rejection of her mother is explained in terms of the decathexis of family bonds and a dramatic attempt at "object removal" (Katan 1937). Yet might not this often violently conflictual dismissal of mother be viewed within the larger picture of pubertal change as a way of altering the mother's *mothering attitude toward her*, a vigorous attempt to change the way mother relates to her in a genuine need to be seen and responded to differently in light of the biological transformations in feelings and appearance she herself is still struggling to accommodate?

If we consider normative biological crisis as a paradigm for growth, then we must understand the physical changes accompanying the arrival of menarche as a sign signaling the need to begin disentangling, not from the fundamental bond with mother herself, but from the infantile forms of this relationship and from the childhood attitudes and patterns it calls up, which must first be repudiated wholesale before they can be relegated to memory, allowing the latency girl to grow into a sexual woman. It is less, then, that the daughter turns to heterosexuality as a defense against the regressive pull back to mother than that she forcefully demands that mother affirm her passage into womanhood. And it is therefore the study of the phenomenology of mother–daughter interactions in the particulars of their complementarity—the phenomenology from *both* sides, and not the study of female adolescence as an abstraction, that will reveal the essential developmental and psychodynamic processes that impact on female identity formation.

From the beginning, the little girl is passionately involved with and observant of her mother: mother's face, her body and movements, her relationships and motives, as soon as words allow, are the source of unceasing curiosity and scrutiny, and it is not long before the subject of reproduction and the female capacity to give birth is broached. Along with the passionate entwinement inherent in this primary attachment, there grows early in the little girl a vaguely felt core, affiliative identification with her mother's maternal function, based on the awareness of *her likeness* to mother, and on the assumption that she too will one day join the ranks of womanhood and beget her own offspring. The significance of playing with dolls is, I believe, self-evident.

Sooner or later, information regarding menstruation is picked up, often in the playground and highly distorted, but characteristically from anyone *but* one's mother. The stories of how many mothers avoid informing their daughters of this upcoming biological reality could probably fill a volume. They fill a chapter of Grasso's (1979) fascinating study of mother–daughter relationships in Italy, a culture still dominated by ancient prejudice and taboo regarding the body, femininity, and sexuality. Interestingly, her main thesis represents a condemnation of the traditional obligatory inter-identifications between mothers and daughters, seen as an impediment to a truly individuated identity.

When the momentous event of menstruation finally happens, the daughter experiences a core primal affiliation extending beyond the personal to the gender at large. For if, as Laufer (1986, after Chasseguet-

Smirgel 1984) suggests, the girl stands in the first place, not for *deficiency* but primordially for *receptacle*, then her menstrual flow joins her to the great tide of women who have menstruated monthly and born the world's babies before her, in a deeply empowering transgenerational kinship that transcends her individual identification with mother. Yet, at the very same time that she is becoming biologically most like her mother, she is required psychologically to separate and differentiate from her. This throws the daughter into a major dilemma, temporarily splitting her identity in two—like/unlike—a biological identification concomitant with a psychological disidentification. To effectuate interpsychic differentiation, she is forced to distance and separate, yet she needs her mother's acknowledgment of her biological change of status and implicitly a shift in the terms of their relationship. It is here that mother's conscious and unconscious dominance, control, attitudes toward sexuality, femininity, and so forth, and the psychological nature and function of her bond to her daughter are most truly revealed, and will impact directly on the daughter's adolescence.

There is more to complicate the picture, however, for a general biological identification is not the same as a fully differentiated sexual identity. Sexuality today is no longer linked to procreation, and sexual activity no longer implies obligatory entry into the entire reproductive sequence; copulation does not have to lead to parenthood. Thus, at menarche, the daughter acquires a biological identification with the procreative capacity and the mothering function, concomitantly with an identification founded on the conventional sexual ideals and images prevalent in her culture. Ritvo (1976) makes reference to this by conceptualizing the young woman's ego ideal as divided into two parts: "one more related to the biological side, and one that is closer to the social side of her life" (p. 136). Her robust banishment of her mother, and particularly of her mother's critical input at this time, is perhaps more selective than immediately meets the eye, having to do more especially with her femininity, her changing body, her budding sexuality and her lively attempts to embellish her appearance in ways that will render her attractive to the opposite sex in a *particularly sexual* way. This then is the component of her identity where mother cannot, and should not, figure at all.

The contoured boundaries of female identity are chiseled out of a paradox of sameness and difference—the former being prerequisite for the latter; the *sense* of identity, writes Greenacre (1958), involves "some emphasis on basic likeness, but with essential attention called to obvious unlikeness" (p. 613). Identity is not a unitary concept, but a fluid, functional one. At the core it is composed of and subsumes many subcomponent representations that are context specific and refer to different aspects of experience originating from different time periods as well as different facets of life. Suffice it to say that although puberty precipitates the need to integrate sexuality into the personality, there is no aspect of female life more personal or private, or one so contingent on highly individualized preference and choice, than sexuality. It is truly a facet of a daughter's existence where mother has no place, and one in which the rapid changes brought about by each successive generation have, in Western society, created huge generation gaps. Unfortunately, for the daughter to develop a florid, highly personalized, and well-differentiated sexual identity—as distinct from her identification with maternity—she will probably pass through a more or less vampish phase, one that will invariably be met with intense opposition from mother.

It is not surprising then that concealment, as Ritvo (1976) noted, is a widespread, if not universal, response to menarche, a time that also coincides with intense rivalry and competitiveness with mother, and the beginning of combative conceit and bitter conflicts. With the arrival of menstruation, the daughter begins fully reclaiming her body, a body that has thus far been nurtured and tended to by mother, but that now has to become subject to her own care and ministrations, her own adornments, use, and self-regulation. This might explain the extraordinary lengths to which adolescent girls will go and the amount of time they allot to fussing with their face and hair, their feet, their nails, their figure, their attire, and the general governance of their body and appearance, which, normally, is calculated to accentuate sexual attractiveness. The need for complete self-regulation might also explain some of the bizarre eating habits adolescents develop.

And here I would disagree with Ritvo (1976), who believed that the uncontrollability by voluntary sphincters of the menstrual flow "contributes to the character traits of helplessness and passivity" (p. 128), for both its accompanying discomforts and irrepressible cyclicity represent, rather, the unequivocal physiological confirmation of the transformation of the girl's body into that of a woman's capable of reproduction. Far from helplessness and passivity, it seems to me, the words *acceptance* and *possibility* (to which should quickly be added *responsibility*) are more appropriate in pinpointing the nature of female psychological adjustment to the inevitability of menstrual flow. The girl is empowered by the bounty of a body that, unlike her male counterparts, can seemingly afford to lose blood. Moreover, it is this event, the advent of menstruation, that pits her against her mother's constraints, creating a conflict of life-and-death proportions—either she or her mother can be "the woman." The simple mother–child equation has to be toppled to become mother–woman, and so the mother of childhood has to be eradicated in psychic terms to make way for the daughter's female flowering. Either the child's mother or the mother's child must die. This then, in the daughter's unconscious, represents the nucleus of this second individuation struggle, experienced by the daughter in terms of mutual exclusivity. The mother's status is seen as blocking the gateway, as it were, to her entrance into adulthood.

From the mother's side there may indeed be some unconscious reticence in acknowledging that her "little girl" has become a woman. The daughter's first menstruation in this sense presages the eclipse of mother's central role and the daughter's ultimate abandonment of the family home for a bond that beckons from the outside world. Gerson (1994) considers the suddenness of menarche—"In one day, the girl cannot and then can, bear a child" (p. 500)—as well as the "profoundly paradoxical" effect that menstruation may exert on young women, "drawing them closer to their mothers in identification with the mother's experience, yet at the same time distancing them as they begin to imagine a new intense relationship field where mother is but shadow, not object" (p. 501). Here too it is undoubtedly the reciprocal interaction between the event and the nature of the response to it that will impress upon the daughter's experience, coloring her attitude toward her hormonal cycle and its integration into her complete female and sexual identity.

Gerson (1994) sites a richly evocative passage from Pogrebin (1991), in which the latter recounts just such an event, which I report in full for its illustrative value:

The day when I first discovered menstrual blood on my panties, I called for my mother to hurry into the bathroom. As soon as she saw the blood, Mommy said something in Yiddish and slapped me across the cheek. Then, she hugged me. I had never been struck before by either parent. I was stunned, but as she held me firm in her embrace, she whispered into my hair, "I'm sorry, darling, but Jews have to slap a girl on her first menstruation to prepare her for the pain of womanhood. Please, God, that slap should be the worst pain you ever know." [p. 29]

Gerson (1994) then asks a well-posited question: "Might this ritual be an enactment of maternal rage over loss and replacement?" (p. 501). The abrupt gesture—like all ritual acts—is polyvalent and multidetermined, effectively conveying and condensing the sudden upsurge of maternal ambivalence that must seize at that moment. In one moment it declares to the daughter, who with this event has just announced her biological equality, "Stay in your place! I'm still your mother! Prepare yourself for a woman's pain! Bless you, congratulations! May your inevitable suffering be mild." Although heavily colored by ethnic overtones, this is nonetheless a wonderful illustration for how indelibly a daughter's female identity is stamped by the traditions that surround her.

It seems to me that the concept of "genital primacy" today has to include the notion of sexual agency and maturation with its own developmental line (Tyson 1982) in that the young woman's attraction to males predates orgiastic capacity and her sexuality goes above and beyond the procreative and maternal role (which will inevitably encompass identifications with mother). Mature female sexuality is separate from and not contingent on biological identifications but rather requires a fully articulated and developed psychic individuation, made all the more difficult, as we have seen, by the tight, undifferentiated quality of the mother–daughter preoedipal bond (see also Balint 1949).

Beginning with Freud (1933), who had already noted the central relevance of the daughter's intense preoedipal attachment to her mother for female development, many psychoanalytic authors since (Balint 1949, Benedeck 1953, Bergman 1982, 1987, Deutsch 1944, Greenacre 1955, 1958, Horney 1934, 1967, Kestenberg 1975, Laufer 1986, Mahler 1981, Ritvo 1976, Schafer 1974, Stoller 1976, Thompson 1964, Tyson 1982) have turned their attention specifically to reconsidering the continuities and discontinuities, the maturational fluctuations, and the complex factors impacting on female development that are directly tied to the nature of the mother–daughter relationship. While broadening and deepening our understanding and expanding on earlier views, with the exception of Mahler and colleagues (1975) and Mahler (1981), there is lacking a sufficiently comprehensive integration of a developmental paradigm shift that effectively accounts for the interactive phenomenology and internal transformations that reflect the dynamics of the adolescent transition. Given the impact on the psyche of early fused internalizations and identifications, one might have hoped for a more radically modified theoretical framework wherein the genetic course of archaic incorporations and introjections was traced in terms of their subsequent repudiation or modification and integration, during adolescence, through either projective mechanisms, disidentifications, or partial identifications, which together form a cohesive sense of self. The final identity, then, writes Erikson (1980), when "fixed at the end of adolescence is superordinated to any single identification with individuals of the past: it includes all significant identifications, but it also alters them in order to make a unique and reasonably coherent whole of them" (p. 121).

Viewed as the recapitulation of an earlier pattern of development, Mahler and colleagues' (1975) separation-individuation paradigm is the developmental model that best accounts for the interactive phenomenology of the adolescent passage. With its phase-specific developmental tasks, each contingent on the outcome of those preceding it, its impetus toward new levels of ego organization and autonomy, its key crisis points and core separation anxiety, it accounts for the pervasive ambivalence as well as for the persistent underlying aggression characteristic of differentiating processes. Again, as in infancy, any closeness to mother is "felt as an actually threatening danger" (Mahler 1981, p. 630) to the young woman who is taking possession of her body and mind, struggling to claim her uniqueness and to find herself. "The very process of separation-individuation" writes Mahler, "is the most eloquent proof, the paradigm, of that constructive use of aggression in development, which, even in the face of considerable odds, is in the service of that which will become structured as the autonomous *individual ego*" (p. 626).

To be sure, this time the contents of the developmental tasks and the nature of the hormonal inducements determining changing aims and object relationships are entirely different. Yet the tensions emanating from the core conflicts of adolescence, which, to coin a term, center around *individuation anxiety*, belong to the same class of impetuous propulsions that typify all human processes of psychological differentiation and growth. The source of this aggression is the maturational process itself, and for this very reason, given the phase-appropriate drive toward total self-governance and autonomy, it gives rise to conflicts of life and death proportions, the referents of which are manifest in the common battle of wills between mothers and daughters.

Only when the integration of a new body image and the subordination of childhood representations have made way for the consolidation of a new sense of self, and the ego, given undue anxiety or interference, has "caught up," as it were, with its newly found independence and strength, can the aggressive momentum subside, thus diminishing ambivalence resulting in sufficient neutralization for a fully developed individuation. We learn from the studies of Mahler and colleagues (1975) that the "gradualness of the intrapsychic process of differentiation . . . is a tortuous route" (p. 226) and that ego structuring results from the reciprocal effects of separation and individuation. "The active aggressive momentum . . . —the individuation thrust—must be invested with neutralized energy without undue impingement by ambivalence" (p. 226) for a smooth consolidation of personality structure to occur, resistive to regressive dissolution, resilient in the face of life's setbacks, and above all autonomously propelled.

The sense of self-definition and well-articulated psychic autonomy is, I believe, what we mean by "identity," although it is well to remember, as Mahler and colleagues (1975) note, that the sense of self is an eminently private, subjective experience, which "reveals itself by its failures much more readily than by its normal variations" (p. 224). With this in mind, I think it safe to assert that the phases and processes of the adolescent passage, as it is lived in contemporary Western culture, correspond to a second separation-individuation process consisting of increased psychic differentiation and intraspsychic reorganization that can occur only over a period of time, thus far unarticulated in simpler or more traditional societies—and therefore that the *psychological birth of the human adult* is not given but found, and is not significantly derived from identifications but is principally acquired through individuation.

Three psychoanalytic theories—the psychosexual, the psychosocial, and the separation-individuation paradigm—have been touched on to render a complete picture of the confluence in adolescence of complex and multifaceted transformative and integrative processes. All three theories, similarly, are needed to account for functions that the ancient rite of passage accomplished in and of itself. In the course of our exploration, I believe some light has been shed on the particular difficulties encountered by mothers and daughters in this society as girls attempt to delimit and define their individuality while still in close proximity to their mothers and without adequate societally defined support. And further differentiations between those identities modeled primarily out of gender and role identifications, versus those contoured by a more fully articulated individuation, have been identified.

With this distinction made, the more general question to which this chapter referred, namely, to understand the difference in *kind* of identity structure yielded by two different solutions to this normative developmental crisis, has been investigated. There remains now, to complete this discussion, the task of comparing and contrasting the qualitative differences between these two diverse manifest routes, in terms of finding their specific divergences as well as their possible latent points of contact. The premise is that, as we enter the arena of formalized performance and prescribed behaviors—that is, the realm of symbolic attitude and action, which is ritual, at once sacred and transmutative—we are observing the externalized expression of profound psychic configurations and transformations as shaped by the simultaneous and reciprocal impact of social and psychological factors wherein we readily recognize equally profound universal human traits about which, as psychoanalysts, we still have much to learn.

I turn now to initiation rites, a topic I believe psychoanalysts have been justly criticized for ignoring (see Arlow [1951] and Bettelheim [1954] as notable exceptions). "Psychoanalytic literature contains many references to individual life crises, but . . . there is practically nothing about the relation of these to rites of passage," writes Kimball (1960, p. xvi). And this, despite optimal opportunities by a method that, as Freud (1917) frequently recommended, was applicable to manifold expressions of the human psyche, linking with "mythology and philology, with folklore, with social psychology and the theory of religion" (p. 389), the comparative study of which he saw as promising important results. In thus proceeding, I am also implicitly taking up Turner's (1967) recommendation to investigators of ritual "to focus their attention on the phenomena and processes of mid-transition" (p. 110), for he believed it was specifically these that "paradoxically expose the basic building blocks of culture, just when we pass out of and before we re-enter the structural realm" (p. 110).

Let me state at the outset that I borrow from anthropological works on initiation rites with no claim to expertise. I take from this vast topic—and some great studies on it—only what may, by way of contrast and comparison, appear conceptually most relevant to the psychoanalyst intent on understanding the subtleties implicit in different forms of identity structuring during adolescence. Comparative anthropological considerations thus serve to give perspective and to bring into sharp relief which adolescent manifestations blossom from universal roots and which are rather the veneers given them by culture. The biology of puberty is universal, but responses to pubertal change are determined by custom, and therefore the adolescent process and the nature of identity structure become intelligible only through an awareness of the conditions offered by the surrounding culture (GAP 1968, p. 785).

For this reason it is particularly important to study, in psychological terms, the process elements of mid-transition. For it is precisely these that most distinctly reveal how cultural device arises to assist the individual psyche in its transformative travail, while, however, exacting a price by simultaneously acculturating the individual in such a way as to assure its own continuity. "Individuality" is thus subordinated to the conforming ethos and tradition of the group. To this end I will focus primarily on the overall form of the ritual process—its elements, its symbolisms, its functions—with specific reference to the *Chisungu*, the female initiation rite of the Bemba of Central Africa, as exquisitely detailed and reported by Richards (1956). I have chosen this particular rite (1) because it is specifically a female rite of passage, and (2) because the Bemba are a matrilineal people practicing matrilocal marriage in a culture in which interfemale relationships—particularly mothers and daughters—will continue to remain central despite marriage, both reasons which seemed particularly germane to the general topic of this work.

"Societies offer, as individuals require, more or less sanctioned intermediary periods between childhood and adulthood, institutionalized *psychosocial moratoria,* during which a lasting pattern of 'inner identity' is scheduled for relative completion . . ." (Erikson 1980, p. 119). In finding this identity, the young adult "gains an assured sense of inner continuity and social sameness which will bridge what he is *about to become,* and will reconcile his *conception of himself* and his community's recognition of him" (p. 120). Erikson criticized psychoanalysis for not having sufficiently considered the fact that such recognition provides "an entirely indispensable support to the ego in the specific tasks of adolescing . . ." (p. 120).

The ritual process serves and facilitates both private and public "adolescing" functions, with an additional element, that of the sacred. Sacrament arises in the formalization of behaviors and symbolic actions performed at a specific time in prescribed ways and with the use of sacred objects. Those participating in the novitiate, by virtue of their transitional or marginal status, are considered to be sacred or holy beings, undefined in social terms, and therefore not subject to the rules or restrictions of society. Their physical segregation from the group or crossing of a threshold separating two distinct areas further marks a ritualized move into a "transitional" condition. "The person who enters a status at variance with the one previously held becomes 'sacred' to the others who remain in the profane state," writes Kimball (1960), and it is this condition that calls for ritualization: "The transitional period is met with rites of passage which cushion the disturbance" (pp. viii-ix).

Van Gennep (1909/1960), who explored the meaning of such rituals in terms of the order of their internal elements, is also generally credited with having first identified a set pattern, or a dynamic *schèma* for *rites de passage,* consisting of three well-delineated phases: separation, transition (or *marge*), and incorporation. The first phase, *separation*, constitutes entrance into a liminal realm demarcating sacred time and space from secular time and space, and consists of symbolic behaviors accompanying a physical separation indicating the initiate's disengagement from an earlier status and a detachment from the group. The second phase marks the transitional (marginal) or liminal period, defining the "passage, wherein the 'ritual subject' (the 'passenger') is ambiguous" (Turner 1967, p. 94), existing in a provisional realm that shares few, if any, of the qualities or attributes belonging to the former or to the future status. And the third phase, incorporation or "re-aggregation," refers to symbolic behaviors and activities indicating reentry into the community of the initiated, who are now recognized in their new status and welcomed back into a group structure with clearly defined rights and obligations. The dynamic or thrust of the rite is expressed through this triphasic design; its *psycho*dynamic impact is accomplished via the externalization of psychological attitudes and processes into formalized symbolic activities. Hence, we distinguish between ceremony and rite, as Turner (1967) asserts, "Ritual is transformative, ceremony confirmatory" (p. 95).

The ritual process exerts its effect in *action* terms through its symbolic form and the particular features of each of its elements. These sequences function by way of encapsulating a concept, conveying an idea or even a constellation of emotions, inciting their contemplation and apprehension through the very execution and performance of the ritual act. The outcome of such articulation, writes Langer (1942), "is not a simple emotion, but a complex permanent *attitude*" (p. 153). Circumscribed, time-bound, and irreversible, the ritual process transmits its "arcane knowledge or *gnosis*" by impressing the neophyte "as a seal impresses wax" (Turner 1967, p. 102) with deeply felt and irradicable new characteristics representing a fundamental change in their essence rather than a superficial acquisition of new knowledge.

Van Gennep (1909/1960) believed puberty rites to be misnamed since their occurrence does not always coincide with the physiological onset of puberty. Yet it is important to remember that they nevertheless do occur at a time when youngsters are still immersed in the "action" mode and are highly impressionable in that they learn by doing: action is the prime means by which adolescents internalize experience. With its mimicry, enactions, songs, ordeals, play, and practice—the "pedagogics" of rites, as Turner (1967) calls them—the ritual form imparts new attitudes while teaching a broad range of ideas, beliefs, dominant social values, and forms of interpersonal relations and responsibilities, as well as defining the passage from an asexual world to one of sexuality and reproduction. By isolating the initiates and gathering them into same-sex groups, divesting them of their previous habits and submitting them uniformly to various ordeals, the ritual process facilitates a breakdown of the old ego, a psychic dismemberment or effacement, as it were, enabling a profound and vital *psychomorphic* transmutation to take place. In this way, society makes the young adult into a reliable carrier of the culture (GAP 1968). Appreciation of the deep developmental function effectuated by the rite is revealed by the usage of certain terms and definitions. Thus, as Turner (1967) comments, in the *Chisungu*, the Bemba speak of "growing" the girl into a woman, viewing the status change as an ontological transformation embodied and transpiring *within* the person (p. 101).

Rites of passage are replete with biological symbolism; life and death, anabolism and catabolism, decay and regeneration are the great archetypal themes of ritual transformation. But initiands are also associated with primary polarities: sun and moon, male and female, nubility and fertility, light and dark, positive and negative, and reversals, as well as the prime substance, earth, since they are simultaneously "dying from or dead to their former status and life, and being born or growing into new ones" (Turner 1982, p. 26).

As we have seen in the course of this chapter, the initial process of disidentification with the old self of childhood and reconsolidation of a new identity arouses emotional attitudes that, in the interim, can indeed evoke overwhelmingly disintegrative and threatening experiences. The difference between the "adolescing" youngster of Western society and the neophyte of ritual process lies in "agency": the former must weather the storm alone and steer a *personal* course of individuation, the latter's individuality is welded to the group's. As the initiands submit to the authority of the elders (representing the entire community) whose speech and riddles wield power and wisdom, they are guided and instructed through their emotional restructuring so that previous sentiments and habits of thought and feeling are vigorously replaced by new ways of acting and thinking whose meanings are assimilated largely unconsciously. Langer (1942) expressed well this form of knowledge acquired in part by way of presentational symbolic acts and in part by representational means:

> Ritual is the most primitive reflection of serious thought, a slow deposit, as it were, of people's imaginative insight into life. [p. 157]
>   . . . human attitudes, vaguely recognized as reasonable and right, are expressed by actions which are not spontaneous emotional outlets, but prescribed modes of participation and assent. [p. 162]

To thus predispose a young and petulant psyche toward conventionality, it seems to me, a particular psychological condition has to be engendered, and it is here that the concept of "liminality," the mid-phase state of rituals so brilliantly elaborated on by Turner (1967, 1969, 1982), is invoked. Neophytes entering the seclusion situation are snatched from attachments, stripped of all the accoutrements that previously defined them. Once aggregated into a homogeneous group, their earlier selves further dissolve as they submit to public mockeries and various degrading or instructive ordeals, conducted, in the *Chisungu*, by female elders embodying the "generic authority of tradition" (Turner 1969, p. 103). Such trials and humiliations as parading half-naked, smeared in earth, before taunting villagers or, as in the *Chisungu*, having to catch water insects with their mouths, climb trees backward, or crawl on all fours backward into the seclusion hut—"to teach the girls obedience" (Richards 1956, p. 74)—are designed not only to disintegrate an old self and discourage regression, but also to test endurance and provide maturational hurdles that psychologically help "prepare them to cope with the new responsibilities and restrain them in advance from abusing their new privileges" (Turner 1969, p. 103).

The neophyte in liminality is no longer defined and not yet classified. Insofar as initiates are "neither living nor dead from one aspect, and both living and dead from another" (Turner 1967, p. 97), they are structurally "dead" or as yet "unborn" and may therefore either be treated as corpses or, conversely, likened to embryos or newborn infants. Undefined in normative social terms, the liminal entity—neither child nor adult—is provided with a sanctioned, time-bound "condition" externalizing much of the often tortuous ambiguity and psychic destructuralization of contemporary adolescence that, paradoxically, despite stringent containment and even the reversal of certain key adolescent tendencies, nevertheless provides a realm of "pure possibility whence novel configurations of ideas and relations may arise" (Turner 1967, p. 97). In the effacing ambiguity and anonymity of this "liminal" state, the neither-girl-nor-woman ritual subject becomes a molten substance, a *tabula rasa*, upon which may freely be "inscribed the knowledge and wisdom of the group" (Turner 1969, p. 103) in those aspects that relate directly to the new status. In order to become receptive to such verbal instructions, and particularly to the numinous symbolisms expressed through ritual sequence and the handling of tribal "sacra"—that is, to the "pedagogics" (Turner 1967) of the rite—initiands have to have entered the cocooned condition of liminality, having acquired those malleable attributes of meekness, humbleness, and submissiveness that characterize obedient dispositions. Here the blatant reversal of the much more typically adolescent attitudes of rebelliousness, irreverent detachment, and aggressive defiance might serve as a source of insight into the *psychologics* of the ritual process. It seems evident that the impact of ritual is obtained in part by a breakdown of the individual ego and primarily by turning into their opposite those very traits that give adolescence its tough individuating impetus. The psychologically taxing and painful separation-individuation process—along with its ambivalence and dramas—is thereby greatly eased. Where there is little choice, little personal adjustment has to be sought and conflict is minimal (Blos 1962), and while initiands, by way of compensation for their restrictions, are granted a certain kind of freedom to feed and adorn themselves at the expense of others, it is a form of liberty prescribed and conventionalized by the community: "Even the *breaking* of rules *has* to be done during initiation" (Turner 1982, p. 42). Liminality then is a "temporal interface whose properties partially invert those of the already consolidated order . . ." (Turner 1982, p. 41) that, despite its time-limited framework and essentially formal character, nevertheless engenders novelty such as "emerges from unprecedented combinations of familiar elements" (Turner 1982, p. 27).

An extensive report of Richards's (1956) beautifully detailed account of the *Chisungu* of the Bemba would extend well beyond the confines and requirements of this chapter, in addition to making demands that go beyond my competence as a psychoanalyst. I will therefore limit myself to grouping under a few main headings what appear to be the elements of this particular rite, the meanings and functions of which correspond to and reflect many of the mother–daughter and adolescent girl's issues I have been discussing. It goes without saying that the character of the features of each rite reflects the special nature of the economic activities, social values, and kinship structure of the tribe, as well as its educational system and unique attitudes toward sex, marriage, relationships, the rearing of children, and social obligations of parenthood. However, from a ritual process with as many as eighteen separate ceremonies lasting continuously for over a month, I will select only those overarching aspects—and the concepts they convey—that most explicitly touch on the adolescent girl's identity formation.

Nubility, fertility, and motherhood are the prime topics of female initiation ceremonies as they may coincide as preliminary to marriage. With the advent of the first menstruation, the Bemba girl, having informed her elders, will prepare for the *Chisungu* initiation rite. Fear of the first period and the dangers associated with the first intercourse, as well as the universality of menstrual taboos, are worth mentioning here. Blood seems to arouse primordial anxieties in men associated with death, birth, weakening, strengthening, life-giving and life-taking forces, and kinship ties. Richards (1956) informs that some of the sentiments expressed during girls' rites are almost universal, engendered by the physiological and bodily changes occurring in girls at puberty. Sexual maturation brings with it the recognition that intercourse now holds the possibility of pregnancy. The first sign of menstrual blood is an indication of possible fecundity; beauty magic and ritual ordeals are now undertaken to test the girl's preparedness for motherhood. The nubility rite prepares the girl for an irreversible change, enabling her to bear children in a socially appropriate way and to beget offspring entitled to a legitimate social status.

Menarche, that is, biological maturity, is thus the sign that adequate preparation for *social* maturity and a change of status must begin. Puberty rites will mark a clear differentiation between the sexes, during which girls will be expected to assume the attitudes and responsibilities of the full female role. It is very interesting that initiands, who as women will generally have to behave subserviently and humbly toward their men, are, in the context of a particularly ventilating ceremony, permitted to dance off their latent hostility and aggression toward the opposite sex, as Richards (1956) recounts, ". . . to swagger, to shout obscenities or to attack the men" (p. 20).

In terms of menstruation, the event signaling the turning of a girl into a woman capable of reproduction, the rite has taken a private occurrence and given it public recognition. Tactfully, it has removed the onus of the ensuing maturational crisis from the family nexus and deposited it into a social arena where it is cause for an entire status change, and where the responsibilities and preparedness for this role assumption are heavily emphasized. In addition, the rite assists in the transition of *body change* and change in *body image* by first stripping girls of all embellishments while simultaneously performing "beauty magic" ceremonies, thereby enforcing the adolescent girl's inherent preoccupation with her attractiveness to the opposite sex, since her appeal will likely lead to swift parentage. While strengthening same-sex loyalties, the rite additionally finds a way for girls to express their ambivalent feelings for boys toward whom they will have to be receptive and submissive. Adolescents are thereby given license to vent their aggression in a relatively channeled way and within the context of a specific situation.

It is common for girls in patrilineal societies to be separated from their families and to join those of their husbands. To soften the pain of separation and cushion a natural resentment toward incursion by the new generation, ceremonies exist during which parents can freely bewail and dramatize the loss of their child, and "cut them away symbolically, make them jump over hurdles, or other barriers, or otherwise convince themselves that their offspring have become full adults and fit to be so considered . . ." (Richards 1960, pp. 20–21). Yet even in this matrilineal society, where the husband will join the bride, a ritual separation—specifically between mother and daughter—and a ritual hiding or "fencing" of the girls paralleling segregation of the mothers, enforces a clearly defined "break" of the childhood tie. *Both* mother and daughter cooperate communally to effectuate this separation, giving external expression to an internal process. It must be emphasized also that the wisdom of the rite puts the burden of the passage squarely on the girl's shoulders in the form of tests of endurance that also "reflect the anxiety of parents . . . as to whether the candidates really are grown up or socially fit for married life" (Richards 1956, p. 123), since it is the girl's *mother* who will be blamed for her girl's shortcomings. Richards (1956) explains that

Chisungu songs stress the challenges of some of these tests, emphasizing the necessity of the girl to succeed in accomplishing "difficult and unprecedented things. They tell her she has to do something she has never done before and accept new demands made on her" (p. 123).

It has already been mentioned that rites contain ceremonies in which the dominant economic and political values, the beliefs and ideology of the social structure, are "taught," and in which shifts in important relationship patterns are conveyed in order to evoke their contemplation. Perhaps it has not been sufficiently emphasized that those elements of custom are transmitted through the use of "sacred emblems" (Richards 1956, p. 59) or "things handed down" such as objects of clay and pottery, figurines of animals and birds, fertility symbols and domestic objects, in ceremonies during which the handling of such "sacra" in prescribed ways consists in practice or play-acting sessions before the "mistress" of the rite. These mimetics, reproducing aspects of domestic or agricultural life, insofar as they are "formalized representations" (Richards 1956, p. 59) of important activities, are undertaken as serious performances. The use of mime and play, or "mock" activities as a teaching means, says something of the experiential nature and "rehearsal" quality of the pedagogics of rite, mimicry being "the natural symbolism by which we represent activities to our minds" (Langer 1942, p. 155), its origins going back to the function of play in childhood.

However, the handling of multivocal symbols, which is "sacra," to the accompaniment of evocative rhythms and riddles does more; it induces contemplation of the *meaning* of each of these scenarios and relationships, and therefore instigates—even cognitively—a far deeper assimilation of their significance. Turner (1967) expresses this idea very well: ". . . the communication of *sacra* both teaches the neophytes how to think with some degree of abstraction about their cultural milieu, and gives them ultimate standards of reference" (p. 108). Rites accomplish this elevation of thought processes promoting the abstraction of ideas by summoning such concepts through symbolic action. In addition, the ritual process brings about an irreversible change, a psychomorphic transformation, resistant to regression, effectuated in experiential terms. However solid this identity might be, it is *not* gained through differentiating and individuating means, as we have seen, but through identification and indoctrination. The separation-individuation process required of Western adolescent girls is not only about joining the ranks of a sex-defined role within society, but of choosing and selecting out of multiple choices that life and lifestyle that most truly reflect the nature of a fully affirmed individuality for which she, and only she, will be made responsible.

From all of the above, I believe, there emerges the multifaceted wisdom of *rites de passage* that, in a time-bound communal framework, externalize, formalize, and give structure and character to many otherwise hazardous inter- and intrapsychic processes. Dilemmas typically arising in the mother–adolescent daughter relationship are bypassed or assuaged by moving their articulation from the family nexus to the social matrix, thereby providing the adolescent with a peer-oriented, socially sanctioned way station that also safeguards the girl from excessive maternal intrusion. The rite thus facilitates the girl's transition into womanhood and her free adoption of the full female reproductive role.

It may seem that I have undertaken a long, circuitous route in the pursuit of deeper understanding of my original question regarding the particular difficulties that appear ever more commonly to arise in mother–daughter relationships as contemporary girls enter the adolescent passage. I was interested in exploring the underlying reasons for the pervasive accretion of verbal and physical aggression and frequent ruptures of this primary bond, and particularly, of grasping the phenomenology or inner experience and the nature of the sentiments swelling within a girl that would compel her to experience her mother's very existence as a threat to her own. I believe that in the unfolding of this discussion, and particularly in the psychologically significant distinction between an identificatory versus an individuated identity structure, some clarity has been found. I might even venture a hypothesis: namely, that by identifying a diagnostically significant typology of identity structures (within the framework of a comprehensive theory of internalization), the etiology of the so-called disorders of the "self" might better be understood and treated by focusing on the developmental pitfalls of this crucial passage. My clinical experience with Mexican, Columbian, Turkish, and Polish young women, all unindividuated in a full adult sense and fixated in various culturally determined ways at points along the adolescent process, leads me to believe that a better understanding of the etiological role of psychic differentiation, or lack of it, would yield valuable theoretical and technical principles.

Throughout the writing of this chapter, the image of a cocoon has persistently pressed itself on my mind, and not surprisingly. As a metaphor of transformation, a symbol of morphological transmutation—which is the psyche in adolescence—there is no vision more apt than the sight of a butterfly making its way out of the remnants of its earlier form to burst freely into flight.

REFERENCES

Aichorn, A. (1925). *Wayward Youth*. New York: Viking, 1948.

Arlow, J. A. (1951). A psychoanalytic study of a religious initiation rite, Bar Mitzvah. *Psychoanalytic Study of the Child* 6:353–374. New York: International Universities Press.

Balint, A. (1949). Love for the mother and mother-love. *International Journal of Psycho-Analysis* 30:251–259.

Benedeck, T. (1953). Some problems of motherhood. In *Women: The Variety and Meaning of Their Sexual Experience*, ed. A. M. Krich, pp. 171–188. New York: Dell.

Bergman, A. (1982). Considerations about the development of the girl during the separation-individuation process. In *Early Female Development: Current Psychoanalytic Views*, ed. D. Mendell. New York: Spectrum.

——— (1987). On the development of female identity: issues of mother–daughter interaction during the separation-individuation process. *Psychoanalytic Inquiry* 7:381–397.

Bernfeld, S. (1938). Types of adolescents. *Psychoanalytic Quarterly* 7.

Bettelheim, B. (1954). *Symbolic Wounds*. New York: Glencoe, Free Press.

Blos, P. (1941). *The Adolescent Personality*. New York: Appleton-Century-Crofts.

——— (1962). *On Adolescence: A Psychoanalytic Interpretation*. London: Free Press.

Chasseguet-Smirgel, J. (1984). The femininity of the analyst in professional practice. *International Journal of Psycho-Analysis* 65:169–178.

Deutsch, H. (1944). *Psychology of Women*, vol. 1. New York: Grune & Stratton.

Erikson, E. (1946). Ego development and historical change. *Psychoanalytic Study of the Child* 2:359–396. New York: International Universities Press.

———— (1980). *Identity and the Life Cycle.* New York: Norton.

Freud, A. (1936/1966). The ego and the id at puberty. In *The Writings of Anna Freud*, vol. 2, rev. ed: *The Ego and the Mechanisms of Defense*, pp. 137–176. New York: International Universities Press.

———— (1958). Adolescence. *Psychoanalytic Study of the Child* 13:255–278. New York: International Universities Press.

———— (1969). Introduction to Kata Levy's "Simultaneous analysis of a mother and her adolescent daughter: the mother's contribution to the loosening of the infantile object tie." In *The Writings of Anna Freud*, vol. 2, pp. 479–483. New York: International Universities Press.

Freud, S. (1905). Three essays on the theory of sexuality. *Standard Edition* 7:125–245.

———— (1917). Introductory lectures on psychoanalysis. *Standard Edition* 15/16.

———— (1933). Femininity. *Standard Edition* 22:112–135.

Friday, N. (1977). *My Mother/My Self: The Daughter's Search for Identity.* New York: Delacorte.

Friedman, G. (1980). The mother–daughter bond. *Contemporary Psychoanalysis* 16(1):90–97.

GAP [Group for the Advancement of Psychiatry] (1968). *Normal Adolescence: Its Dynamics and Impact* 5(68).

Gerson, M. J. (1994). Standing at the threshold: a psychoanalytic response to Carol Gilligan. *Psychoanalytic Psychology* 11(4):491–508.

Grasso, L. (1979). *Madri e figle: specchio contro specchio.* Florence, Italy: Nuova Guaraldi Editrice.

Greenacre, P. (1955). The prepuberty trauma in girls. In *Trauma, Growth and Personality.* New York: Norton.

———— (1958). Early physical determinants in the development of the sense of identity. *Journal of the American Psychoanalytic Association* 6:612–627.

Horney, K. (1934). Personality changes in female adolescents. In *Feminine Psychology*, ed. H. Kelman, pp. 234–244. New York: Norton.

———— (1967). *Feminine Psychology.* New York: Norton.

Jones, E. (1922). Some problems of adolescence. In *Papers on Psychoanalysis*, 5th ed. London: Balliere, Tindall & Cox, 1948.

Katan, A. A. (1937/1951). The role of displacement in agorophobia. *International Journal of Psycho-Analysis* 22.

Kestenberg, J. S. (1975). Menarche. In *Children and Parents: Psychoanalytic Studies of Development*, ed. J. S. Kestenberg, pp. 285–312. New York: Jason Aronson.

Kimball, S. T. (1960). Introduction. In *The Rite of Passage*, ed. A. van Gennep, pp. 5–19. London: Routledge & Kegan Paul.

Kincaid, J. (1996). *The Autobiography of My Mother*. New York: Farrar, Straus & Giroux.

Langer, S. K. (1942). *Philosophy in a New Key: A Study in the Symbolism of Reason, Rite and Art*. Cambridge, MA: Harvard University Press.

Laufer, E. (1986). The female Oedipus complex and the relationship to the body. *Psychoanalytic Study of the Child* 41:259–276. New Haven, CT: Yale University Press.

Levy, K. (1969). Simultaneous analysis of a mother and her adolescent daughter: the mother's contribution to the loosening of the infantile object tie. In *The Writings of Anna Freud*, vol. 5, pp. 379–391. New York: International Universities Press.

Mahler, M. (1981). Aggression in the service of separation-individuation. *Psychoanalytic Quarterly* 50:625–638.

Mahler, M., Pine, F., and Bergman, A. (1975). *The Psychological Birth of the Human Infant: Symbiosis and Individuation*. New York: Basic Books.

Pogrebin, L. C. (1991). *Deborah, Golda and Me*. New York: Crown.

Richards, A. (1956). *Chisungu*. London: Faber & Faber.

Ritvo, S. (1976). Adolescent to woman. *Journal of the American Psychoanalytic Association Supplement* 24(5):127–138.

Schafer, R. (1974). Problems in Freud's psychology of women. *Journal of the American Psychoanalytic Association Supplement* 22:459–487.

Spiegal, L. A. (1951). A review of contributions to a psychoanalytic theory of adolescence. *Psychoanalytic Study of the Child* 6:375–393. New York: International Universities Press.

——— (1958). Comments on the psychoanalytic psychology of adolescence. *Psychoanalytic Study of the Child* 13:296–308. New York: International Universities Press.

Stoller, R. (1976). Primary femininity. *Journal of the American Psychoanalytic Association Supplement* 24:59–78.

Thompson, C. (1964). *On Women*. New York: Basic Books.

Turner, V. (1967). *The Forest of Symbols*. Ithaca, NY: Cornell University Press.

——— (1969). *The Ritual Process*. New York: Aldine de Gruyer.

——— (1982). *From Ritual to Theater: The Human Seriousness of Play*. New York: Paj.

Tyson, P. (1982). A developmental line of gender identity, gender role, and choice of love object. *Journal of the American Psychoanalytic Association* 30:61–86.

van Gennep, A. (1909/1960). *The Rite of Passage*, trans. M. Vizedom and G. Caffee. London: Routledge & Kegan Paul.

Whitmont, E. C. (1982). *Return of the Goddess*. New York: Crossroad.

6

Demeter and Persephone Revisited: Ambivalence and Separation in the Mother–Daughter Relationship*

Molly Walsh Donovan

The story of Demeter and Persephone is generally seen as the archetypal Greek myth of mother love. I would like to go beyond that one dimension and consider it here as a myth rich in meaning about the mother–daughter relationship in all its complexity. As with all myths, there are many versions of this one. Here is a brief telling of the basic story synthesized from several sources (Bolen 1984, Graves 1955/1992, Spitz 1992, Young-Eisendrath and Wiedeman 1987):

One day, Demeter's beautiful daughter, Kore (later to be named Persephone), was out playing with other young maidens, picking flowers in a lush meadow. Her eyes fell on a narcissus flower, placed there by the goddess Gaia, to please the god of the Underworld. It was a flower of

---

*An earlier version of this chapter was presented at the Spring Meeting of the Division of Psychoanalysis of the American Psychological Association in New York, April 18, 1996.

exquisite beauty and fragrance, and was designed to entice the lovely young maiden. It was irresistible, and Kore reached to pick it. As she did, the earth opened and Hades appeared in his magnificent chariot with his two strong horses, placed Kore in the chariot, and rode off with her to his kingdom, the Underworld.

After Kore's disappearance, Demeter roamed the earth, grieving and searching for her daughter. Her search was long and arduous, involving much travail. When she finally learned of her daughter's whereabouts, she pleaded with Zeus to return her daughter to her. Zeus refused and Demeter brought a great famine over the land by withholding fertility from the earth, refusing to let any crops grow. When Zeus saw what was happening, he relented and agreed to arrange Kore's release, sending Hermes to the Underworld to bring her back. During her stay under the earth, Kore had refused all nourishment, but before her departure, Hades discovered that she had eaten some pomegranate seeds in his garden. Upon her reunion with her daughter, Demeter first questioned whether Kore had consumed anything while in the Underworld. Because she had eaten while there, Kore was bound to Hades, and had to return to the land of the dead as his wife, Persephone, to reign as Queen of the Underworld for a third of the year. For the remainder of the year, she would be able to be with her mother on the earth. While Demeter and Persephone are together, the earth produces life; while Persephone is with her husband in the Underworld, the earth is bare. Thus are the changes of seasons explained.

This is a very rich and complicated myth, with many intricate details about the abduction of Kore and about Demeter's search; it is not possible to elaborate on those details here. Traditionally, the emphasis in interpreting this myth has been on Demeter's grief at losing her daughter, Persephone, and on her search. Recent writers (Herman 1989, Spitz 1992, Young-Eisendrath and Wiedeman 1987) have highlighted the themes of separation and reunion and the relationship between this mother and daughter and what leaving meant for Persephone in relation to her mother and to her development of self.

Before her abduction by Hades, Persephone was Kore, a word meaning sweet maiden or young girl, tied to her mother. The trap set for her, a narcissus flower, can be seen as a symbol of self-love (Young-Eisendrath and Wiedeman 1987) or a wish to add something to the self (Spitz 1992); it was only when she reached for this irresistible flower that the earth opened and Hades whisked her away to his kingdom, the Underworld. Her picking the flower could thus be seen as symbolizing an openness to other aspects of the self that will take her away from the world she knows, that of being with her mother. Demeter's grief at her daughter's disappearance led to her neglect of the earth; she turned herself into an old woman roaming the world, and ultimately threatened Zeus with world famine if Persephone were not returned to her. Zeus was persuaded only by this threat and Persephone was returned to her mother, but not until after she had eaten six pomegranate seeds in Hades' kingdom. The pomegranate is "redolent of heterosexual union with its seeds and blood-red juice" (Spitz 1992), and she is bound to him by this act. Thus, when she was returned to her mother, she was no longer a young maiden but a woman who had tasted sexuality; she had become separate from her mother.

For Jungian writers Young-Eisendrath and Wiedeman (1987), the myth is a tale of separation and individuation mediated by the animus, the male principle. Zeus and Hades have colluded in this stealing away of the maiden, have aided in her separating from her powerful mother, Demeter, and becoming a distinct person. Kore, the maiden, becomes Persephone, Queen of the Underworld, and as such appears in subsequent myths as a powerful and compassionate presence, a guide for visitors to the Underworld.

In most versions of the myth Persephone is abducted, taken against her will. However, I recently became aware of what was referred to as a "pre-Hellenic" version of the myth (Estes 1991) in which Persephone was drawn away by her curiosity and wandered off and into the Underworld. She was not a passive victim in this leaving, but an active investigator of the darker aspects of life, away from the protection of mother. However, even in the predominant version of the myth in which Persephone is abducted, the eating of the pomegranate seeds provides another moment in which in some versions Persephone is cast as a passive victim who is forced or tricked to eat them and in other versions as a willing participant who is offered the seeds and accepts. Each version of the story points to a different resolution of the mother–daughter symbiosis.

Caldwell, in his 1990 essay "The Psychoanalytic Interpretation of

Greek Myth," says, "Decomposition (or splitting) . . . essentially the differential representation of the ambivalent relationship between child and parents, is one of the major structural principles in Greek myth . . ." (p. 353). It is in the nature of Greek myths to represent psychic struggles in very dramatic, primitive, graphic ways, ways that convey the power of the conflicts. That is their beauty; they speak to us in ways that rational, more "realistic" discourse cannot approach. So it is in this highly charged story of Demeter and Persephone that the Greeks portrayed the strength of the mother–daughter bond and their difficult task of separating and individuating while remaining connected.

In our time also the mother–daughter bond has been acknowledged as one of an intensity so great that the relationship is extremely difficult to navigate. The psychoanalyst Doris Bernstein (1993) wrote of this relationship: "All mothers [of daughters] share one common experience: the mother sees herself in the body of her infant daughter" (p. 23).

Another well-known psychoanalyst, Joyce MacDougall, speaks of the intensity of the mother–infant connection, saying, "The infant's first reality is the mother's unconscious." These were the first words I ever heard MacDougall utter at a lecture many years ago, and they made an indelible impression. They say that we cannot know the first, and perhaps the most powerful, influence on us in any directly comprehensible way.

The contemporary writer Adrienne Rich (1986) writes, "Probably there is nothing in human nature more resonant with charges than the flow of energy between two biologically alike bodies, one of which has lain in amniotic bliss inside the other, one of which has labored to give birth to the other. The materials are here for the deepest mutuality and the most painful estrangement" (pp. 225–226).

And in *The Second Sex*, Simone de Beauvoir (1949) says, "In her daughter, the mother does not hail a member of the superior caste; in her, she seeks a double. She projects upon her daughter all the ambiguity of her relation with herself" (p. 488).

These are powerful statements about a basic truth: mother and daughter are inextricably linked by their like biology and their conscious and unconscious psychology, so their relationship is fraught both with possibilities and with pitfalls. While there is the potential for great empathy and closeness, there is also the potential for great difficulty in the process of differentiation and individuation. And this is true even in the best of relationships between mother and daughter. Achieving a measure of separateness and differentiation while keeping a connection requires consciousness and internal work at some level from both members of the dyad. In the myth, Demeter and Persephone each had her own experiences while separated. This can be seen as each attending to her own internal processes around the separation. This allowed them each to grow and to come together able to accept each other as separate.

This chapter considers some of the vicissitudes of the mother–daughter relationship, a relationship in which individuation is difficult and threatening and merger is maintained only at the price of a real relationship and of the daughter's growth and development, and that of the mother as well. Many women I see have troubled relationships with both their actual mothers and their internalized mothers that involve alternating patterns of merger and rejection. This situation is antithetical to the development of empathy and to authentic individuation in both members of the mother–daughter pair.

What I would like to describe and illustrate clinically is what I see as a reverberating cycle of envy and rejection in the troubled mother–daughter relationship, in which differentiation is taken as rejection and differentness leads to envy and to attempts to sabotage the growth of the other and reestablish the merger. The mother's envy of her daughter's potential and freedom, and her feeling of rejection as her daughter appropriately moves away from her, can be communicated to the daughter in many, often unconscious ways. This can lead to the daughter's inhibiting herself or to guilt about surpassing her mother. From the other side, the daughter's envy and resentment of mother's power, her attachment to and dependency on mother, and her need to define herself can lead to angry rejection of the mother, perhaps alternating with attempts to reconcile by renouncing her differentness. In this scenario neither mother nor daughter can flourish.

CLINICAL VIGNETTES

Sasha

Sasha sits in my office racked with sobs. She can barely talk. The words that come are about feeling guilty, feeling unable to make it right, unable to get it right. She sees her mother's unhappiness, her mother's inability to get her life right, the pain that her mother denies and drowns in drink—always has. Her mother says that her life is fine, that she is happy, though she allows at times for what she says is the slight exception of her husband's treatment of her, his belittling remarks and his angry outbursts at her. In their frequent phone conversations Sasha hears her mother's self-deprecating remarks and becomes mute, knowing from years of experience that she cannot make her mother stop—stop putting herself down, stop drinking— and that trying to stop her mother drains her. Even to hear these comments drains her, making her feel responsible, helpless, furious, and guilty for her own life.

Sasha is a bright, successful, 40-year-old attorney in a high-level government job. She is married to a man twenty-five years her senior, and says that she has felt consciously guilty about this relationship vis-à-vis her mother for a long time. She feels, she says, her mother's envy of her relationship, adding that her husband is about the same age as her mother. Sasha speaks of herself as greedy—she feels as though she could eat someone up—and feels very ashamed of that. She sees herself as bad for wanting things and trying to get them for herself.

I have been seeing Sasha for about a year. I think of her as feeling tremendous ambivalence about her achievements and about her relationships, coming out of her hitherto unconscious awareness of her mother's envy. Sasha's mother did not recognize her envy of her smart, lovely, high-achieving daughter, and acted it out. She was not able to give her daughter the supplies Sasha needed to become independent without undue fear of loss of her connection to her mother. Sasha spent her childhood trying to be good, trying to do everything she could think of to bring happiness into the family. She has not been able to fully let that go and this dynamic gets played out in her present-day relationships in which she tries to please in order to keep things peaceful, and she feels guilt when she tries to discover and express her own needs. Despite this, she has achieved much, both professionally and in her relationship life, but has great difficulty allowing herself to be truly pleased with that.

Lee

Another patient, Lee, also an attorney in her forties, whom I have been seeing for over ten years, spent many years before therapy and many years while in therapy wanting to make her mother's life okay so she could go on with hers. She felt her mother's envy in her mother's disapproving comments about her life, about how she chose to live her life, to spend her money, to have a profession. She had felt this as a girl and recalled her mother's difficulty in allowing her as a teenager to have relationships with friends and then with boyfriends; she did not feel she was allowed to have anything separate, anything of her own. Lee did manage to locate herself a thousand miles away from home for college, and has not lived near home since then. As an adult, her attempted solution to the guilt she felt for leaving had been to buy things for her mother that she assumed her mother felt deprived of and to offer to take her mother on trips abroad. Her mother never went on the trips and the gifts were never right. From Lee's point of view, nothing would make up for her having the relative freedom she had and for choosing a different way of living from her mother's—and she was right. As long as her happiness was dependent on her mother's becoming happy, she was stuck. These issues came into the transference early in the work, with Lee expressing concern for my feelings about what she did in her life. She would become anxious thinking I might be angry at her for leaving me by going on trips, for having relationships, or for doing anything that would differentiate her from me. After many years of working in the transference, Lee is now in the termination stage of her therapy, quite happy with her life, and having recently married for the first time in her life. These issues have, of course, arisen in our relationship once again as we approach termination, though now Lee's ambivalence about separating can be experienced as a natural and expectable feeling given our long and intimate association, and not as a source of anxiety and peril. She also knows that I share some of those mixed feelings.

These two women present themselves and their issues very differently, yet there are similarities in their dynamics. Both have been inhibited by what they have experienced and what, together, we have labeled as their mother's envy. Both their mothers were in unhappy, long-term marriages in which they were belittled and treated by their husbands as if they were there only to serve and to listen to them. (This is not unlike Demeter's treatment by Zeus before she threatened him with famine on the earth if he did not listen to her.) Neither mother worked outside the home, and both did in some way see their daughters as special. They were also very ambivalent about their daughters' leaving them—both physically and emotionally—and unconsciously communicated to their daughters, in some subtle and some very blatant ways, their envy of them and resentment about their own plights. This is inevitable when feelings go unrecognized and is confusing to both sender and recipient of the communication. This has led, for these daughters, to an inhibition of themselves, especially in their capacity for joy and creativity. Although both are accomplished women in their professions, they do not feel this accomplishment as an integral part of them nor do they feel happy about their lives (though Lee has been able to reach this point). Their anhedonia seems to be a way of staying merged with their depressed mothers and reducing their guilt and, in fantasy, their mother's envy and thus the danger of punishment for happiness. If mother has seemingly not been able to achieve a measure of happiness and if mother appears to have no pleasure in her life, then feeling happy or experiencing pleasure can feel dangerous to these women because it breaks "the taboo of any real separation" (Herman 1989, p. 272), causing anxiety and a pulling back from these experiences and a retreat into the original merger.

ENVY AND PROJECTIVE IDENTIFICATION

Melanie Klein (1957) saw envy as innate and essentially limits her discussion of it to the infant's envy of the mother. Winnicott, while not having published an account of his criticism of Klein's theory of envy, seemed to have seen her view as limited and as dismissing the importance of the environment and of the unique mother–infant bond. This interpretation of Winnicott is supported by his paper *Hate in the Countertransference* (1947/1975), in which he speaks of the mother hating her infant. Harold Boris (1994) presents a very clear, helpful, and provocative look at this dark emotion in his book entitled, simply, *Envy*. Envy, he says, needs to be considered as a relationship. It is an awareness of oneself and others as to who has what. It is, fundamentally, an emotion that is a response to disparity. To compare and to find oneself wanting leads to envy.

In this fiercely competitive culture of ours, envy as defined by Boris must be a near-universal experience that we routinely process— both our own and others' envy. One way we do that, Boris (1994) says, is "the maneuver by which people try to mitigate their envy by converting differences into similarities" (p. 81). In the parent–child relationship, though envy is not the dominant feeling that most parents have toward their children, it is unavoidable that parents will sometimes envy their children—envy their youth, their opportunities, even, sometimes especially, envy the parenting they receive. In the person for whom envy is a major problem, however, the awareness of disparity is a constant presence as is the awareness of lacking something. And in the mother who has been frustrated in her own development, and who has remained unconscious about that aspect of herself, envy of a child will be communicated in some way, for example, by a lack of generosity, by disparaging remarks, or by inhibiting a child's expressiveness. One of the ways this unconscious feeling may be communicated is through projective identification from mother to daughter.

I find projective identification a useful concept, both intrapsychically and interpersonally, and believe it to be a ubiquitous phenomenon. Many writers, notably Ogden (1982), have extended Klein's original concept, seeing projective identification as a mechanism present in most intense relationships and acting reciprocally. Family therapy literature sees projective identification as a basic mechanism used in families to influence their children's identities (Knapp 1989). Knapp writes that, in a two-person system, the more vulnerable identity is likely to be more influenced by the other's projections; thus children are more susceptible to parents' projections than the reverse. Knapp adds that "in addition to the vulnerability of the recipient, . . . the intensity in the interaction and the states or power of the projector, determine the extent to which the projection becomes accepted as an aspect of identity" (p. 54).

In the mother–daughter relationship, projections ricochet back and forth, unconscious and unverbalized. While I believe that there is certainly envy of the mother by the little girl—envying mother's freedom, power, competence, her developed body—and that this is projected into the mother by the daughter, projection in that direction (daughter to mother) does not have the power that mother to daughter projection has, at least in the child's early life. In the child, whose identity is developing, and who is totally dependent on her mother, projective identification from mother has enormous power. (This is not to say that children's projections into parents do not have great power; they do. In becoming a parent, one opens oneself to being affected in that way.) It is arguable that at some point in their lives the power may shift to become equalized or even skewed in the opposite direction.

The task of individuation in this relationship between two like bodies in which mother's projective identifications have much power to define the daughter is difficult at best for both mother and daughter. At the Oedipal stage, at puberty, and again at young adulthood, the issues of separation and individuation are sharply in focus. As Bassoff (1988) understates it in talking about separation at these stages, "Such leavetakings are not usually cordial; rather they are clumsy, disruptive, bewildering, and, at times, cruel" (p. xi). Mother's protectiveness at these stages is often experienced by the daughter as inhibiting of her independence and sexuality, and as pressure to be like her. The daughter, for these many reasons, may feel the need to pull away adamantly and angrily in order to assert her autonomy. The daughter's rejection can be very painful for the mother, especially for the mother who cannot identify with those feelings and experiences them as solely about her and defining of her. The daughter's acts of self-assertion and movements into her own self-development may call into question for the mother all the values she has tried to live by. Kim Chernin (1985/1994) speaks of the daughter's guilt for surpassing her mother and her need to stop herself from doing that. She speaks specifically of eating disorders as a way of doing that, but there are many ways to inhibit development. The mother–daughter relationship is one in which competition is routinely denied or avoided and mothers can feel personally rejected by statements of differentiation. This can lead to the daughter's feeling guilty about hurting her mother, and lead her to deny the difference in order to repair the felt rift between them.

CONCLUDING VIGNETTE

Another brief vignette illustrates this mother–daughter dynamic and how it got played out in the transference.

Kate

Upon moving to Washington to live with her boyfriend, Kate, a 26-year-old journalist, had been given two names by her New York therapist: mine and a male therapist's. She had had a very positive experience with her prior therapist, a man, and decided she wanted to work now with a woman therapist.

Kate seemed from the first session like a motherless child—not waiflike as that word could connote, but on the contrary, very well put together, everything precisely put together, as if she'd been keeping everything together for a very long time. She is quite striking with her dark, casual good looks, her long straight brown hair and brown eyes that look directly out at the world. There was an adamancy to her stance—her put-togetherness and her directness—that suggested a defense was at work.

Indeed, Kate confirmed this impression in the early sessions, talking about how alone she had felt as a child, and how she always had felt she was wrong. Her parents divorced when she was 6 years old and her brother was 4, her mother remarrying when Kate was 8. Kate lived with her mother and stepfather, receiving much criticism and little nurturance. Her mother, who was quite self-deprecating, seems as if she was anxiously caught up in keeping her second marriage together, and neglected the children, particularly Kate, to whom she seems to have been antagonistic. This became markedly worse around puberty.

In the therapy, Kate formed a positive, somewhat idealizing transference rather quickly. She responded to any affirming statement on my part or to my remembering something she had told me with great appreciation and much feeling. She talked through her tears about how rare it had been in her family for her to be listened to and acknowledged in any positive way. We came to talk about her as having "raised herself," looking for nurturance where she could find it. Several months into the therapy, she came to a session wearing an outfit that was quite similar to the one I was wearing that day. She noted it in a very pleased way, saying that she now dresses like me. This session was followed by one in which she was quite pulled back and silent, and it became clear over the next couple of sessions that her silence had been the result of her feeling that she had stepped over a line with me in saying she was like me in that way, and she was frightened that I would feel that she wanted too much from me. This brought up memories of having to care for herself in many ways, and to memories of being called "selfish" by her mother when she wanted some attention or asked to do things that would involve time, money, or effort on her mother's part.

This dynamic was repeated in a very striking way in a session of group therapy. After a year and a half of individual sessions, Kate entered a therapy group, in addition to her individual sessions. She had been in the group for about eight months when the following occurred: the group had been doggedly focusing on one member who had brought up an issue and the discussion seemed to be circling around some other issues that were in the room but not being addressed. I made a general statement to the group to that effect. A bit later on in the session, Kate reported feeling that my statement had been directed at her, and that I was saying that she should keep quiet. Other group members expressed surprise at her reaction and were curious about it; they also reassured her that they often appreciated her comments, and that her comments that day had been very on point. Later in the session I said to Kate that she often said things in the group that were quite powerful and that I felt that she had difficulty recognizing her power and the importance of her statements to others. Again, she heard me as telling her that she was too much and should shut up. This was clearly a distortion of what I had said, and it was helpful to her to have the group affirm this so she could look at her fear that, as she expressed herself more and as she began to feel more effective and powerful in group and in her life and relationships, she would lose her connection to me, as she had with her mother when she asserted her needs or her self.

Kate has grown and moved on from that place and has been able to establish a relationship with her mother in which both try to be fairly open and direct with the other about their feelings, positive and negative. Her mother still has a difficult time really celebrating Kate's triumphs and successes, so Kate has learned to go to others for that reaction and tell her mother only later, when she doesn't need her to respond in a particular way. To their credit, they are both still working on the relationship and it is still evolving.

CODA

The myth of Demeter and Persephone is a rich one and is a story that gets reenacted in every culture in many different ways. It serves as the basis for a book of poetry by Rita Dove (1995) called *Mother Love*, which provides an unsentimental, though sympathetic, look at the mother–daughter relationship, trying on different interpretations of the myth and casting it in modern terms. Dove looks not only at Demeter's loss, but at Persephone's complicity in her leaving. She dedicates the book "FOR my mother, TO my daughter," thus invoking the inevitable repetition of this scenario in each generation. These are the last few lines of her poem "Missing."*

> . . . Now I understand she can never
> die, just as nothing can bring me back.
>
> I am the one who comes and goes;
> I am the footfall that hovers.
>
> [p. 62]

---

*Reprinted from "Missing" in *Mother Love* by Rita Dove, copyright © 1995 by W. W. Norton & Co. Used by permission.

REFERENCES

Bassoff, E. (1988). *Mothers and Daughters: Loving and Letting Go.* New York: Penguin.

Beauvoir, S. de (1949). *The Second Sex.* New York: Bantam, 1961.

Bernstein, D. (1993). *Female Identity Conflict in Clinical Practice.* Northvale, NJ: Jason Aronson.

Bolen, J. S. (1984). *Goddesses in Everywoman: A New Psychology of Women.* New York: Harper & Row.

Boris, H. (1994). *Envy.* Northvale, NJ: Jason Aronson.

Caldwell, R. (1990). The psychoanalytic interpretation of Greek myth. In *Approaches to Greek Myth,* ed. L. Edmonds, pp. 344–389. Baltimore: Johns Hopkins University Press.

Chernin, K. (1985/1994). *The Hungry Self: Women, Eating and Identity.* New York: HarperCollins.

Dove, R. (1995). *Mother Love.* New York: Norton.

Estes, C. P. (1991). *The Creative Fire.* Tape recording. Boulder, CO: SoundsTrue Recordings.

Graves, R. (1955/1992). *The Greek Myths.* London: Penguin.

Herman, N. (1989). *Too Long a Child: The Mother–Daughter Dyad.* London: Free Association Press.

Klein, M. (1957/1984). *Envy and Gratitude and Other Works 1946–1963.* New York: Free Press.

Knapp, H. (1989). Projective identification: Whose projection—whose identity? *Psychoanalytic Psychology* 6:47–58.

Ogden, T. (1982). *Projective Identification and Psychotherapeutic Technique.* New York: Jason Aronson.

Rich, A. (1986). *Of Woman Born.* New York: Norton.

Spitz, E. H. (1992). Mothers and daughters: ancient and modern myths. *Analytic Reflections* 2(1):32–48.

Winnicott, D. W. (1947/1975). Hate in the countertransference. In *Through Paediatrics to Psycho-Analysis,* pp. 194–203. New York: Basic Books.

Young-Eisendrath, P., and Wiedeman, F. (1987). *Female Authority.* New York: Guilford.

PART III

MARRIAGE
AND MATERNITY

Most authors agree that it is difficult for girls to emancipate from the mother and turn to men because their ties with the mother are deeply rooted in bodily isomorphism. Such moving away is often accompanied by symptoms until the woman becomes a mother herself (Tyson and Tyson 1990). The use of somatization (Pines 1993) is observed as a method to avoid conscious affects and fantasies that are overwhelming to the ego. An ill-defined sense of guilt may lead to unconscious punishment in the choice of partners or miscarriages. Benedek (1970) states that permanency in marriage is dependent on ego organization that is not discouraged by changing aspects of love. The advent of motherhood, personality changes, and so forth, all contribute to new challenges.

Benedek has shown that we need to perceive the family as a psychological field. Marriage, she says, offers the opportunity of being loved, being attached, not being alone. Heterosexual love is a complex attainment. For the wife, she is content that she has satisfied her husband's needs; for the husband, his personality and achievements satisfy the woman he has loved even though she has become more of a mother. This ego organization lays a good foundation to have children.

Any infant is an enigma at birth, but the infant is a total object for the parents' needs. The narcissistic investment of the loving parent represents a demand on the child for support of the parents' self-esteem. Turrini and Mendell (1995) speak about the concept of "maternality," which is defined as the total of intrasystemic psychic components that inform maternal thoughts, affects, and behaviors. There is not only a biological symbiosis but an emotional symbiosis that grows from reciprocal interactions through processes of introjection and identification. Parents unconsciously relive certain parts of their developmental problems; depending on their nature and intensity, pathology may result. Joel Bernstein addresses the conditions that contribute to the development of maternal feelings while Robert Gordon discusses how rage can extinguish a mother's love of her children when resentment against the husband, or former husband, takes over.

Fenchel (1986) suggests that maternal unavailability becomes strain trauma and echoes through several generations. Children repeat unsolved problems in succeeding generations. Daughters who have been victimized exhibit a sense of loyalty and identify with the abusing parent. Clinical histories reveal a series of strain traumas. While trauma derivatives find expression in symbolic form, they are mostly observable in the context of intimate relationships. Such persons relate to reality as if reality itself caused traumatic conditions. Maria Bergmann (1985) reminds us that preverbal strain traumas become character traits that influence attitudes toward the external world through the superego and the ego ideal.

Anna Freud (1970) describes how the mother may be experienced as "rejecting" when she misunderstands the child's needs or does not adapt to the child's rhythm and speed. Indeed, lack of love for the husband may be extended to the child. The worst scenario is when a mother wavers between rejection and possessiveness. Repeated rejections by separations produces individuals that are dissatisfied, shallow, and promiscuous in their relationships. The deteriorating process between mother and child is described as a sadomasochistic one resulting in endless quarrels.

Turrini and Mendell state that mothers reported withdrawal, depression, child abuse, and flight when they could not live up to their maternal ego ideals. The birth of a child activates in the mother the longing to reestablish the fantasy of the early dyad with her own child. Diane Barth demonstrates how daydreams and fantasies about the child will influence the bond between mother and child upon birth and then onward. If the mother's anxiety or anguish takes over, rage is experienced and results in a "good-bad" dichotomy to protect the early cherished maternal ideal. The child represents to the mother the external representation of self, spouse, and grandparents. The child's accomplishments—or lack thereof—affect the mother's self-esteem regulation.

Maria Bergmann illustrates in her chapter the consequences for girls who suffered disturbances in the symbiotic phase. She mentions in particular specific cases of role reversals. In such instances, the daughter mothers the mother and the mother becomes the child. She believes that such reversals are defensive, adaptive processes to safeguard the cohesion of the self. Basic to such defense is the fear of abandonment. Such women who mothered their mothers also show bisexuality and alternate in their object relationships between idealization and disillusionment. Dale Mendell's paper focuses on the distortion of the Oedipus complex. Such women utilize sex and men for ungratified symbiotic longings.

An interesting observation on energies fueling mothering is made by Dr. Bernstein. Speculating about vanity and voyeurism, Bernstein focuses on the fate of homosexual libido in women. He believes that mothering depends on desexualized homosexual libido to a large extent, which also energizes female companionship and "sunny dispositions."

REFERENCES

Benedek, T. (1970). The family as a psychological field. In *Parenthood—Its Psychology and Psychopathology*, ed. J. Anthony and T. Benedek, pp. 109–136. Boston: Little, Brown.

Bergmann, M. (1985). Character resistances: current clinical views. *Issues in Ego Psychology* 8:7–16.

Fenchel, G. (1986). Maternal unavailability as intergenerational trauma. *Issues in Ego Psychology* 9:25–31.

Freud, A. (1970). The concept of the rejecting mother. In *Parenthood—Its Psychology and Psychopathology*, ed. J. Anthony and T. Benedek, pp. 376–386. Boston: Little, Brown.

Pines, D. (1993). *A Woman's Unconscious Use of Her Body*. New Haven, CT/London: Yale University Press.

Turrini, P., and Mendell, D. (1995). Maternal lines of development: an aspect of gender identity. *Psychoanalytic Inquiry* 15:93–111.

Tyson, P., and Tyson, R. L. (1990). *Psychoanalytic Theories of Development*. New Haven, CT: Yale University Press.

7

Mothers and Daughters:
Daydreams and Mutuality

Diane Barth

In a recent session a young analysand, pregnant with her first child, laughingly reported a conversation she had had with her husband while lying in bed the night before. "We talked about what our baby would be like, what characteristics we wanted and what we didn't." She chuckled as she went on to list the qualities they had chosen: "my neatness, his sense of humor, my hair, my intelligence, his savvy. . . ."

Fantasies about unborn children frequently precede the births of those children by years, even decades. Daydreams about oneself as a parent and as a member of a family group other than the one in which one grew up are part of the developmental process, whether the dreamer is 5 years old, 25, or 55. Although both men and women frequently have daydreams about both male and female children, since the subject of this book is mothers and daughters, we will focus in this chapter on daydreams in the mother–daughter dyad. Much of what is said here, however, can be applied to many other significant relationships, including father–daughter, mother–son, and sibling–sibling.

Before a girl is born her mother has usually had many contradictory fantasies about her, including her gender (even in cases where a mother knows her baby's gender, she often has daydreams about the possibility that the technicians made a mistake), her looks, her personality, and her future. Contained within these daydreams will also be ideas about the relationship a woman will have with her daughter—among other things, how it will be both similar to and different from her relationship with her own mother. It is often taken for granted by psychoanalysts that these daydreams can have a powerful, if subtle, influence on the daughter, and a significant amount of work can involve an analytic effort to tease out just what this impact has been.

While this pursuit can be extremely useful, it can ultimately lead to an unbalanced analysis. A more integrated approach needs to take into account the knowledge that the information being explored is filtered through both the daughter's and the analyst's perceptions of the mother, each of which contains numerous daydream images. For example, images of the analysand's mother as experienced by the analysand coexist in the consulting room with visions of that mother as imagined by the analyst. At the same time, the room is filled with ghosts of other mothers: the analyst's perceived, longed for, and experienced mother; both analyst's and analysand's fantasies of the analyst as mother (which can occur whether the analyst is male or female); cultural, professional, and personal archetypes of ideal, flawed, and bad mothers; and so on. It is extremely beneficial to include exploration of some of these daydreams in any woman's analysis, but unfortunately such exploration does not always occur. Far too often, reported images of and experiences with parents, particularly negative reports about mothers, are viewed simply as reality by an individual and/or her therapist and, as though observable reality does not have intrapsychic meaning, they are not explored for the multiple, complex meanings they may contain. Viewing this material as daydream data should not be used to negate actual experience, but it can open up inquiry into intrapsychic and interpersonal meanings and allow access to hidden and unexplored aspects of these experiences.

Current infant research has underscored the mutual interplay between parent and child, offering strong evidence that although the relationship between mother and child is not equal, neither is it a one-way street. In other words, a daughter's response to and attitude toward her mother can have a significant impact on the relationship between them as well as on each member of the dyad's experience of her or himself, alone and in a relationship. Benjamin (1992) has highlighted this often neglected aspect of parent–child relating: the interactive cycle of mutual responsiveness and mutual understanding that develops between parent and child and that influences *both* members of the pair. Stern (1995) and Turrini and Mendell (1995) have noted that a mother's self-esteem is often closely tied to her sense of competence as a mother, and who can reflect how well she is doing better than her child? (These reflections, however, will be filtered through the mother's value system, expectations, and assumptions—in other words, through her daydreams about what is normal, what is good, and what is bad.)

While many analysts have applied these ideas to the concepts of transference and countertransference, few have directly linked them to parent–child dynamics. Yet this is not a new idea. Erikson (1959) wrote that the child, in the process of being raised by a family, also raises the family. Loewald (1980) also addressed this interweaving of intrapsychic and interpersonal in his eloquent discussion of the complex factors that contribute to "the waning of the Oedipus complex" (p. 384).

Mother–daughter daydreams often reveal many of the elements of mutuality and mutual recognition described by Beebe and Lachmann (1992), Benjamin (1992), Olesker (1990), and Stern (1985). When such daydreams are explored in the analytic work, they act as powerful conduits not only to intrapsychic and interpersonal dynamics, but also to the interface between the two, an area of intrapsychic experience Ogden (1986) has called "dream space." The interplay of mutual daydreams is a lifelong process, beginning very early in the relationship and continuing through every stage of life. Opening this world of beliefs, longings, and fears to analytic investigation can pave the way to potential integration of a variety of contradictory and confusing experiences and imaginings.

At this juncture it would be useful to define the term *daydream.* Singer (1975), one of the earliest researchers on the subject, wrote:

. . . daydreaming has long been recognized as a wispy, mysterious and yet intriguing facet of our behavior. Because of its completely private nature it is impossible to formulate a generally agreed upon definition of this act. Probably the single most common connotation is that day-dreaming represents a shift of attention *away* from some primary physical or mental task we have set for ourselves, or *away* from directly looking at or listening to something in the external environment, *toward* an unfolding sequence of private responses made to some internal stimulus. The inner processes usually considered are "pictures in the mind's eye," the unrolling of a sequence of events, memories or creatively constructed images of future events which have varying degrees of probability of taking place. Also included as objects of daydreaming are our awareness of our bodily sensations, our emotions and our *monologues intérieurs*, those little inner voices we hear talking to us somewhere in our heads. [pp. 3–4]

Raphling (1996) calls daydreams "waking fantasies" and agrees with Singer that one of the difficulties inherent in analyzing them is that they are narratives "not usually revealed to anyone" (p. 534). Frequently daydreams have never been articulated, even to the dreamer, so that they are often part of the "unthought known" described by Bollas (1987). Although daydreams are mentioned by a number of analysts (e.g., Bollas 1987, Freud 1900, 1908, Winnicott 1982), until recently they have seldom received detailed examination in the analytic literature (e.g., Barth, in press, Raphling 1996). This may be partly due to the overtly conscious nature of daydreams, as opposed to the unconscious dynamics seen in sleeping dreams and fantasies, as well as to Raphling's (1996) reported finding that daydreams are seldom spontaneously, directly, reported in analysis. However, in my experience, once a therapist brings up daydreams as a topic of interest, analysands frequently respond with daydream material as well as anxiety, embarrassment, and resistance. Investigation of both content and defense can lead to valuable dynamic work in and out of the transference.

Daydreams can provide access to symbolic thought even in clients who tend to focus on the concrete rather than abstract aspects of their experience. They can help analysands understand something of the "as if" nature of analytic work, and they can be useful instruments for learning to "play" (Winnicott 1982) in psychotherapy.

They offer "a place from which to become aware" (Winnicott 1982, p. 27n) of one's internal world, a transitional space with which to discover the world of symbolic meaning. For example, in mother–daughter relations, both daydreams and actual interpersonal patterns often have a tendency to become static and rigidified. Exploration of the symbolic meanings contained in these calcified images can be invaluable, but for some individuals the abstract meaning remains beyond reach. Although they may be intelligent and articulate, these individuals experience what Benjamin (1995) called a "foreclosure of symbolic space" (p. 203). Daydreams can provide an important transition from concrete to abstract so that, for example, unrecognized or unacknowledged childhood traumas can become available for conscious working through and also explored for their personal meaning. Daydreams often make it possible to question rigidly maintained childhood interpretations of early experiences, to reexamine them from an adult perspective, and eventually to integrate new understanding with old. Exploration of this material can lead not only to greater self-awareness, understanding, and flexibility, but it also often opens the door to new aspects of old daydreams and to new daydreams altogether. Such new daydreams can then lead to significant shifts in actual patterns of interacting between mother and daughter, with concomitant shifts in both intrapsychic and interpersonal shifts in *both* individuals. The following example will illustrate some of this complex, multifaceted, and fascinating process.

THE CASE OF ELISA

Elisa had no concept of symbolic meaning when she began therapy with me. Although obviously intelligent, she was extremely concrete in her thinking. While almost everything she did seemed to have a number of unconscious meanings, they were beyond her comprehension or interest. She was in her late twenties when she came to me for help with a severe eating disorder. At five feet seven inches tall, she had gone from one hundred forty to one hundred and five pounds in six months, and she was eager to shed more weight. The idea that her compulsive quest for thinness might have psychological meaning was anathema to her. As she put it, she had felt fat all her life, and now she finally felt that she had her size under control. She had come into therapy only because her boyfriend was concerned and had told her that if she did not get help, he did not think he could stay with her. She casually mentioned that her parents, particularly her mother, had also expressed some worry about her physical and emotional condition. "But," she added, "my mother has always wanted me to be thin. I don't know why she's so upset."

In response to this comment, I asked Elisa to tell me what she imagined was going on in her mother's mind. "How do I know?" she insisted at first. I soon discovered that Elisa did not like to think about things unless, as she put it, she "knew they exist in reality." Elisa's difficulties with "as if" experiences made it hard to explore her resistance to knowing about her own daydreams, so I simply explained to her that I view these "inner pictures" as clues to our emotional and psychological world, where we try to make sense of what goes on in and around us. I also told her that I was not testing her, that there was no right or wrong in this process, but that we might learn something important about her experience if she allowed herself to begin to play with some of her images. Nervously, but with obvious interest, she gradually began to try to put into words some images of her mother and her mother's ideas and feelings about her. Her daydreams provided an entrance to a variety of other significant areas of Elisa's experience, but I will restrict my discussion here to those related to her mother.

Elisa told me that she and her mother had battled over her weight and what she ate ever since she could remember. "I grew up feeling like a chubby kid," she told me, "but when I look at pictures of myself as a little girl, I wasn't really chubby at all. A little round, maybe, but not *fat*. But my mother was always telling me not to eat certain things. She told me that I was built like my grandmother, her mother, and that I would have to watch myself or I'd end up getting really heavy. And she'd tell me I couldn't have mashed potatoes, and then she'd serve my brother an extra helping." Numerous other images of her mother followed this theme, so that in this early phase of the work it might have been tempting to interpret Elisa's eating disorder as a reaction to her mother's intrusion and criticism around food, weight, and many other aspects of Elisa's life. We could also have drawn some conclusions about Elisa's competitive strivings with her brother and her feelings about what appeared to be her mother's preferential treatment of him. But although each of these hypotheses seemed to have clinical validity, none of them captured the more complex and confusing aspects of what made Elisa who she was. A more enigmatic and ultimately meaningful picture was gradually revealed as Elisa struggled to articulate more and more of her daydreams.

For example, when Elisa spoke about her diet and her wish to lose more weight, I asked her to tell me about her daydreams about what it would be like to be as thin as she wanted. "I'd be sexy," she answered immediately. I asked her what "sexy" meant to her. "Men would find me attractive." Her answers were brief, but they were indicators of some of the stories she told herself—her fantasies, hopes, beliefs, and expectations. They were as much as she could talk about in the beginning of our work together, so I did not push her to tell me more about them. In fact, I was not sure that she knew more about these images herself, so I simply encouraged her to pay attention to the details of these stories whenever she could. I also gave her some examples of questions to ask herself: How and why would being thin make her feel attractive? What would she have when she was thin that she did not have when she was heavy? Why?

Daydreams about her mother quickly entered the conversation. For example, Elisa described her mother as tall and thin, beautifully dressed, extremely feminine. Although Elisa was also tall and thin, she dressed in baggy sweat clothes and spoke disparagingly of her body: "I'm not very tall, and I'm kind of dumpy. I have all this cellulite on my thighs and my butt." She felt that her mother was critical of and disappointed in her. As I encouraged her to think and talk more about this daydream, she discovered that she had several contradictory pictures of both her mother and herself. In one, for example, she viewed her mother as disdainful of her and herself as rebellious at her mother's overemphasis on looks, while in another she saw her mother as incompetently trying to teach Elisa how to "be a woman." (Only years later were we able to explore the possibility that Elisa had overeaten and underdressed in part out of revenge. It seemed an excellent way to punish her mother, not just refusing to live out what she imagined was her mother's daydream of her, but making her mother fail as well; in this early stage of the work, however, Elisa did not have enough of a sense of agency to examine her own motivated behavior toward her mother.)

Elisa also began to elaborate on fantasies about her mother's preference for her brother. Sometimes she believed it was because her mother preferred men to women, a daydream for which Elisa could offer great amounts of evidence. Other times she imagined that her mother preferred her brother because he "took after her," whereas Elisa was said to be more like her maternal grandmother, with whom her mother had a difficult relationship. Eventually, as we explored numerous situations and Elisa's daydreams about them, Elisa began to construct a more complex and empathic picture of her mother—and a concomitant one of herself. Such images alternated with other, more critical portraits of both her mother and herself. As her daydreams of her mother and herself became more multifaceted, so too did her relationship with her mother. Elisa became aware of some images of her mother that she had always suppressed—for example, that her mother was mildly phobic. As we explored this material, Elisa commented, "I guess I needed to see her as strong and critical. I just couldn't bear thinking of her as frightened."

Elisa, like many of us, maintained a daydream of her mother as the omnipotent, powerful mother archetype. In order to keep this image alive, any adult must simultaneously close off other information about a real mother. Because daydreams are conscious, it is often possible to begin to explore charged material without disrupting necessary defenses. At the same time, the analyst's interest in and use of daydreams communicates a belief in multiple and symbolic meanings, and often engages an analysand in the pursuit of these meanings. As Elisa became more conscious of her own contradictory images of her mother, she also began to be curious about some of her mother's different images of her. She wondered if her mother had more than one picture of her. She was learning to explore and "play" with her fantasies, but she also asked her mother directly (although she was not convinced that her mother always gave her honest answers). Interestingly, she found that while she was often irritated by her mother, she felt much less vulnerable to her mother's criticism and as a result became less hostile to her. In turn, Elisa reported major changes in her mother's behavior. "She's not so critical of me anymore," she told me. When I asked how she explained this phenomenon, Elisa replied that her mother must have finished menopause "or something." While this interpretation may well have been accurate, my own hypothesis (daydream) is more in line with Basch's (1980) comment that "when adolescents and young adults with the benefits of insight won in therapy cease to demand what the parents cannot give psychologically, the relationship improves and is placed on a different footing" (p. 82).

While Elisa may never know the full truth about her mother's inner pictures of her, the exploration of her own daydreams about those images and about her mother opened up both her internal and her interpersonal worlds so that she could find new and more satisfying ways of being, in relation to her mother and in other relationships as well. Elisa's experience is not uncommon. When women are helped to explore their daydreams about their mothers, they often discover that they have many contradictory images of this important figure. A mother can be viewed as helpless and incompetent in one daydream and as potent or terrifying in another. Contrasting memories, which are also, in effect, daydreams, can exist side by side, as when a woman has images of her mother in violent rages and also as comforting and loving. Exploring the daydream content does not mean denying the "reality" aspect of these experiences, but it does mean making room for the many mothers that every woman has: for example, the wished-for mother as well as the experienced mother; the mother of different moods and abilities as well as the consistently known or represented mother; and even the same mother viewed from the perspective of a child as opposed to that of an adult.

As Schafer (1983) pointed out, it is extremely important for the therapist to keep the many images of mother in mind even when the analysand cannot, and gradually to help the analysand come to see some of the other images she splits off or ignores. Eventually most women analysands will find in themselves some of the very qualities they have criticized in their mothers. If they have not looked at these dynamics with some degree of empathy, they will have difficulty when the time comes to integrate them into their own self-image. As a woman mourns not only her mother's failings but also the traumas, losses, pains, and inadequacies of her own childhood, she will gradually be able to look at her mother from a more adult perspective. Daydreams of an omnipotent mother may diminish and be replaced by surprising shifts in her real relationship with her mother.

As every therapist knows, the process leading to this shift is long and difficult. Although, as I have noted elsewhere (Barth, in press), the concept of daydreams is often less threatening than that of "fantasy," it can nonetheless elicit anxiety and discomfort. Analysands may be concerned that their daydreams are uninteresting or that they will reveal too much. Like Elisa, they may not always be able to capture daydreams or distinguish them from "fact." Furthermore, both analyst and analysand may have a stake in remaining ignorant of certain daydream material about their mothers. As is always the case, such resistance serves important purposes and should not be viewed as volitional or negativistic. Exploration of the anxiety that accompanies the thought of daydreams, as well as whatever daydream material is available to the individual's conscious awareness, will gradually help the analysand become more comfortable with the process and lead to rich and useful work.

Not surprisingly, many daydreams also capture significant issues in the relationship between analyst and analysand. In the following example an analysand worked through in the transference some of the tremendous pain she felt as her daydreams of an idealized mother diminished. At times, daydreams of mother and analyst merged so that the transference meaning was particularly vivid. At other times, as she put it, "I'm having to feel the pain twice. Not just about you, and not just about my mother, but about both of you."

THE CASE OF MARGARET

Margaret began therapy in her mid-twenties, several years after graduating college. I will not go into detail about our early work together, as the focus of my discussion is in the later phase of the work. Two points from the initial period are, however, important. First, Margaret came to therapy for help with career direction. She felt she was drifting along without a purpose, working as a secretary to a physician while she tried to decide what to do with her life. However, she was worried that she would spend the rest of her life in this state of limbo. She saw herself as like her mother, a frustrated artist who had never been able to pursue her dream of being a working painter. Margaret's father encouraged his wife to continue to paint, but she complained that she could not pay attention to the children and do her work. When Margaret and her two brothers went to school, her mother attempted to return to her artwork, but with little success. The second point about the early work with Margaret is that her initial description of her mother as a loving but unhappy woman soon shifted to daydream images of a volatile, angry, and sometimes explosive "witch."

For some time I encouraged Margaret to explore the daydreams that resided in these descriptions. As she opened up images of an all-powerful, sometimes frightening and ungiving mother, Margaret also began to explore thoughts about herself as "powerless, intimidated, frightened, demanding." She experienced herself and was described by her family as "greedy and selfish" when she argued with her mother or asked for something for herself. I suggested that this sounded like she was breaking an unspoken family agreement not to upset her mother, based on a family portrait of her mother as both fragile and dangerous. As these ideas triggered still more daydreams, Margaret began to question her own image of her mother. Was she as strong or dangerous as Margaret had always believed? Was she as fragile and incapable of giving as the family seemed to think?

These questions emerged slowly and with great trepidation. Margaret experimented with being more direct and less confrontational with her mother, acting as though she expected her mother to be equally rational. Although this led to several explosive battles, Margaret found that neither she nor her mother fell apart as a result and, while not always successful, this approach gradually led to a significant change in the interactions between Margaret and her mother. Margaret felt that her mother was more respectful and caring, and that they had more of a "real" relationship. Not surprisingly, these changes caused shifts within the family system, and other issues began to emerge both within the family and in the analytic work. However, in order to maintain the focus of this discussion, I will not go into these changes here but will focus on a specific development in the transference.

Margaret initially viewed me as a benign but omnipotent figure. She was extremely grateful to me for being so helpful, and for some time she idealized me and looked unquestioningly to me for advice and guidance. Over time, however, as she made significant advances in her life, she began to articulate daydreams that I was feeling competitive with her because she was younger and more attractive than I, and because she had her future ahead of her. It was fairly simple to make the connection to her mother, who Margaret now viewed as incompetent, unsatisfied, and potentially envious of Margaret's successes. Like her mother, Margaret had always taken pleasure in painting and other visual artwork, but she was tremendously conflicted about pursuing a vocation that had been so difficult for her mother. Again, I will not go into detail about the work that we did, other than to say that we explored a number of variations of daydreams about both her mother's and my reactions to her if she were to pursue this career. Over time, Margaret decided to apply to a graduate school where she would be able to do fine art and also obtain a degree in teaching in order to support herself if she could not do so with her art alone. She felt both pleased with this decision and worried about her mother's response. She was also conflicted about asking her parents for financial assistance. "I don't know if they'll give it to me. Maybe it isn't even fair to ask. It's sort of like rubbing my mother's nose in it. I'm doing what she could never do, *and* I'm asking her to pay for it." Her daydreams included a fear that both mother and father would be furious with her for making her mother support her as she pursued this mutual interest of theirs.

Margaret thought that I would not be competitive over this particular issue, because she imagined that I was very satisfied in my career. In fact, with some discomfort, she was able to articulate her own envy of my professional competence. She was, however, afraid that I would be angry at her for leaving me, since the schools to which she had applied were all quite some distance away. I asked her to talk about her daydreams of what it would be like for her if I were angry at her. Spontaneously she replied, "I'd feel terrible." Then she stopped and looked at me in surprise. "It's true. I'd feel terrible. But mainly I'd feel bad because it would be such a surprise, coming from you. And it wouldn't make sense. I'd probably get mad at you and tell you to cut it out." Margaret was surprised and pleased to think that she was imagining treating me and being treated in return as though she was my equal. In the next session, however, she was uncharacteristically silent. Finally, she blurted out, "I don't want to be your equal! I can't stand it." Sobbing, she continued, "I don't want to be grown up. It feels so . . . so lonely. If you're not the adult and my mother's not the adult, then I'm on my own. It's terrifying."

Margaret was unusually verbal about this issue, but it is my experience that even when analysands are not so verbal, they often experience a period of mourning as they become aware of their growth, even when they are feeling generally more content. Kohut (1971) made a tremendous contribution to psychoanalytic theory by showing that idealization is not only a normal characteristic of human development, but also often a crucial attempt to maintain a cohesive sense of self. However, he believed that if loss of idealization is painful, then it is not a healthy process. Loewald (1982) on the other hand, suggested that growing up involves the painful destruction of the idealized, omnipotent parent. I would suggest that at times both individual and what appears to be contemporary cultural anger at maternal failure is derivative of the nearly universal daydream of an omnipotent, omniscient mother who can protect us from all pain and harm. Although anger is often a part of the mourning process, it can also defend against the painful loss of a sense of safety and security concomitant with deidealization. In either case an analysand's daydreams can be powerful tools in the exploration of the dynamics involved.

When daydreams are viewed as potential expressions of the many sides of experience, they can be used to explore a variety of interpersonal and intrapsychic dynamics. In this last part of the chapter I would like to discuss how this can occur when the analysand is a mother who is having difficulties with a daughter. While Winnicott (1982) suggested that a parent must survive a child's attempt to destroy her or him for the child to move to the level of mature object usage, Loewald (1980) suggested that something in the parent is in fact destroyed by the child's growth. Basch (1980) on the other hand believed that the change from dependent child to independent adult can be a relief for some parents, freeing them from unmanageable burdens. I have found each of these formulations to be true, sometimes singly and sometimes in combination. When contradictory and potentially troubling emotions of a variety of forms can be explored with the help of daydream material, both mother and daughter can be freed from rigidly maintained attitudes, and the mother–daughter system opened to new forms of interaction.

Just as a daughter's images of her mother are generally a mixture of reality and the meanings the child attributes to her experiences of and with her mother, so too are a mother's images of her daughter also a mixture, including responses to *something* coming from the child, even if it is a misinterpretation of what is perceived. A classic example of this phenomenon is the variation of ways that a baby's biting behavior can be interpreted. While one mother may feel that when her baby bites her breast while nursing it is a sign of anger, another may interpret the same behavior as part of the baby's exploration of the world, an attempt to explore qualities of the breast other than those that can be found through sucking, a need to relieve teething discomfort, or a desire to find out how her new teeth work. In the same way that a daughter's perceptions of her mother's daydreams about her will affect both the interactions between them and the daughter's sense of herself, the mother's perceptions of her daughter's images of her will have an impact on the relationship and on the mother's feelings about herself. It is therefore crucial to try to understand some of the multiple and often elusive meanings of these intertwined daydreams for mother as well as daughter. (Once again, although we are focusing on the mother–daughter dyad in this chapter, this point can be made for parents and children of both sexes.)

Although it is often difficult to tease out the origins or accuracy of these deeply interwoven daydreams, I am not suggesting that mothers and daughters must or even should be in therapy together. In the examination of the daydreams of women analysands, an analyst should be sensitive to the complex layering and compound nature of mother–daughter daydreams. A daughter's images of her mother have many meanings as does a mother's daydreams about her daughter. In the therapeutic process, the many facets of the intrapsychic and interpersonal dynamics should be at least acknowledged, at best explored and understood. If the process works, not only the analysand but also her relationship and, frequently, the other member of the dyad will undergo significant changes. The following example illustrates one way this can occur when the analysand is a mother of a daughter with whom she has a difficult, troubled relationship.

THE CASE OF LOUISE

Louise was in her late thirties when she came to see me. Recently divorced, she was afraid of how she was going to deal with life as a single mother. In particular, she was worried about coping with her youngest daughter, Samantha. As Louise put it, "If I'd had her first, I'd never have had a second child." She described Samantha as a difficult child who had been angry since birth. As a baby and even now as a 7-year-old, Samantha was difficult for Louise to comfort, control, or relate to. Louise commented that she "knew" that her younger daughter thought she was a bad mother. "She tells me that she hates me. She refuses to allow me to help her pick out clothes or do her homework or anything. She says, 'You don't know anything about it,' when I ask why I can't help." I asked Louise to try to spin out the daydreams that both of her daughters had about her. "Well, I know Samantha thinks the hospital made a mistake when they gave her to me. She's told me that she's sure that I'm not really her mother, and she tells me about her fantasies about where her real mother is and when she's going to come and get her."

I asked Louise if she thought that a child's daydreams of having a different mother meant that she was a bad mother. She paused for a moment, then said, "Well, when you ask me that question, my first reaction is 'of course not.' But I think in my gut I must really believe that it does, at least in Sam's case." My question set off other daydreams, some of which Louise had always discounted. There is not room to describe the many different images of herself, her daughters, and her own parents that occurred to Louise, as well as her thoughts about how each of these individuals viewed her. These daydreams were myriad, and they allowed us to open up many different aspects not only of Louise's relationships with both of her daughters but also of herself in relation to other significant people in her life. As she put these pictures of herself into words, Louise began to consider the possibility that each of her daughters had more than one image of her.

For example, she realized that Alexa, her older child, sometimes had daydreams with far more negative content than Louise had ever thought; and she also saw that Samantha sometimes actually had positive daydreams about her. For example, one day when they were going to the dentist, Samantha said, "Mom, I'd like to have some special time alone with you." Louise told me that she was completely stunned. She could not remember another time that Samantha had requested such a thing. "She told me that she really likes being with me," Louise continued. Hesitating, she added, "You know, it's not true that she's never said anything like that before. It's just that I never really believed her. It never occurred to me that she might have a mixture of good and bad feelings about me. But I *do* remember times that we've really had a good time together. I guess I never made room for that part of our relationship before. I was so focused on her negative thoughts about me that I couldn't imagine that she might have positive, loving ones, too." As she made room for her daughter's mixed images of her, Louise found herself more aware of her own mixture of feelings about both of her children.

Benjamin (1992) suggests that despite infant research demonstrating the bidirectional or mutually influential nature of mother–infant relationships, there remains a tendency for analysts to focus on mother as object and child as subject. In some instances this stance simply and subtly perpetuates many of the dynamics that are contributing to an analysand's difficulties. When the mutual impact of mother–daughter daydreams is explored, some of the complex nature of these relationships can be addressed and acknowledged. In Benjamin's (1992) terminology, this allows for an examination and maintenance of optimal tension between opposites—for example, fantasy and reality, intrapsychic and interpersonal, connection and separation—which can lead to a sense of self and a sense of other, an ability to be intimate while maintaining a cohesive sense of self. Opening up daydreams that mothers and daughters have about one another helps analysands to manage this tension. It makes it possible to eventually avoid unhelpful parent-blaming, splitting, and defensive feelings of victimization and allows for eventual analysis of hidden identifications with the negated aspects of mother. It allows both parent and child to mourn the dreams that have never been met, to accept loss of omnipotence and omniscience, and a chance to be among the fortunate parents and children who may eventually achieve "some sort of balance, equality or transcending conciliation" (Loewald 1980, p. 395) with one another and within themselves.

It is not my intention to suggest that exploration of daydreams is the ultimate analytic technique. Like everything else in the psycho-analytic process, daydreams are only one component of complex and often confusing dynamics. In mother–daughter relationships, day-dreams are often used to close down and maintain unhappy interactions. They can, however, be used to teach analysands to "play," and thereby to open up these relationships in important and highly meaningful ways. They are powerful tools for exploring the many facets of the complicated intrapsychic and interpersonal worlds of our analysands.

REFERENCES

Barth, F. D., in press. Using daydreams in psychotherapy. *The Clinical Social Work Journal.*

Basch, M. F. (1980). *Doing Psychotherapy.* New York: Basic Books.

Beebe, B., and Lachmann, F. M. (1992). The contribution of mother–infant mutual influence to the origins of self- and object representations. In *Relational Perspectives in Psychoanalysis,* ed. N. J. Skolnick and S. C. Warshaw, pp. 83–117. Hillsdale, NJ/London: Analytic Press.

Benjamin, J. (1992). Recognition and destruction: an outline of intersubjectivity. In *Relational Perspectives in Psychoanalysis,* ed. N. J. Skolnick and S. C. Warshaw, pp. 43–60. Hillsdale, NJ/London: Analytic Press.

——— (1995). *Like Subjects, Love Objects: Essays on Recognition and Sexual Difference.* New Haven, CT/London: Yale University Press.

Bollas, C. (1987). *The Shadow of the Object.* London: Free Association Press.

Erikson, E. H. (1959). *Identity and the Life Cycle.* New York: International Universities Press.

Freud, S. (1900). The interpretation of dreams. *Standard Edition* 5.

——— (1908). Creative writers and day-dreaming. *Standard Edition* 9:141–155.

Kohut, H. (1971). *The Analysis of the Self.* New York: International Universities Press.

Loewald, H. J. (1980). *Papers on Psychoanalysis.* New Haven, CT/London: Yale University Press.

Ogden, T. H. (1986). *The Matrix of the Mind: Object Relations and the Psychoanalytic Dialogue.* Northvale, NJ: Jason Aronson.

Olesker, W. (1990). Sex differences during the early separation-individuation process: implications for gender identity formation. *Journal of the American Psychoanalytic Association* 38:325–346.

Ralphling, D. (1996). The interpretation of dreams, I. *Journal of the American Psychoanalytic Association* 44:533–547.

Schafer, R. (1983). *The Analytic Attitude*. New York: Basic Books.

Singer, J. L. (1975). *The Inner World of Daydreaming*. New York: Harper Colophon Books.

Stern, D. N. (1985). *The Interpersonal World of the Infant*. New York: Basic Books.

———— (1995). *The Motherhood Constellation: A Unified View of Parent–Infant Psychotherapy*. New York: Basic Books.

Turrini, P., and Mendell, D. (1995). Maternal lines of development: an aspect of gender identity. *Pyschoanalytic Inquiry* 15:92–111.

Winnicott, D. W. (1982). *Playing and Reality*. London/New York: Tavistock.

8

The Effect of Role Reversal on Delayed Marriage and Maternity*

Maria V. Bergmann

In recent years, an increasing number of women have come to psychoanalytic treatment near the end of their fertility cycles. They are childless and afraid to remain so. They have postponed marriage and maternity in favor of professional opportunities and social and sexual freedom. As a rule, they have several college degrees, secure professional status, and a lifestyle that permits independence from men. They have had intense relationships, primarily with older or younger men—rarely with peers. In most cases the men did not want children—because they already were fathers.

Not infrequently these patients had previously been in treatment with attractive male therapists. Apparently, seductive aspects of the father–daughter relationship were repeated in an erotized transference (Blum 1973) but ended in disappointment and remained unanalyzed.

---

*Reprinted from *Psychoanalytic Study of the Child*, vol. 40, copyright © 1985 by A. J. Solnit, R. S. Eissler, and P. B. Neubauer, Yale University Press. Used by permission.

The choice of the second analyst had been "researched." It had to be a woman who had accomplished combining marriage, maternity, and a profession. These patients disclosed various fears and anxieties: whether a woman can have both a child *and* the man she loves; whether she can have a child and yet retain her profession. A few women expressed a wish to have a child without a mate. Or there was anxiety about maternity as a "trap," or a "conviction" that a woman who has become professionally successful will be regarded as "masculine" and no man will want her. The unconscious doubt in their capacity to produce a child had resulted in their "unintentionally" becoming pregnant: the majority of the patients studied had had one or several abortions prior to treatment. These women presented a characteristic picture with conflict derivatives from various stages of development. What stood out were incestuous feelings toward their fathers—feelings that had not been repressed following the oedipal period—and a deep yearning for closeness with their mothers.

Freud (1931) believed that becoming a wife and mother was a complementary process: the wish for a child stemmed from the earlier wish for a penis, and marriage and motherhood supplied a woman with her mature sexual identity and fulfillment. It is my impression, however, that the wish for the penis and the wish for a child are not as unified as Freud thought. Penis envy also can lead to a wish for a penis in heterosexual love but without integration of other adult goals.

Among my patients were women who enjoyed sex but whose unconscious conflicts prevented them from achieving motherhood; for others, maternity was decisive, but their sexual pleasures were inhibited. None of these patients had been able to unite the separate currents of maternity, sexuality, and professional activity. In terms of severity of psychopathology, these patients were no more disturbed than those who marry in order to have a child or stay in an unhappy marriage or settle for a lasting love relationship without children. They all suffered from essentially neurotic disturbances.

In this presentation I draw on the analyses of six women who differed in many respects, but who had a cluster of specific features in common: their difficulties began during their preoedipal period when their mothers failed to let the girls outgrow the symbiotic phase; there were narcissistic problems leading to a reversal of the role of mother and daughter; object relationships were disturbed early in life; and the fathers' seductive attitude toward the little girls was prominent. For reasons of discretion, no individual case history can be given.

I suggest that this cluster of specific features constitutes a "central psychic constellation," which Silverman and colleagues (1975) define as "a psychic organization possessing sufficient cohesion and stability to maintain a significant impact upon the course of further development" (p. 155). These authors attempted to isolate phase-specific elements of character development related to the choice of defenses, affects, and the role of a given environment by the time a child is 3½ years old. The Oedipus complex was reviewed within a developmental continuum.

In this essay, data related to developmental lines (A. Freud 1963) and to the central psychic constellation were obtained through reconstruction. Solnit (1982), Escoll (1983), and others have observed the reappearance of early object relationship themes in the transference and their significance for genetic reconstruction. In my patients, the central psychic constellation constituted a core of early psychic characteristics that became a predictable motivational system in adulthood and aided in the understanding of recurring problems related to marriage and maternity.

In this chapter, the concept of the basic psychic constellation is used as a tool of reconstruction. In view of the similarity of some decisive specific data, it may become a tool of prediction within carefully specified limits in the treatment of adults who have certain related problems.

THE WISH FOR A SYMBIOTIC RELATIONSHIP

As these women approached the end of their fertility cycle, the wish for a child surfaced with particular urgency, reviving lifelong dormant wishes for closeness with mother. This yearning included symbiotic and later restitutional wishes in relation to the mother. Symbiotic wishes were preconscious: the patients hoped for an intimate relationship with their own wished-for infants—one that would provide this yearned-for feeling they themselves had lost too soon or never fully replaced by later intimate experiences with their mothers. Symbiotic wishes surfaced as transference fantasies early in treatment, or when a current love relationship had come to grief. Family romance fantasies sometimes disguised underlying symbiotic yearnings; several patients expressed the wish to be the analyst's only child and exclusive love object.

The childless women had erected strong defenses against fears of reengulfment by their mothers (Mahler and Gosliner 1955) and against fears of abandonment by either parent. These anxieties also appeared in the transference as strong ambivalent swings and difficulties in regulating closeness to and distance from another person. At the same time, these women expressed yearnings for a father who would exclude the mother from father–daughter intimacies. During the preoedipal period, a need for exclusive dyadic object relationships had become firmly anchored (Abelin 1980, Mahler 1971). In adulthood, triadic relationships were tolerated only with inner conflicts and sometimes ended in divorce following the birth of a child.

As the childless women approached the end of the fertility cycle, their intense unfulfilled symbiotic wishes resurfaced with particular urgency. These wishes formed one of the strands in the central psychic constellation.

THE EMERGENCE OF "ROLE REVERSAL" AS A GENETIC TURNING POINT

In the course of normal development, most children reverse the roles of mother and child in both fantasy and play activities. In the women described here, however, the reversal of roles occurred in reality. The mothers' neediness forced these girls to alleviate the mothers' distress—by attempting to mother their mothers.

Every one of the patients was the oldest child in her family. She found herself mothering younger siblings as well as her mother. This was poignantly relived in the transference neurosis: when the analyst suffered from a minor visible injury, these patients became oversolicitous and competed in their caregiving fantasies with the analyst's family, particularly the husband. It became apparent from dreams and fantasies that in childhood (and to this very day), when the mothers had been ill, troubled, or unavailable, the little girls became helping caregivers in the family, a role encouraged by the fathers, who were frequently absent—actually, emotionally, or both. (In the generation now 40 years and older, most fathers had served in World War II.)

Each girl, perceiving her mother's neediness,[1] had become a mother to her own mother and siblings before she had had enough time to experience the protection, security, and pleasures enjoyed by children who had received adequate mothering. The mothers in turn had made these girls part of their narcissistic and anxiety-laden world by their demands on them. Memories of being the "child-mother" were relived with painful affects and vivid imagery.

In states of anxiety or stress, mothers had difficulties with impulse control. Discharge of stress temporarily led to a loss of personal communication with the child as a child, as if the mother had lost sight of the respective roles of each. The child in turn felt impelled to take care of the mother. In reliving early longings for the mother's emotional presence in the transference, the patients said they felt *unrecognized, ignored, overlooked*; one patient described her feeling as "emotionally disconfirmed."

Being unable to communicate rage reactions about being overlooked led to a structural regression with weakened self-esteem and a transitory loss of differentiation from the mother as caregiver. The withdrawal of the mother's object cathexis from the child "as a child" led to a disruption of self-constancy, with an accompanying fantasy of *role reversal* shared by mother and child. This fantasy creates a temporary hiatus in the *real* relationship between them, and the child's self-cathexis is temporarily weakened in the service of maintaining the tie to the object. This disturbance in the cohesiveness of the child's developing self-representation and self-constancy causes fragmentation of the child's developing self-image. A diminished self-cathexis will prevail until the child's inner representation of self corresponds again to the conscious experience of herself as a child or, seen from the object's point of view, until the mother regains her maternal role. Role reversal serves to prevent loss of relatedness between mother and child and thereby preserves some continuity within the child's self-representation. Thus, in spite of its damaging effects, role reversal

---

1. Freud (1923): "The ego is especially under the influence of perception, and . . . speaking broadly, perceptions may be said to have the same significance for the ego as instincts have for the id" (p. 40). See also Mahler (in Panel 1958) and Spitz (1965).

is a defensive operation in that it preserves the cohesiveness of the child's self. The child, rescued by a move toward lesser differentiation from the object but unsure of the object's "staying power," may, however, begin to experience separation anxiety and become phobia-prone.

In many instances these girls exhibited a "quasi-parental precocity" that circumvented the emergence of sibling rivalry and characterologically gave way to precocious altruism and surrender toward those who were needier or younger (A. Freud 1936). Reversal of the role of mother and child—both in reality and in fantasy—interfered with identification with the mother as a predictable, child-caring object.

A patient said, "When I remembered in my last hour that I saw my younger sister being nursed, I also remembered the first time my mother was home. It was after my sister was born. I had a nurse's outfit, and my doll was injured and bandaged all over and needed special attention. I thought that my mother had never been there for me *alone* because she didn't stay home until the younger children came. She taught me how to be a mother, how to take care of all the things she had to do and of the younger children. As long as I can remember, I tried to make life easier for her. Yet she feels a victim to this very day! I was always an adult and by the time I was grown up I had had it about being with children." This patient had picked lovers according to the model of serving helpless younger children. Her relationships had come to grief, however, because each time she had hoped in vain for reciprocity and protection from her mate as she originally had from her preoccupied mother.

When the mother experiences the child as a distant part of herself, "what is left out" of the relationship is never fully cathected, nor is it repressed (Burlingham 1935). Thus, self-perception, self-constancy, internalization, and identification with the mother remain underdeveloped. Fear of abandonment assumes a central role (Brodey 1965). *What is left out* will be left out again in the transference relationship, whether the analyst is in the role of parent or child. Instead, feelings of not being understood will be expressed (and often be correct) until words for "what was left out" have been found jointly by analyst and patient. In the transference, role-reversal fantasies appeared as fears of complete abandonment, if the patient would not comply by taking care of the analyst (mother) first (Fleming 1975).

Patients remembered not being allowed to be rageful or needy. One patient said, "No wonder I don't want a baby. *She* is my baby. She is either a child or a queen." From early on, whenever the mother abdicated her role, the girl took care of her younger siblings. One patient commented, "I never understood that it took me so long to have wanted a child because I never felt I was allowed to be a child long enough myself." Another said, "I feel like a child or like a mother, but not as *me* with a continuing feeling of me." Or: "My mother loves me when I am her mother, but I want a mother too; I thought of you [the analyst] as my mother." This patient continued, "I feel so rejected when my mother can't cope, and at such moments I hate the idea of having a child."

I was struck by another feature that these women had in common—in all six cases there had been interferences with the girls' ability to engage in doll play. In normal development this activity provides opportunities for testing a variety of roles in fantasy—the child can play at being father or mother or sibling or baby. My patients, however, having actually been "little mother" to siblings and to their own mothers, showed significant disturbances in doll play. They recalled playing with the toys of siblings; of younger siblings being *their* "doll children," for whom they often created toys and games. They envied girls who had lovely dolls or children they visited whose mothers participated in doll play.

Almost without exception, memories predominated in which dolls were taken apart or destroyed. As younger siblings were their play objects, these girls had little emotional space for owning a doll on whom they could bestow love, about whom they could fantasy, and whom they could endow with unique features they did not have to share with anyone. I wondered whether this was a sign of disturbance in the mother-child intimacy that prevented these patients from experiencing first their mothers as unique, and later a man as unique and irreplaceable. The disturbance that resulted from the reversal of the roles of mother and child in reality seemed to have eliminated the desire to give fantasies free reign in doll play.

The disturbances in doll play had other repercussions. Doll play has been described as basic to the development of the female body image, including internal vaginal body cathexis (Kestenberg 1968, 1971), and as crucial in overcoming fears of object loss, particularly in relation to the mother (Blum, in Panel 1976). Hence the lack of doll play interfered with these developments.

While the parental attitudes had created difficulties, they also seemed to be responsible for specific strengths in these women. Both parents had considered their daughters special children and imbued them with high hopes for future achievements. These children became "exceptions" (Jacobson 1959), and role reversal became a source of gratification for them. Yet these girls felt helpless and weighted down by the emotional burdens placed upon them. They lost the sense of a carefree childhood too quickly: feeling both special and helpless created an oscillating self-cathexis. Symbolically, by reversing roles, these little girls became the mothers they never had had. Role reversal represented a defensive substitute for separation-individuation in the sense that the children acted precociously as "independent adult helpers," thereby creating a fantasied identity. But role reversal also defined these girls' place in the family: they could feel secure because they were needed.

These children grew up to become caregiving women, task-oriented and responsible in their object relationships. The capacity "to take it" and the praise for being "special" promoted initiative, courage, and a sense of adventure. The ability to fight for something in spite of pain constituted a conscious motivational asset in solving inner conflict.

The disturbances of role reversal I describe here constitute a specific variant on a theme of narcissistic pathology (Bergmann 1980). As Brodey (1965) observed, if mothers have not resolved their earliest fear of abandonment, they are unable to cathect the child as a separate libidinal object. The child must "conform to expectation to prevent severe psychological decompensation in the parents" (p. 183).

Kernberg (1975) has described narcissistic patients who adopt a stance of coolness or self-preoccupied distance toward people they feel close to in order to control hostile feelings. This attitude enables them to maintain continuity of self-cathexis and to avoid fragmentation of the self. These disturbances are also reminiscent of Bach's (1980) description of adults who cannot maintain subjective and objective self-awareness simultaneously, an incapacity that implies not accepting two children simultaneously: mothers who make a mother of the older child may then treat the younger child as a child.

What I have, for brevity's sake, labeled *role reversal* formed another, most important strand in these women's central psychic constellation, making them prone to subsequent disturbances in self and object constancy, namely, problems of internalization and identification with the mother's *maternal* aspects, and experiencing separation as total abandonment. Another strand of the central psychic constellation derived from a precociously sexualized father–daughter relationship.

THE FATHER'S ROLE

The threatening end of these women's childbearing capacity ushered in a turning point in the life cycle. Heightened incestuous guilt that emanated from the unmarried state and unconsciously affirmed the tie to the father surfaced at this time in life and added to inner pressures.

Inconsistent protectiveness by an emotionally unpredictable mother led to an intensification of the relationship between the little girl and her father. (Abelin [1980] described the father as "a second specific attachment object . . . [but] the toddler will most likely turn to *her mother for comfort*" [p. 155, my italics].) In most cases the patient had early memories of being close to her father whenever he was at home, probably earlier than the toddler's first discovery of him as a delightful companion following differentiation.

In these patients the preoedipal tie to the father was characterized by a surge of wishes for security and protection from him, and he in turn took on a maternal role when the mother abdicated her functions. The intense mutual love between father and daughter and the aura of seductive fantasies that characterized their relationship from early on led to omnipotent feelings, created a sexual precocity, and made it difficult for the girl to delineate her realistic place in the family. Early love for the father along with increased ambivalence to the mother interfered with the resolution of the rapprochement crisis and intensified separation problems (Abelin 1980, Mahler 1966, 1975). Identification with the father was based on a need for security and nurture, which strengthened the incestuous tie to him and intensified a need for sustenance that sometimes assumed an addictive quality in adulthood. In analysis this need appeared concurrently with oral wishes, upon which penis envy was superimposed.

The sexualized tie to the father consolidated oedipal precocity and, in combination with role reversal, concretized the fantasy of having *had* babies with father; upon mother's withdrawal, externalization and role play assumed a concreteness and an aura of reality. Thus incestuous guilt became a permanent source of internal conflict, paid for by the childlessness. When identification with the maternal father produced the wish, "I want a child," it represented a bisexual and narcissistic wish for self-completion. In adulthood an independent wish for a baby increased separation anxiety and fears of abandonment. Identification with the mother did not include a wish for a baby, but identification with the maternal and oedipal father did.

The mother was recognized as being father's sexual mate, and the identification with her *sexual role* carried the girl into heterosexuality during adolescence. However, the mother also was devalued as "the child." At times of parental marital tensions these patients felt the need to protect their mothers, but secretly they sided with their fathers. This concretized and externalized the oedipal fantasy of being father's "other woman," a role that seemed much more desirable than that of the married mother, who was in danger of being abandoned. The mistress fantasy represented not only an oedipal victory over the mother but also a "preoedipal victory," that of remaining father's little girl at the same time.

Some of the women did not progress developmentally beyond the "mistress phase" without analysis, much as they wanted to be married. They experienced sexual closeness with a mate and feelings of revenge and narcissistic triumph over their mothers. Oedipal feelings for the father were relived in analysis, sometimes with an unusual amount of pain that stemmed from the concreteness of the tie and from far-reaching disappointment in the childhood "love life" that ended by his becoming the girl's "lost lover." The father remained an idealized object of love and identification; there was much less ambivalence toward him than toward the mother. However, there frequently was a guilt-laden fantasy that professional prominence based on cognitive or intellectual capacities would make a woman "masculine" and cause infertility. The one-sided identification with mother and the depth of preference for father made it difficult to overcome bisexual wishes. In adulthood this led to anxiety about marital commitment.

The early sexualization of the relation to the father and the impaired capacity to separate from him formed another strand in the basic psychic constellation. The oedipal father fixation produced the fantasy that the little girl *had had* a baby with him and that she *had been* his "other woman." Unconscious themes of oedipal *and* maternal victory over the mother interfered with the postadolescent capacity for the transfer of love feelings and wishes for a baby to a man of her own who was a peer in adulthood.

THE NEGATIVE OEDIPAL CONSTELLATION

In these patients the negative oedipal phase seemed short-circuited. As indicated, symbiotic wishes surfaced early in the treatment, either directly in fantasies or vigorously defended against, so that mother as the patient's "girl baby" was cared for lovingly or rejected with considerable frustration and rage.

The girl's identity formation was inhibited. Mahler (in Panel 1958) describes two pivotal stages of identity formation: the separation-individuation phase and the phase of resolution of bisexual identification. The integration of body-image representations with pregenital concerns depends on successful identification with the parent of the same sex. In addition, "affirming emotional attitudes of both parents to the child's sexual identity" are of paramount importance for "distinct feelings of self-identity" and the solution of the oedipal conflict (p. 138).

Blos (1974) pointed out that the negative oedipal conflict survives in a repressed state until adolescence. My patients never fully experienced the negative oedipal conflict and therefore did not repress it in Blos's sense. It remained in a developmentally rudimentary form, amalgamated with revived symbiotic longings, seemingly from the time of its appearance until its reappearance in the transference.

I believe that normally the girl's hostility to her mother after the discovery of the sexual differences is mitigated and the love relationship with her safeguarded if the mother allows her little girl to be a "little woman" (and can accept her penis envy at the same time). The little girl allowed to apply her mother's cosmetics, strutting about in mother's high heels, and laughing with impish delight, symbolizes phallic-exhibitionistic self-expression. Permission to express her need to show off her body, to perform, to be a tomboy without having to forfeit her simultaneous feminine development, and to play mother's role helps the girl to feel physically loved as a female child. This approval counteracts her lowered self-esteem due to penis envy and promotes oedipal in favor of pseudo-oedipal relationships with each parent. It helps her to accept her clitoris and vagina as adequate organs. When her feminine body image becomes anchored as lovable, the little girl feels able to reach the oedipal phase with mother's permission. She can then value her mother in spite of her "penislessness."

The mother's affirmation of the girl's femininity promotes identification with, and idealization of, the mother. The girl child needs this affirmation. The preoedipal as well as the oedipal girl needs mother–girl intimacy, which grows out of sharing and loving "feminine things" and "women's concerns"; if a mother allows participation in her world and a girl can *play* being an adult woman, the girl feels she is permitted to remain a child. Insufficient consolidation of the love tie to the mother during the negative oedipal period will prevent repression of incestuous feelings toward the father during and following the oedipal phase and will continue into latency. A struggle to possess the mother exclusively will be avoided. Under more favorable conditions the incest barrier is maintained because the oedipal mother belongs to the father. In my cases the incest barrier was not sufficiently affirmed: the mother always seemed too childlike to be experienced fully as a mother, and the father was too available as an incestuous love object, so that far-reaching characterological adaptation against threatening bisexual wishes and incestuous stirrings became urgent.

Many of these mothers preferred to share personal feelings with their daughters rather than their husbands, thereby exposing the fathers to the daughters' seductive wishes and behavior which led to precocious oedipalized intimacies with the fathers. During the negative oedipal phase, the reemerging symbiotic wishes became sexualized, and wishes for separation from the mother failed once more.

Concrete wishes and fantasies directed toward the analyst became central early in the transference to fill a gap left open by disturbances of identification with the patient's mother. There was an unstated pressure on the analyst to help the patient overcome narcissistic self-devaluation stemming from her childless, unmarried state.

Thus I see another trend forming the basic psychic constellation in the mother's lack of responsiveness to the girl's feminine and bisexual tendencies, which did not permit a sufficient flowering of the negative oedipal love tie and its subsequent repression. The sense of feminine identity was infirm and the girl was unprotected against sexualization and overstimulation in the oedipal father–girl relationship.

SPECIFIC PROBLEMS IN LATENCY AND ADOLESCENCE

Normal oedipal experiences strengthen the incest barrier and induce the growing child to differentiate identification from love. Internalization of the parents as oedipal objects promotes superego structuring and later oedipal mourning. Loewald (1973) has observed that under favorable conditions oedipal relationships are transformed into internalized, intrapsychic, depersonified relationships. Internalization as a completed process fosters emancipation from the original object.

In the women I have described this process did not take place. The new objects, therefore, were experienced as incestuous. Analysis had to bring out the extent to which both love and idealization were still attached to the figure of the father. The intrusiveness of both parents continued into latency and puberty, interfering with phase-specific needs for separation and autonomy.

During adolescence the fathers tended to supervise the girls' attire—not, however, as one would expect, in the direction of greater modesty but in ways that would enhance the girls' seductiveness and sexual appeal. For instance, hairdos were discussed or sweaters that would make growing breasts protrude. The mothers on the other hand tended to join the girls in the excitement about their dates but were also most inquisitive. In analysis we discovered that the excessive interest in the girls' dates on the part of each parent confirmed once more the strength of the tie and the fear of losing the daughter. This in turn interfered with the girls' growing attempts to find a love object who was a peer.

It is more difficult to describe the positive results of role reversal as they emerged in postadolescent sublimations since they had not appeared as complaints. The patients assumed adult responsibilities for their parents, particularly for the mother, which consolidated in latency but became even more apparent in adolescence. Characterologically, this strong sense of responsibility disposed them toward a certain asceticism and fostered the capacity from adolescence on to delay gratification and to yield to others. These girls often became counselors or advisors to *other* girls in love. They frequently became interested in the helping professions or in caring for other women's children. As adults, for instance, they tended to become ideal mothers to children of divorced boyfriends.

Jacobson (1964) has pointed out how instability of the superego interferes with identity formation and self-constancy. Although she does not use the term *self-constancy*, she describes persons whose sense of identity alters when the object relationships change from positive to negative affects and back again—when they vacillate between love and hate. Object constancy and reality testing are interdependent, but the constant object implies a firm libidinal cathexis of the object representation, a realistic perception of the object, and a resultant capacity to sustain love (Bak 1971).

In these patients, unfulfilled incestuous wishes surfaced again during adolescence and interfered with peer relationships and the choice of a mate. Their relations to men showed the imprint of the failure to resolve oedipal issues. Typically, initial idealization was followed by disappointment. This pattern became part of the character structure and resurfaced in their adult relationships to men. Alternating idealization and disillusionment also characterized the transference neurosis.

In masturbation fantasies, dreams, and in the transference two topics predominated: primal scene fantasies in which the patient would replace the analyst's husband, and torture fantasies attesting to the extensive sexual overstimulation during childhood. They were narrated with excruciating pain, an irrevocable sense of exclusion from the parental couple, and intense narcissistic injury.

ADULTHOOD AND MARRIAGE

When the core of the infantile neurosis has remained intact, there is only partial separation from the original objects in adulthood. Adult love relations can be sustained only as long as their unconscious connection to the original, ambivalently loved oedipal objects is maintained and as long as revenge fantasies can remain dissociated or repressed.

As the unconscious incestuous tie to the father continued into adulthood, adult love relationships were playful, seductive, but not nourishing for the patient or her mate, except at the beginning. Before analysis, some of the women were frigid or could reach clitoral orgasm only by stimulation. The vagina remained excluded, sometimes unconsciously "saved" for father. There were typical fantasies that prevented orgasm: the women suspected the men to be primarily interested in themselves; at the same time, they felt obliged to satisfy their mates sexually, but often at the expense of their own sexual needs. This was another way in which role reversal in childhood interfered with orgasm in the adult woman.

It was as if in adult love relations oedipal themes had become actualized, thereby burdening the adult love relations with incestuous guilt. On an unconscious level these women had difficulties in differentiating lovers from their fathers, and their own sexual role or that of a mate from the relationship between mother and father.

The adult love relations repeated the pattern of the oedipal conflict. For a period, the adult love relationship drew its strength from the narcissistic triumph of circumventing the incest taboo. Initially, infantile grandiosity and narcissistic strivings found satisfaction in the love relationship. During the early phases of the relationship, parental idealizations were displaced upon the lover. A web of fantasy was spun around him, with unconscious hopes for assuaging childhood injuries and conscious wishes to realize adult life goals.

Unconsciously, the lover needed to become the seductive parent, required to commit incest, which gave the love tie an addictive quality (Blum 1973) and made it "very special." Uniqueness not experienced with mother early in life was thus temporarily found in some of the relationships via the unconscious incestuous fantasy that held the relationship together. The living out of incestuous oedipal wishes gave the relationship its special "magic." During the incestuous and narcissistically gratifying phase, the woman remained the child, actively seeking good mothering but able to accept it only from a member of the opposite sex with whom she identified (Bergmann 1982).

An intensive search for a husband took place ostensibly only and concealed a wish to find "the good mother of symbiosis" in the union with the lover. These women's love relationships lacked the depth of postoedipal commitment. The lovers alternately played the roles of parent and child, at times giving the analyst the impression that they were "playing house."

When parents have been prematurely disappointing, narcissistic gratification cannot be obtained later in life without the assistance of another person. The women therefore needed to keep their lovers in the role of a narcissistically gratifying parent; at the same time the initial success in the adult relationship revived the conflict about losing the incestuous ties to each parent and led to overt anxiety. Separation from the mother seemed impossible: it implied not only forfeiting the symbiotic tie to her forever but also being saddled with feelings of guilt about leaving the mother who needed the daughter as a permanent caregiver. It was easier to have an adult relationship and divide commitment and love between father and adult lover.

For a time these women succeeded in staving off separation anxiety and incestuous guilt, but the anxiety about separating from the *real* parents and the fear of making a commitment to marriage and maternity brought the unconscious conflict to the fore. In fact, analysis revealed time and again that the adult woman unconsciously still preferred her father to her lover or husband. As the woman unconsciously already "had had" her oedipal child with the father, the wish for a baby was pushed into the background.

In the second phase the idealizations gave way to disappointments because of unrequited childhood fantasies. Symbiotic and incestuous longings that had nurtured the love tie were transferred from the parents to the lover or husband only temporarily: disappointment brought the relationship to an end.

MARRIAGE

The achievement of marriage and maternity hinges on coming to terms with losses. Some women do not feel impelled to marry and have children; for a variety of reasons they settle for an older or younger permanent mate—perhaps a series of them. My patients, however, wanted marriage and maternity, both of which were felt needs. Having been "special" and idealized children, they wanted to build a family of their own to experience and represent the parents as an ideal couple that truly cared for a child. Such deeply conscious ideals helped the analytic process.

Nevertheless, marriage was unconsciously equated with losing a part of the self that in fantasy represented a part of a parent as well. One patient dreamed: "I am marching down the aisle to get married and my future husband waits for me. I become frozen and cannot walk. I wake up." Unconsciously, the frozen stiffness represented the father's phallus and the patient could not marry lest she lose the nourishing tie to the father by not remaining his phallic extension. That the patient herself personified the paternal phallus by becoming frozen emerged as a reconstruction after an adolescent recollection made this connection clear to both the patient and myself (Lewin 1933). Anxiety over object loss also may have caused the patient to awaken.

Another patient viewed marriage and motherhood as a "prison or trap." Her commitment to her lovers was tenuous and marred by overwhelming anxieties while at the same time the tie to her parents remained a strong and active force. She commented that marriage was "the worst fear of my life."

As a rule it took several years of intensive analytic work for these women to relinquish incestuous, ambivalent ties to the parents, to feel free to fall in love with a peer, and to get married. Typically, after being sure of marriage, these patients proceeded to plan for a child. This demonstrated that they had at least partially forgiven their mothers.

MATERNITY

The repetition compulsion prevented these women from being able to tolerate triadic relationships without fears of abandonment, which in turn interfered with the wish to have a baby. Blos (1974) stresses that adult mothering is possible only if the young woman attains a postambivalent relationship to her mother.

It became apparent in analysis that just as the real and prospective mothers were not differentiated, the patient recalling her childhood could not differentiate herself from a fantasied prospective child. In both versions, mother and child were merged; the lover became the "good mother" (of symbiosis) while the "bad mother" image was displaced onto the real mother, her substitutes, such as the lover's wife, or a prospective child. The patients were fearful that the baby would replace them once again by being considered first. Unconsciously, the prospective child was identified with a sibling or parental oedipal rival.

The child also represented the paternal phallus, and childbirth became linked to a castration fantasy and to early narcissistic disillusionments. Feelings of revenge for not having been permitted to remain the child were sometimes displaced in fantasy onto the would-be future child; moreover, these feelings sometimes merged with jealousy toward a sibling, particularly if he was male.

One patient said, "I can't have a baby because then I would have to lose my mother. To keep my child out of her life would kill her. It is as if I had kept her alive by letting *her* be my baby. If I had a real baby, I would have to give up my mother. I have such guilt toward her that I have to keep her alive." And another woman: "When I think of getting married, I have the image of a little girl holding the hand of a big man. I idealize someone I don't love as an adult woman. I obviously don't want to have a baby. It seems as though I had always been waiting for Daddy."

When contemplating having a child, many of these women demonstrated an incapacity to rely on the baby's father and to trust him. One patient said, "I have a fantasy of being alone; a cold wind is blowing. I am isolated and poor. I have no job and I am alone with a baby. If I get married and have a child, I shall be a wife and mother without a career and without money." This was a frequently recurring image. Another patient said, "I imagine having a baby and there's just nobody out there who cares. I have no parents and no husband—I am trapped! How am I going to rear this child alone and ever get back to my profession? Who is going to pay the bills? I feel all alone. It is a nightmare." Abandonment appeared to be a punishment for having abandoned the "child-mother."

Some of these women passed the child-bearing age without having achieved maternity. They then went through a period of intense mourning for not having been able to produce a child. The lost child represented the patient herself as well as the loss of a symbiotic union with her own mother.

SUMMARY

Role reversal is a phenomenon that appears not only in the interactions discussed here but in other types of relationships. Nor is it to be found only in this particular group of patients. When the wish for a child is too conflict-laden by fixation on the fantasy of a libidinally nourishing father and by the hope of finding the *real* mother, the establishment of an independent adult self is less likely.

The conflicts I focused on have previously been assigned to pregenital and incestuous oedipal fixations. Role reversal, if present, adds the dimension of narcissistic pathology, self-constancy, and the development of object relations from childhood to adulthood.

The capacity to continue a profession, be a lover to a mate and mother to children initially necessitates—as does analytic work itself—the giving up of a considerable number of infantile gratifications. This process is encumbered by the weight of parental models who strove for infantile and narcissistic gratification themselves, not leaving enough room for the child to express and fulfill phase-specific infantile needs. Thus new identifications have to be created in adulthood.

In my patients a central psychic constellation with role reversal as its most prominent feature remained active throughout the life cycle. They had intense symbiotic longings that propelled them toward a lifelong search to find the symbiotic mother in lover, husband, and baby. Only by achieving this could they forgive their own mothers for sporadically abandoning them emotionally.

The fantasy "once there was a baby no one would take care of" had its root in memories of childhood role reversal and in unconscious incestuous ties that did not permit separation from mother without superego punishment. The central experience of emotional abandonment led to impermanence of self and object constancy.

Reversing roles, the daughter became her mother's mother and identified with her father. A preference for dyadic over triadic relationships characterized unconscious conflicts. Role reversal lent conviction to the sense of having *had* a baby with father and being his "other woman," thereby intensifying an incestuous fixation.

The alternating currents of the oedipal conflict persisted in these women's adult love relationships in which they lived out an incestuous fantasy, sometimes addictive in character but also consummated with heightened separation anxiety, whether the lover represented the patients' mother, father, or the self. Due to insufficient repression and superego structuring, these relationships could not become permanent.

These women could be described as "prisoners of childhood." Many of the clinical features they presented could be subsumed under "fate neurosis" (Deutsch 1930). Psychoanalytic treatment enabled them to overcome some of the effects of role reversal. The giving up of erotized relationships via the analysis of the erotized transference (Blum 1973, Freud 1915) was the most decisive step that led these women from being mistresses to independent womanhood.

REFERENCES

Abelin, E. L. (1980). Triangulation. In *Rapprochement*, ed. R. Lax, S. Bach, and E. J. Burland, pp. 151–166. New York: Jason Aronson.

Bach, S. (1980). Self-love and object-love. In *Rapprochement*, ed. R. Lax, S. Bach, and E. J. Burland, pp. 171–196. New York: Jason Aronson.

Bak, R. C. (1971). Object-relationships in schizophrenia and perversion. *International Journal of Psycho-Analysis* 52:235–242.

Bergmann, M. V. (1980). On the genesis of narcissistic and phobic character formation in an adult patient. *International Journal of Psycho-Analysis* 61:535–546.

——— (1982). The female oedipus complex. In *Early Female Development*, ed. D. Mendell, pp. 175–201. Jamaica, NY: Spectrum.

Blos, P. (1974). The genealogy of the ego ideal. *Psychoanalytic Study of the Child* 29:43–86.

Blum, H. P. (1973). The concept of erotized transference. *Journal of the American Psychoanalytic Association* 21:61–76.

Brodey, W. M. (1965). On the dynamics of narcissism. *Psychoanalytic Study of the Child* 20:165–193. New York: International Universities Press.

Burlingham, D. T. (1935). Empathy between infant and mother. In *Psychoanalytic Studies of the Sighted and the Blind*, pp. 52–70. New York: International Universities Press, 1972.

Deutsch, H. (1930). Hysterical fate neurosis. In *Neuroses and Character Types*, pp. 14–28. New York: International Universities Press.

Escoll, P. (1983). The changing vistas of transference. *Journal of the American Psychoanalytic Association* 31:699–711.

Fleming, J. (1975). Some observations on object constancy in the psychoanalysis of adults. *Journal of the American Psychoanalytic Association* 23:743–759.

Freud, A. (1936). *The Writings of Anna Freud*, vol. 2: *The Ego and the Mechanisms of Defense*. New York: International Universities Press.

———— (1963). The concept of developmental lines. *Psychoanalytic Study of the Child* 18:245–265. New York: International Universities Press.

Freud, S. (1915). Observations on transference-love. *Standard Edition* 12:157–171.

———— (1923). The ego and the id. *Standard Edition* 19:3–66.

———— (1931). Female sexuality. *Standard Edition* 21:223–243.

Jacobson, E. (1959). The exceptions. *Psychoanalytic Study of the Child* 14:135–154. New York: International Universities Press.

———— (1964). *The Self and the Object World*. New York: International Universities Press.

Kernberg, O. F. (1975). Normal and pathological narcissism. In *Borderline Conditions and Pathological Narcissism*, pp. 37–45. New York: Jason Aronson.

Kestenberg, J. S. (1968). Outside and inside, male and female. *Journal of the American Psychoanalytic Association* 16:457–520.

———— (1971). From organ-object imagery to self and object representations. In *Separation-Individuation*, ed. J. B. McDevitt and C. G. Settlage, pp. 75–99. New York: International Universities Press.

Lewin, B. D. (1933). The body as phallus. *Psychoanalytic Quarterly* 1:22–47.

Loewald, H. W. (1973). On internalization. *International Journal of Psycho-Analysis* 54:9–17.

Mahler, M. S. (1966). Notes on the development of basic moods. In *Psychoanalysis—A General Psychology*, ed. R. M. Loewenstein, L. M. Newman, M. Schur, and A. J. Solnit, pp. 152–168. New York: International Universities Press.

———— (1971). A study of the separation-individuation process. *Psychoanalytic Study of the Child* 26:403–424. New Haven, CT: Yale University Press.

———— (1975). On the current status of the infantile neurosis. *Journal of the American Psychoanalytic Association* 23:323–333.

Mahler, M. S., and Gosliner, B. J. (1955). On symbiotic child psychosis. *Psychoanalytic Study of the Child* 10:195–212. New York: International Universities Press.

Panel (1958). Problems of identity. D. Rubinfine, reporter. *Journal of the American Psychoanalytic Association* 6:136–139.

———— (1976). The psychology of women. E. Galenson, reporter. *Journal of the American Psychoanalytic Association* 24:105–108.

Silverman, M. A., Rees, K., and Neubauer, P. B. (1975). On a central psychic constellation. *Psychoanalytic Study of the Child* 30:127–157. New Haven, CT: Yale University Press.

Solnit, A. J. (1982). Early psychic development as reflected in the psychoanalytic process. *International Journal of Psycho-Analysis* 63:23–37.

Spitz, R. A. (1965). *The First Year of Life*. New York: International Universities Press.

9

Vanity:
Of Mothers and Daughters

Joel S. Bernstein

INTRODUCTION

In classical analytic theory, narcissism is explained as a libidinal cathexis of the ego (Freud 1914). Initially it appeared that this primary narcissism existed as a primal reservoir of drive and energy (Freud 1915–1917). Later it appeared that it may have been a kind of object libido divided into narcissistic libido and object libido proper (Freud 1924). No matter, for, in whatever case, whether of reservoir narcissism or object narcissism, narcissism is sexual. (It is of no minor significance that most major theories of narcissistic disorders omit their libidinal, sexual origin.) Narcissus looked into the pool and fell in love with the image of a beautiful young boy.

Freud wrote clearly and completely about homosexuality and its origins (1920, 1922). One of its explanations depends upon narcissism (Freud 1914, 1915–1917). The child, boy or girl, chooses a sexual object on the basis of the similarity to himself or herself, so that a homosexual object choice is effected on the basis of an underlying narcissistic object choice.

This state of affairs does obtain: narcissism can affect homosexuality.

But the opposite state of affairs obtains as well: homosexuality can affect narcissism.

It is not hard to account for this development. If there is a need to defend against homosexuality, one way that libido can be disposed of is to redirect the homosexual libido back to the ego (Freud 1915) and the original narcissism, and now that narcissism is homosexualized and increased (intensified).

Thus a major shift in libido distribution has occurred: object libido, homosexual object libido, is redirected back to the ego and intensifies narcissism. (We might more accurately speak of homosexual or homosexualized narcissism.) Also, when there is a major vicissitude (shift) of libido (Freud 1915), very often the partial instincts follow the shift (Freud 1905). In our particular discussion, I am interested in the vicissitude of the instinct of looking, variously regarded as scoptophilia or voyeurism.

In line with the "original" outer-directedness of the homosexual object libido, voyeurism, or the sexualized looking at the other, falls in the same direction. With the redirection of the homosexual object libido onto the ego, the voyeurism too follows and turns itself back upon the ego. And now, following the vicissitude of the libido, and turning itself upon the "narcissized" ego, voyeurism takes the ego as the homosexualized object of its looking.

As a consequence of homosexual object libido being turned back upon the ego, there is an increase in narcissism.

As a consequence of voyeurism following the lead of object libido and turning its focus on the narcissized-homosexual ego, there arises vanity. (As Freud [1915] points out in "Instincts and Their Vicissitudes," instincts can have more than one opposite or reciprocal: one reciprocal of voyeurism is exhibitionism; another, as pointed out here, is taking oneself as the object of looking.)

Vanity, or the preoccupation with one's own looks, can indeed have several causes, but large among them is the redirection of homosexual looking back onto oneself.

Men indeed can be vain, but often their vanity is narrow and restricted, connected as it is to castration and penis equivalents, with homosexual interest duly, but secondarily, affected, whereas, women's vanity is often broader, deriving, as it does, from the primary attachment to the mother and the entirety, the expanse, of the mother's body. (More on this later.) We can say that vanity is particularly characteristic of the relationship between mothers and daughters.

THREE CASE HISTORIES

Her mother was a Holocaust survivor (as was her father). Her father was virtually absent, working long hours and sleeping much of his time at home. The mother was extremely infantile: she would demand the daughter's attention, service, and obeisance, or would otherwise rage at her, accusing her of selfishness, and then proceed into a depressive, long-term silence.

As an adult, the patient was a sweet and giving person, but with a strong, paranoid feeling of being unappreciated and criticized. When, in treatment, the paranoia fell away, she became preoccupied again with the size of her breasts (way too large) and her weight. (She had been preoccupied with these matters since early adolescence.)

One could not tell if her breasts were too big; she seemed to be at a reasonable weight. No matter. She was obsessed about her breasts and her weight and suffered extreme social anxiety.

Reality held no sway until we came upon her homosexual feelings toward her mother. Her mother herself had large breasts and was fat: she would dress in the bedroom and the bathroom with the doors open. Yes, the patient was quite drawn to her mother's breasts. It turned out that the family home was funeral, mausoleumlike. It was dark and silent for much of the time. The mother's rages were welcomed as a break in the lonely, unremitting silence. And the mother's breasts and fat body could be related to sexually—not affectionately, but at least sexually.

With the recognition of her homosexual feelings toward her mother, the patient's preoccupation with the size of her breasts and her weight literally disappeared.

*   *   *

In the beginning she bragged how she did not have sex with men, regardless of how much they wanted her. But soon it was clear she was unable to: she did not like kissing and she did not like intercourse. And, difficult as it was to say, she did find women's breasts quite attractive. Her own breasts were ugly, pendulous, and this condition was one of the reasons she did not want to have sex: the men would see her ugly body.

Soon she was recalling how her mother walked around the house: in a diaphanous housedress that revealed her entire body, her breasts and her rolls of fat. It was clear that the patient had been sexualized by her mother. Her preoccupation with her breast size and her "ugly" body increased. She had breast reduction surgery (according to her physician the reduction was appropriate) and the preoccupation with her breasts receded.

Now the patient focused on her anus and anal odors. (This shift had already begun before the surgery: she had likened her breasts to a penis and to feces.) First she spoke about the odors of others but soon she focused on her own body odors. She hated to bathe—though she did—because, she admitted, she wanted to smell. As it is, she likes to stay in her clothes—the same clothes—as long as she can.

Coming to treatment early one morning, she had the thought that she wanted to stick her finger in "everybody's asshole." She spoke of this reluctantly (surely I was to be an early morning recipient) and then the floodgates opened. (Interestingly, the word "gate" comes from the Indo-European "ghed" and means to void, to defecate.) She spoke of her analization by her mother. Her mother checked her bowel movements and wiped her. Her mother gave enemas and took anal temperatures with gobs of Vaseline well beyond the time when the child protested. Her mother would scream about the father's fecal odors even though the mother's odors, particularly her urine odors, were piercingly offensive.

At this point the world appeared to the patient as anal. She revealed that when she went to public bathrooms she would check the toilets to see if she could find any unflushed feces. A robber had defecated in her toilet and left it unflushed. She thought of that often and was pleased to learn that that is not uncommon for robbers to do.

Clearly her anal interests were connected to her mother's

provocative anality. Throughout, during the time when she was concerned with the ugliness of her breasts and then with her anal odors, she was afraid of being physically close to her mother. She admitted that she had overwhelmingly strong impulses to touch her mother sexually.

I will not go on with this case, except to tell you that as the patient began to immerse herself in her own anality and accept it, she began to feel increasingly strong sensations in her vagina, connected to thoughts about men.

Both of these cases demonstrate clear elements of homosexuality in their vanity. They also demonstrate clear elements of negativism. But vanity always shows elements of negativism. Think of the woman who looks in the mirror and likes what she sees. But still she looks in the mirror. She looks often because she is intent on finding flaws, imperfections, ugliness.

* * *

She was a beautiful model, oft photographed. She had soft creamy skin, blonde hair, and beautiful blue-green eyes. (She was quite bright, eventually obtaining a Ph.D. in physics.) She was quiet and shy and very smart. And she had an extraordinary talent: she literally could make men "come" in their pants. She would gently scratch her arm and look at a man and he would wet himself.

She was, with all these talents, vain: she spent hours with the mirror. She practiced her "ejaculatory skills" and she practiced looking beautiful. (She could cry beautifully, with the tears running down her cheeks in synchrony.) She noticed every feature and examined it as to its beauty.

Historically, her father and brothers had paid a great deal of attention to her whereas her mother had not: her mother suffered from characterological depression bordering on clinical depression. However, she watched her mother intently and could describe her every feature. She related to her mother through vanity.

Negativism is demonstrated in this case by the hours in front of the mirror, looking for blemishes and imperfections.

We can say that vanity is homosexualized narcissism with an element of negativism or hostility in it. But the vanity is not essentially a hostile vicissitude, it is more of a libidinal-homosexual vicissitude. The negative element is comprised of two components which are usually fused. First there is what I call negative vanity (see below). Second there is the hostility that was originally involved in the homosexual object choice. Thus, in the case above, we learned that the patient had an obsessive thought, whenever she came upon a knife, to stick it into one of her family members.

VARIETIES OF VANITY

There are many varieties of vanity and all involve the transmutation of homosexuality into narcissism, along with the minor elements of negativism. There is, among them, body vanity, positive or negative, relating to size, weight, and shape. The homosexual element is demonstrated by the fact that often among those who "sculpt" their bodies in gymnasiums and fitness centers homosexuality breaks out. We should regard this as a "return of the repressed" (Freud 1896). Then there is artistic vanity, intellectual vanity, athletic vanity. The homosexual involvement in these is indicated by the tendency to venerate a "master" of the same sex.

Negative Vanity

In the unconscious, contradictions exist (happily and easily) side by side (Freud 1911). That is equivalent to saying that opposites too exist side by side. And actually opposites define each other and often come from the same word root (Freud 1910). Thus, in the unconscious, opposites are virtually equivalent.

In the conscious, of course, with the help of the reality principle, opposites are understood to be at categorical extremes.

In the psyche a number of phenomena depend upon opposites. These include, among others, reaction formation, turning (as in turning back upon the self or projecting out upon the other), idealization, depreciation, part–whole representation (Freud 1911). And I include another, which is implied in all of these opposites: "negatization" (Bernstein). Negatization is the turning of something positive into its negative, for defensive purposes. But, as with all defenses, the defended-against impulses still show through (Fenichel 1945).

Now we can speak of negative vanity. Negative vanity is the positive vanity of high self-regard turned by negatization into its opposite, the vanity of low self-regard. (The word *regard* is used in its literal sense, of looking, and in its figurative sense, of respecting.) Note that in both positive vanity and negative vanity there is looking. That is what is essential, the looking, homosexually derived as it is; and the sign of the looking, plus or minus, positive or negative, is of no unconscious consequence.

So that, for the purpose of homosexualization of narcissism in vanity, whether a woman regards her breasts as beautiful or ugly is of no unconscious significance: only that she regards (really, overregards) is of significance.

Negative vanity would include all of the negative self-regards that permit of opposites (those that run along a continuum): facial ugliness, big "nosedness," baldness, bad hair color and poor hair texture, bad skin, body ugliness, ugly "pedal extremities," as Fats Waller calls them in his song "Your Feet's Too Big," and all kinds of physical awkward-ness: cloddishness, two-left-"footedness." And the negatives about intellectual abilities and various talents: stupidity, dumbness, inability to draw (can't draw a straight line), inability to carry a tune and tone deafness, poor sight and the need to wear glasses (blind as a bat). Note how many negatives have their own names and expressions: their own appellations show how noteworthy they are.

One might argue that these negatives are not just positives of another name, in disguise, but are true negatives. I agree and remind that I have said that vanity (positive vanity) is marbled with hostile elements. But it is hostility that rides the coattails of vanity, not vanity that rides the coattails of hostility.

Once we arrive at appreciation of negative vanity we are very close to appreciation of shame and embarrassment. We refer again to our appreciation of opposites to fund our understanding. One opposite of negative vanity is vanity proper (that is, positive vanity); just so, one opposite of shame and embarrassment is exhibitionistic pride (Bernstein). Hidden in the withdrawal and covering-up of shame and embarrassment is exhibitionism: the embarrassed or ashamed person always ends up drawing attention to himself. And now we can understand why the ashamed or embarrassed person will not tell us what he or she is embarrassed about: we might not disapprove but rather accept, and then he or she would be deprived of his or her negative exhibitionistic fantasies.

But we must note this difference: the opposite pairing of shame-embarrassment and exhibitionism does not necessarily involve homosexual libido as does the pairing of negative vanity and vanity.

Negative Vanity Continued:
Another Resemblance

Just as negative vanity relates to shame and embarrassment, so does it relate to the superego (or superego functioning), but perhaps on a greater and more significant scale.

In vanity per se one looks at oneself (really, one looks oneself over) and likes what one sees. In negative vanity one looks at oneself and finds imperfections and does not like what one sees. As I say, vanity and negative vanity are virtually identical in the unconscious, but, through negatization, and with some hostile elements, there is some true negativism to negative vanity.

Now let us look at the superego and guilt. The superego looks over the ego to find imperfections too (not imperfections of the body but imperfections of the psyche) and lets loose with its negativism, guilt.

It would seem that these are literal (not poetic) parallels: vanity is the negative (or potential negative) view of the body and guilt is the negative (or potential negative) view of the psyche. (We say that the superego rewards the ego when it behaves well but really the superego looks for imperfections. That is why the concept of the ego ideal was developed [Freud 1914, 1933].) Moreover, just as vanity involves homosexual libido, so does the superego (Freud 1914): in that the superego predominates with same-sex identifications (Freud 1923), it depends upon large amounts of homosexual libido.

I am not maintaining here that vanity, embarrassment-shame, and superego guilt are all the same, but rather that they depend on many similar mechanisms, particularly negatization.

MOTHER, DAUGHTERS, AND VANITY

Freud observed that for both boys and girls the first object (the first libidinal object) is the mother (Freud 1931, 1933). Thus, for boys, the first object is a heterosexual object and for girls the first object is a homosexual object. Freud goes on to explain some of the factors involved in the girls' arduous transition from the homosexual object of the mother to the heterosexual object of the father.

Most little girls do make the transition from the mother as primary libidinal object to the father as primary libidinal object. But still a great deal of homosexual libido remains (is retained) and is handled (desexualized) in various ways by the ego.

A great deal of desexualized homosexual libido is involved (retained) in women's considerable affection for, and overall involvement with, other women. Women variously hug and kiss and laugh and generally enjoy each other. (Most men—although it is changing—stay at a distance from each other, warily admiring the closeness of women.)

Another great deal of desexualized homosexual libido is involved (retained) in women's vanity. "Vanity, thy name is woman." As explained above, in vanity the considerable homosexual object libido directed to the mother is blocked and is redirected back upon the ego, thereby intensifying and homosexualizing narcissism.

A third amount of desexualized homosexual libido is absorbed in the woman's sunniness or sunny disposition. This trait has been referred to as female hypomania but it is not hypomania. Rather, it can be used defensively to create hypomania. Sunniness is a major trait of woman: when men imitate women, they often show sunniness, though greatly exaggerated. That exaggeration (burlesquing) of sunniness by men suggests a considerable envy thereof.

It is probable in my mind that considerable desexualized homosexual libido is retained in the ego of the female generally, and is retained specifically in at least camaraderie, vanity, and sunniness, for the task of mothering. Mothering requires an inordinate amount of energy, and that energy is derived from desexualized, female homosexual libido (Bernstein).

ETYMOLOGY OF THE WORD "VANITY" AND ITS SIGNIFICANCE

The word *vain* comes from the Latin *vanus* and means empty or void (Simpson 1968). Although this original definition would seem to be somewhat understandable in terms of the popular, "conscious" definition of vanity, it would seem to be much more comprehensible in terms of its "unconscious" definition. Unconsciously, vanity refers to homosexual object love turned back upon the self, particularly the physical self. But the homosexual object love is turned back upon the self because it is blocked off from its object—repressed—and creates an emptiness within the self that must be filled. Moreover, formation of the superego depends upon lost (external) objects being replaced in the ego and the superego and then attacked in the ego (Freud 1917, 1923).

Thus the emptiness of classical vanity (the word in its Latin meaning) is of major significance in the unconscious formation of vanity and the superego.

ANOTHER TYPE OF HOMOSEXUALITY

Freud said that there are two causes of homosexuality (1920, 1922): homosexuality from constitutional factors and homosexuality from environmental, social factors. (And since it was Freud's [1915–1917] concept of a "complemental series" of factors, we can assume that he also implied interaction of the two factors.)

I would consider both of these factors direct or dynamic factors because they impact on the sexuality itself, whereas I would consider this next factor nondirect or nondynamic because it impacts not on the sexuality itself but on the choice of sexuality. (In structural terms [Freud 1923], I would say that the first two factors impact on the id while the next factor impacts initially on the ego.)

I am speaking here of the mother's wish, conscious or unconscious, of the child's sexual orientation. So that, beyond the actual (sexual) dynamics of the home and the child's innate disposition, the mother's wish of sexual orientation may be an overridingly strong factor.

If the mother's grand stores of homosexual libido are not sufficiently desexualized in vanity, camaraderie, sunniness, and mothering, but are also not directly sexualized (that is, homosexualized) in her own sexual orientation, then they can act as a great wish force that the child feels compelled to fulfill.

The little girl retains her homosexual object choice or switches it but with a homosexual base; the little boy retains his heterosexual object choice but with a homosexual base or switches it to a homosexual object.

I would call this kind of homosexuality "homosexuality complaisant."

SUMMARY

Vanity depends upon homosexual object libido that is initially directed outwards toward an object, and expressed voyeuristically, being turned back upon the ego, particularly the body ego. Now, instead of taking the original homosexual object as the object of voyeurism, the person takes himself or herself as the object of his or her voyeurism. In the process, narcissism is intensified and homosexualized.

Although it superficially appears that vanity involves a strict "loving" of oneself, actually vanity shows a strong element of negativism in it, looking oneself over constantly for flaws.

The negativism in vanity depends upon two factors. First, the hostility involved in the original homosexual object choice, but second, and primarily, negativism created by the defense "negatization." "Negatization" depends upon the unconscious equivalence of opposites to turn conscious elements into their categorical opposites while leaving them equivalent in the unconscious.

There is a considerable amount of desexualized homosexual libido in the female. I speculate that this is stored for the lifelong, arduous task of mothering. Mothering depends considerably on desexualized, homosexual libido. Otherwise, that considerable desexualized homosexual libido is channeled into vanity, female camaraderie and affection, and the sunny disposition, sunniness.

Men indeed show vanity, but, relative to the fundamental,

same-sex relationship of mothers and daughters, vanity is particularly characteristic of women.

REFERENCES

Bernstein, J. S., in preparation. Some Small Truths.

Fenichel, O. (1945). *Psychoanalytic Theory of Neurosis.* New York: Norton.

Freud, S. (1896). Further remarks on the neuro-psychoses of defense. *Standard Edition* 3:159–185.

———— (1905). Three essays. *Standard Edition* 7:125–245.

———— (1910). The antithetical meaning of primal words. *Standard Edition* 2:153–161.

———— (1911). The two principles of mental functioning. *Standard Edition* 12:213–226.

———— (1914). On narcissism. *Standard Edition* 14:67–102.

———— (1915). Instincts and their vicissitudes. *Standard Edition* 14:109–140.

———— (1915–1917). Introductory lectures. *Standard Edition* 15, 16:3–482.

———— (1917). Mourning and melancholia. *Standard Edition* 14:237–258.

———— (1920). The psychogenesis of a case of homosexuality in a woman. *Standard Edition* 18:145–172.

———— (1922). Some neurotic mechanisms in jealousy, paranoia and homosexuality. *Standard Edition* 18:221–232.

———— (1923). Ego and the id. *Standard Edition* 19:3–66.

———— (1924). Economic problem of masochism. *Standard Edition* 19:157–170.

———— (1931). Female sexuality. *Standard Edition* 31:223–243.

———— (1933). New introductory lectures. *Standard Edition* 22:3–182.

Simpson, D. P. (1968). *Cassell's Latin Dictionary.* New York: Macmillan.

10

The Medea Complex and the Parental Alienation Syndrome: When Mothers Damage Their Daughters' Ability to Love a Man

Robert M. Gordon

When doing custody evaluations, I am often struck by the frequency with which mothers aggress against fathers by turning their children against him. In the process, they do great harm to the children. As a therapist, I am often struck by the resistance of patients who as children were brainwashed against a parent. I believe that brainwashing by a mother is both more common and more powerful than that by a father, since the child's bond with the mother is more intense and primitive. Such brainwashing and alienation usually leads to a lifelong problem with establishing and maintaining a healthy intimacy. The mother's perception and definition of the father, if programmed at an early age, becomes a core fundamental belief, and if questioned, the person's core sense of reality seems shaken: "If my mother lied to me about my father, then can I trust her love for me?" Thus there is a great deal of resistance to the awareness of having been brainwashed.

In this chapter I discuss the mother–daughter bond, the Medea complex (the mother's revenge against her former husband by depriving him of his children), brainwashing and the parental alienation syndrome (the children's pathological unconscious wish to please the "loved" parent by rejecting the "hated" parent), the subsequent disturbed intimacies that the brainwashed child suffers later in life, and a case history of three generations of parental alienation syndrome and its unusual resolution.

In this chapter I bring together two separate issues: the Medea complex and the parental alienation syndrome. To my knowledge, I have not seen these two concepts brought together. I believe that the Medea complex in divorcing mothers is a frequent cause of parental alienation syndrome.

THE MOTHER–DAUGHTER BOND

Mothers are more likely than fathers to be alienators and brainwashers (Gardner 1987), more likely to take out their aggression on their children. Selma Kramer (1995) refers to Steele's research (1970) in stating that children are more physically abused by their mothers, and sexually abused by their fathers. Women may have few means of expressing power, and thereby may use their own children as scapegoats.

The mother's brainwashing of a daughter is particularly powerful due to the daughter's identification with the mother. Juni and Grimm (1933) in their study of adults and their parents found that the strongest relationships were between mother–daughter and father–son dyads. Troll (1987) found that mother–daughter relationships "appear to be more complex, ambivalent and ambiguous than do other parent–child configurations" (p. 284). Olver and colleagues (1989) found that "first born women had the least separate sense of self and reported the greatest degree of maternal involvement and intrusiveness. . . . Men showed a more separate sense of self than women" (p. 311). They also found that mothers were reported to be more highly involved with and intrusive in the lives of their daughters than of their sons. Gerd Fenchel in this volume points out that the mother–daughter relationship is a primitive latent homosexual one that is intense and ambivalent, one that requires first fusion, then separation, for the proper development to occur.

When the mother encourages her daughter to see her father as bad, this may become an oedipal fixation in that the daughter may be attracted to men who will mistreat her, or she may mistreat them. The daughter will also have problems with separation from the mother and with attachment and abandonment with subsequent love objects. The son has his mother as his oedipal love object, but is aided in his separation from her when he must go to his father for his male identity. The daughter is more closely tied to her mother as both a primary love object and the source of her identity. Her oedipal drive toward the father fosters development in helping her to separate from her mother and to master the outside world that father represents. If the mother devalues the father, and sees separation as betrayal, the daughter does not make that necessary break from her mother. The daughter remains with a parasitic mother, insecure and dependent.

Fathers are very important to their daughters' feminine development. Biller's research review (1971) supports that girls who had positive relationships with their fathers were more likely to have satisfying heterosexual relationships. When a mother poisons her daughter's love for her father, she is also compromising her daughter's ability to maturely love any man. The mother is programming her daughter to be her ego extension without a will of her own, and to be with her and no one else, narcissistically bound.

Although both boys and girls are greatly harmed when they are turned against a parent, the harm is often different. Studies indicate that boys suffer the most harm when they are stuck with mothers who express hostility toward their fathers—the source of their male identity (Hodges 1991, Kelly 1993). This chapter, however, will focus only on the mother–daughter bond in the parental alienation syndrome. Although the daughter's self-esteem may not suffer as much as the son's, her ability to deal with separation and mature relationships with men is very deeply affected. Wallerstein and Corbin's (1989) ten-year longitudinal study of girls from divorced families found that the nature of the mother–daughter relationship and the daughter's identification with her mother were predictive of the daughter's ability to address the tasks of her relationships with men later on. Daughters who identified with hostile mothers had the poorest adjustment.

A woman has two internal sexual love objects: the mother representation–the original love object—and the father representation—the later oedipal love object. Both affect object choice. The boy has a narrower band of "chemistry." His love for a woman will always be affected by his internal mother representation. He has his mother as his ever-powerful love object. His father is a latent homosexual love object and source of identification that does not play the same gyroscopic object role as does the mother. A man will not marry a woman like his father. A woman, however, will choose a man in reaction to her mother or her father. If the daughter is brainwashed against her father by a hostile paranoid mother (which is often the case), the daughter has internally two core love objects, the hostile mother and the devalued father. These internal objects will guide her love choices and her behaviors in relationships with men. By picking, provoking, or distorting, she will try to repeat her emotional past with men. I caution the reader about the distinction of "emotional past" versus "actual" past. Our neuroses may be based on real events as well as on false perceptions and fantasies. For example, in the parental alienation syndrome the "hated" parent may in fact be loving and the "loved" parent may be very disturbed and unloving. This sets up a complex system of layering of object relations in the ego. At one level the child is traumatized by the perceptions and not the reality of the "hated" parent and consciously hates that parent, yet at the unconscious level the child often secretly loves that parent, who was in fact loving. The "loved" parent may be loved on the conscious level, but feared and hated on the unconscious level. The patient may start therapy claiming that she was traumatized by her father, and later in therapy realize that her trauma was based partly on the image of her father, and largely on her mother's exploitation and hostility. The patient who was brainwashed will not present this as a problem, and has special defenses to guard against this awareness.

Why would a mother do this to her own children? The story of Medea may help us to understand such motives. The Greek drama served a purpose not just to entertain, but to provide a catharsis for the collective unspoken traumas and pains of the audience. These classic stories express most beautifully powerful human conflicts characteristic of our universal psychology.

THE MEDEA COMPLEX: THE MYTH

Euripides wrote *Medea* around 400 B.C. It is a story of intense love turned to such intense hate that Medea kills her own children to get back at her husband for betraying her. Medea is so madly in love with Jason that she tricks her own father, King Aeetes, who guards the Golden Fleece, and kills her own brother so that Jason can steal the Golden Fleece. (Jason might have done well to consider how she treated her father and brother before he married her.) Jason leaves Medea to marry yet another princess. Medea plans her revenge. The chorus blames Aphrodite for causing all the trouble, for having intense passion turned to hate. (The Greeks often displaced their psychodynamics onto their gods.) Medea offers the bride gifts of a beautiful robe and chaplet. When Jason's new bride puts on the gifts, her head and body burst into flame and she dies a horrible, painful death. When her father embraces her corpse, he too bursts into flames and dies the same tortured death. Medea then takes her sword and kills her and Jason's two children. The chorus, amazed at the degree of Medea's vengefulness, doubts that anything can rival a mother's slaughter of her own innocent children. Medea escapes Jason with a dragon-drawn chariot. She taunts Jason, not allowing him to embrace or bury his sons, and rejoices at having hurt him so.

Fred Pine (1995) refers to Medea as an example of a particular form of hatred found in women.

> Medea's internal experience is a compound of a sense of injury—a sense that builds to imagined public humiliation and a sense of righteousness. . . . The righteousness implied here in "the wrong they have *dared* to do to me" has struck me clinically. It is a frequent accompaniment of hate and hate-based rage. I think it stems from something self-preservative ("I have been so mistreated that I have this right . . .") and some flaw in the superego, possibly based on identification with the child's experience of the rageful mother's giving herself full permission—and without subsequent remorse—to express her rage toward the child. [p. 109]

That is, Pine suspects that for a mother to be so destructive to her own children, she herself must have been exposed to her own mother's unremorseful hostility.

Jacobs's (1988) paper entitled "Euripides' Medea: A Psychody-namic Model of Severe Divorce Pathology" views the Medea mother as a "narcissistically scarred, embittered dependent woman . . . [who] . . . attempts to sever father–child contact as a means of revenging the injury inflicted on her by the loss of a self-object, her hero-husband" (p. 308). Jacobs's idea is that the Medea mother is so dependent that she cannot deal with the loss, and thus holds on with hate.

Medea certainly has a flaw in her superego. We know this early on when she betrays her father and kills her brother to help Jason steal from them. But she not only kills his new bride and her father, but her own children. Her love turned to hate is so passionate that she destroys that which intimacy between them produced. The hate goes beyond her instinctive need to protect her own children. Medea must make Jason suffer more than she suffers for it to be a punishment with revenge.

Jason: You loved them, and killed them.
Medea: To make you feel pain.

The Medea complex involves a mother who is still pathologically tied to her (ex)husband. She has a great deal of rage, probably, as Pines (1995) suggests, from her interactions with her hostile mother. This rage is rooted in part in a wish to destroy the children, whom at some level she resents being stuck with, and this may turn her rage into overprotectiveness as a reaction formation. She is unable to let her children separate from her. She tells them the harm that will befall them when they are out of her control. When the mother wishes to punish the father by turning their children against him, she is also aggressing against the children. In her unconscious, both the children and the husband represent the same thing (others that did or might betray), and destructiveness is wished on them both. In short, a mother who brainwashes her children against their father has a Medea complex. She probably has paranoia or at least paranoid features within a borderline or psychotic character structure. She cannot deal with the loss, and remains tied to her (ex)husband in an intimate hate, and keeps her children tied to her out of fear.

A Medea mother must kill off her own femininity in order to be destructive to her own children. As Lady Macbeth prays so that she will be able to help murder:

> Come, you spirits
> That tend on mortal thoughts! unsex me here,
> And fill me from the crown to the toe top full
> Of direst cruelty! [*Macbeth* I, v]

BRAINWASHING AND PARENTAL ALIENATION SYNDROME

I agree with Gardner's (1987) assessment that most mothers in custody disputes do some form of brainwashing. I have done custody evaluations for over fifteen years. I have found that mothers' attempts to turn their children against their fathers in custody disputes are very common. I have also found that this is by far the most destructive aspect of divorce on children. I now consider brainwashing children against a parent as a form of child abuse, since it leads to enduring psychopathology.

Kelly's (1993) longitudinal research of children's postdivorce adjustment found that the majority of children adjust to divorce, and older children express relief. Most symptoms last six months to two years postseparation, and usually involve only adjustment disorders. Only about 10 percent of divorcing couples with children fight over custody. Of this group, at least one parent often has hostile and paranoid features. In a study of MMPI's given to parents in custody evaluations, the MMPI's of the parents who lost the custody dispute had significantly higher scores in Psychopathic Deviant (hostility), Paranoia, and Mania (narcissistic and impulsive tendencies) than parents who won the custody dispute (Otto and Collins 1995). Children do adjust to divorce, unless a disturbed parent uses them as pawns to punish the other parent. This traumatizes the child, and its effects may be lifelong, often passed on generation after generation.

Gardner (1987) stated, "Although the mothers in these situations may have a variety of motivations for programming their children against their fathers, the most common one relates to the old saying, 'Hell hath no fury like a woman scorned.' . . . Because these mothers are separated, and cannot retaliate directly at their husbands, they wreak vengeance by attempting to deprive their former spouses of their most treasured possessions, the children. And the brainwashing program is an attempt to achieve this goal" (p. 87). Gardner also feels that these mothers are aggressing against their own children by brainwashing them against their fathers. "These mothers exhibit the mechanism of reaction formation, in that their obsessive love of their children is often a cover-up for their underlying hostility" (p. 87). "And when these mothers 'win,' they not only win custody, but they win total alienation of their children from the hated spouse. The victory here results in psychological destruction of the children which, I believe, is what they basically want anyway" (p. 88).

Brainwashing consists of conscious acts of programming the child against the other parent. But Gardner went on to describe what he refers to as parental alienation syndrome. The concept of the parental alienation syndrome includes the brainwashing component, but is more inclusive. It includes not only conscious but unconscious factors within the programming parent that contribute to the child's alienation from the other parent. Furthermore, it includes factors that arise within the child, independent of the parental contributions. The child may justify the alienation with memories of minor altercations experienced in the relationship with the hated parent. These are usually trivial and most children quickly forget them. These children may even refuse to accept evidence that is obvious proof of the hated parent's position. Commonly these children will accept as 100 percent valid the allegations of the loved parent against the hated one. "All human relationships are ambivalent . . . the concept of 'mixed feelings' has no place in these children's scheme of things. The hated parent is 'all bad' and the loved parent is 'all good'" (Gardner 1987, p. 73).

Dunne and Hedrick (1994) in their research found that parental alienation syndrome "appeared to be primarily a function of the pathology of the alienating parent and that parent's relationship with the children. PAS did not signify dysfunction in the alienated parent or in the relationship between that parent and child" (p. 21). This study supports Gardner's definition of parental alienation syndrome as a pathological reaction to a parent, and not a conflict arising out of the real relationship with the rejected parent.

Gardner also refers to factors arising within the child that contribute to parental alienation syndrome, such as the fear of losing the love of the alienating mother, since "the loved parent is feared much more than loved" (p. 90). Additionally, oedipal factors are sometimes operative in the parental alienation syndrome. A daughter may resent the father's new female partner, and may identify with her mother's jealousy and rage, and the daughter may exact revenge by rejecting him.

DAMAGED ABILITY FOR SEPARATION AND INTIMACY

A daughter has first her mother as the primary love object, and then shifts to her father as the oedipal love object. These two internal objects guide her attractions and patterns of intimacy. If she had in fact a rejecting father, but a healthy loving mother who does not turn her against the father, the daughter will have damaged relationships with men. But she has a good prognosis for overcoming this problem. Since her mother was healthy, the daughter can form love relationships built on that basic love relationship. If, however, her mother has a Medea complex—that is, she turns her daughter against her own father out of revenge—the daughter is more likely to have a damaged ability to love maturely. Both her primary love object (the mother) and oedipal love object (the father) are internally driving her to self-defeating relationships. To love a man is to betray her mother. And she can only love as she has been taught and shown. The daughter will find unconscious ways to undermine relationships. She can unconsciously undermine them in three ways: picking, provoking, and distorting.

Picking

Denise comes from an upper-middle-class family. Denise's mother refused to let her father visit her after their separation when Denise was 5. By the time the court ordered shared custody, Denise's mother had brainwashed her against her father. Denise refused to go with him. When she did go, the parental alienation syndrome was so entrenched that she provoked fights so bad that eventually her father discontinued the shared custody. She had seen very little of her father since, and remained very close with her overprotective paranoid mother. Denise and her mother were very symbiotic. Denise was also very protective of her mother, sensing her mother's need for her. When Denise entered treatment at 34, she had not been married, nor had she been able to be in an intimate relationship with a man for more than two years. She had chemistry only for men who were of a lower social class who were rejecting or abusive. She often suffered from depression and anxiety. She had trouble separating from these men. Denise was attracted to men who represented her mother's and her own image of her father as a "bum." Her attraction was also based on her attachment to her mother, who was exploitive and destructive to Denise. These two love objects—her mother's view of the father, and the hostile mother—formed her attraction to men. Denise fell in love with men who were in fact both her mother and her fantasized oedipal father, tainted by the mother. She alternately saw me as the overly controlling mother or as the rejecting, abandoning father. As she worked through the transference in treatment, she began to realize how her mother had distorted her father to her, and how her mother had used and injured her. I actively confronted her trivial complaints against her father as evidence of parental alienation syndrome. Toward the fifth year of analytic treatment, Denise was able to feel deep attraction to and fall in love with a kind and reasonable man. When she felt irrational aggression toward him, she was able to defuse it with insight into her past programming. Denise also reconciled with her father, and enjoyed a new relationship with him.

Provoking

Lora came to treatment for phobias and general anxiety. She had little psychological-mindedness, and at 37, though very attractive, had only rationalizations to explain why she had only short-term unhappy relationships with men. She spoke about men as a typically disturbed gender. Her parents fought bitterly until their separation when Lora was 10. She lived with her mother, who told her that her father was mentally ill and often made fun of him. She saw little of her father, whom she devalued as ineffectual and crazy. When Lora would be in a relationship with a man, she would tell him that she is easygoing and gets along with everyone. Yet she would find the most outrageous ways to provoke everyone, particularly her boyfriends. Even the most submissive would be provoked to outrage, at which point Lora would distort the events and project the blame for the conflict onto the boyfriend. She would tell him that he had distorted everything because of his personal problems, but that she could love him anyway. Lora would commonly enact this with me. She would act out. I would interpret her behavior to her, and she would somehow rewrite history and complain, "You are projecting your personal problems on to me. How can I get better if you don't have your own head on straight?" Lora was able to repeat her emotional past by provoking conflicts in her relationships. She resisted any interpretations into her own aggression, or that she was seeing me, and men, as crazy and ineffectual. Lora was too tied to her mother's ego to be objective. She constantly tried to provoke fights with me. The transference was very rocky, and she remained provocative and insightless. She soon dropped out of treatment, thinking that I was more disturbed than her, thus repeating her usual pattern.

Distorting

Sue entered treatment at 46, with two failed marriages and many failed affairs. Sue's mother was diagnosed with schizophrenia and was hospitalized several times when Sue was a child. Although her parents remained together, it was a very conflicted relationship. She did not feel close to her cold father. Her mother was unpredictable and was often paranoid about her father. Her mother viewed Sue's developmental stages as separations and betrayals, and guilt induced Sue for her attempts at separation. Her mother was very hostile to her father and men in general, who were considered the sole source of women's suffering. (Although in this chapter I define the Medea mother in the context of revenge in divorce, the Medea complex can exist in marriage where the mother has the paranoid perception of her husband as psychologically abandoning her. She will turn the children against him and damage them just the same as would a divorced mother.) I considered Sue to be a high-functioning borderline. She is very intelligent and functioned very well in her profession, and had some close friendships. She regressed in intimacies, however, and became paranoid and depressed in her relationships with men. She would become extremely jealous, demanding, intolerant of separations, and controlling, and would have fits of rage as a reaction to imagined insults. She would drive even the most tolerant men away, and come to the conclusion that her mother was right about them all along. She distorted the men in her life to justify her rage. She became like her paranoid mother when she was with men. Although Sue in her six-plus years of treatment made great progress in her self-esteem, and became less likely to fall into deep depressions, she still had the tendency to regress in intimacy. Like most borderlines, she stayed better compensated outside of committed intimacies. Her reality testing remained good, except in intense committed intimacies, where the pressure to distort men became overwhelming. This distortion is rooted not so much in her relationship with her distant father, but more on her terrifying relationship with her very disturbed mother. Distorting her perceptions of men allowed her to act out and escape from terrifying intimacy, which she unconsciously feared would engulf her as did her mother. Destroying her relationships with men also helped keep her psychically tied to her mother.

People can repeat the emotional past by *picking* someone who is likely to fit within their internal object world, by *provoking* someone to act in a way consistent with their internal object world, and by *distorting* so that the person at least temporarily seems part of their internal object world. Although I have presented the ways that people repeat their emotional past as three separate psychological mechanisms—picking, provoking, and distorting—they almost always occur together. Many people seem healthy if they have picked a sicker partner. Yet if they are with a healthier partner, they may have to do more provoking and distorting to make them fit within their internal object world. More disturbed individuals provoke and distort more than higher functioning individuals who mainly repeat their past object relations by whom they pick.

I have found that those people who have been brainwashed against a parent in childhood will have very disturbed relationships. If they are to have a chance at healthy relationships, it will happen only if they can work through their distorted objects in the transference in the analytic frame of a committed intimacy with the therapist. The causal frame and nature of supportive counseling is much too superficial to work through the deep damage to early object attachment and development. Also, many nonanalytically trained individuals, not working with unconscious distortions, take at face value the patient's complaints and memories and thereby reinforce the brainwashing and the psychopathology. Patients who have parental alienation syndrome will frequently try to divorce the therapist, using the same or similar complaints as the brainwashing parent. The Medea mother is unconsciously feared and she becomes a sacred cow. The adult patient will at first feel guilt at any feelings of aggression toward the mother, and often blames the therapist for feeling the aggression. After confidence is built that the therapist is neither destroyed nor destroying, the patients will be able to take on their deeper feelings about their mothers and work them through.

However, when working with children with parental alienation syndrome, the work is more concrete and reality based. Rather than working through the transference, a form of "deprogramming" is necessary. This is a deviation from the usual neutral analytic stance. Young children need to idealize their parents as a source of self-esteem. This idealization needs to be protected; however, "errors" that the mother makes must be overtly pointed out to the brainwashed child. The alienated parent is objectified through reality clarifications, and should eventually be brought into treatment with the child.

THREE GENERATIONS OF PARENTAL ALIENATION SYNDROME: CASE STUDY

I offer this particular case study to (1) illustrate how the Medea complex can continue for generations, and (2) provide a highly unusual example of a successful deprogramming.

Richard's parents were the firstborn of their gender from divorced parents. Both his mother and his father were turned against their fathers by their mothers, who prevented them from seeing or having a loving relationship with their respective fathers. Richard's mother also eventually cut off her relationship with her mother as well. Richard was raised by two parents with parental alienation syndrome, he would marry someone with parental alienation syndrome, and his children developed parental alienation syndrome. His father was cold and distant. His mother was very hostile and paranoid. Richard's normal stages of separation were interpreted by his parents as betrayals. Their parental alienation syndrome expressed itself in their transference that he was the abandoning father. Once Richard moved out of his home after high school, he too cut off his relationship with his family of origin.

Richard met Kathy in college. Kathy came from divorced parents, and from very much the same family dynamics as Richard's mother. Although Richard felt he was attracted to someone from a very different social and religious background, he was nevertheless picking someone like his mother, who would treat him as did his mother. Kathy's father was an alcoholic and her mother was paranoid and provocative. Her mother would provoke the father to punish the children, but when he beat them she would act helpless, and later align with her children against the father. She constantly included her children in her suspicions that their father was engaged in affairs. The mother used these suspicions to have an affair to which she felt entitled. Kathy told her father about the mother's affair, which ended the marriage. They divorced when Kathy was a teenager. Kathy's experiences with her mother were very similar to Richard's mother's experience with her mother. Kathy had no relationship with her father after her parent's divorce. She remained ambivalently tied to her mother, both hating her and feeling dependent on her, and had parental alienation syndrome with her father.

Although she felt very dependent on Richard, Kathy was unable to express love and affection to him. Soon after they married, Kathy accused him of having affairs, and scapegoated him for her fears and insecurities. She, like Richard's mother, never said that she loved Richard, and Richard never seemed to notice it. After four years of marriage, there were two unplanned pregnancies that gave them a daughter and then two years later a son. Kathy was very overwhelmed by this second pregnancy. She regressed and became very hostile to Richard. She feared having children, and told Richard that she was afraid that she might abuse them. Richard took an active role with the children, but Kathy began to interfere with his time with them. She would manage to schedule activities during the times he was to be with his children. During his analysis, Richard was able to accept that his mother was unable to love him, and that he had picked someone who also would scapegoat him and be unloving. When Richard asked Kathy what she felt toward him, she admitted, after ten years of marriage, that she never did love him or could love him, that she was unable to love anyone. She admitted that she could only feel hate for him. This was enough for Richard to finally leave the marriage. Although they had agreed to joint custody of their son, who was 2, and their daughter, who was 4, as soon as Richard found a loving relationship and was happy, Kathy told him that he would have to go to court if he ever wanted to see his children again.

By the time of the home study, ordered by the custody officer, the children had been brainwashed against Richard. He had always been very involved with his children, but during the interim visits the children were clearly more distant and cool to him. The social worker who had done the home study had been recently divorced and was bitter and wrote her report in favor of the mother, taking her complaints against Richard at face value. Richard petitioned the court to have Richard Gardner be the court-appointed impartial evaluator. Gardner told Richard that he was biased in favor of mother's having custody since the mother's bond with the children was stronger. Gardner told him that he would have an uphill fight for 50 percent physical custody. Richard claimed that Kathy was paranoid and resented his happiness, and that she was bent on destroying his reputation and his professional practice, turning his children against him, and driving him out of town. Richard provided evidence of Kathy's lodging a false ethics complaint against him to his local professional group and spreading false rumors to his referral sources to destroy his practice. When Gardner asked the daughter, then 6 years old, why she had to move from her home, she replied, "Because my mother was afraid that Daddy would come and knock it down. Mommy said that she could never be happy until he was dead. Mommy hoped he was the one shot at the bank that was robbed" (referring to a mass shooting at a local bank). Both the daughter and the son went on with their mother's brainwashing against the father, all with the view that their father was immoral, evil, dangerous, and should not be trusted or loved.

Gardner noted that the father was warmer and interacted more comfortably with the children and understood better than the mother their emotional needs. He stated that Kathy showed signs of paranoid delusions, that she was a fabricator and was brainwashing her children against their father. He also stated that if it weren't for the father's prior frequent and positive involvement with his children, the parental alienation syndrome would have been complete. He suggested that Richard have full legal custody and 50 percent physical custody.

In the years that followed, Kathy did not get involved with men and continued to undermine Richard's relationship with his children. When his children reached adolescence they refused to see him or talk with him. They both provoked and distorted in ways that the father would appear consistent with the mother's view of him. Richard had been sending both the children for therapy. The therapist had inadvertently reinforced many of the children's perceptions of the father, taking many of their complaints about him at face value.

Richard finally asked their therapist if he could be included in joint sessions with his children. Each child had a long list of secret complaints they had not verbalized to their father, echoing their mother's perceptions of him as a bad person. Consistent with parental alienation syndrome, these perceptions took on a mental life of their own. The complaints were trivial or false memories. The children's therapist immediately saw the unfairness and distortions in their complaints. For example, his daughter claimed that one Christmas when she was 6 her father gave her coal for Christmas. His daughter said, "You thought this was funny. I tried not to show my hurt, but I was very hurt." The father firmly stated that this never happened. This denial was evidence, according to the children, of their father's defensiveness. Richard gave his daughter the phone number of his former girlfriend who was there at the time so that his daughter might ask her if he ever had given her coal for Christmas. His daughter avoided the phone call, unconsciously needing to maintain her view of her father. The father told the therapist that he had videotaped much of their childhood, and said that he was certain that he had recorded the Christmas in question. Richard brought a small TV/video player to the next session. He first played a scene about an incident recalled by his son, who claimed that Richard was brainwashing him against his mother while playing a board game that he distinctly remembered ten years ago when he was 4 years old. His son reversed the source and aim of the brainwashing, thereby protecting his mother. When his son saw the very scene on the tape, he was struck by how young he seemed. He seemed confused that not only did the incident not occur as he had remembered it, but that his father was being very supportive and sensitive to his needs, and that he was clearly enjoying his father. The Christmas scene showed both children excitedly opening many presents and playing with their cherished toys with utter delight. There was no coal. Both children were amazed by what they were watching. They had been certain of their vivid memories of ten years ago, when they were small children, and were also certain that their father was a liar. Now they stated that they could have been wrong. In the next session Richard read the section of Gardner's report stating that their mother had brainwashed them against him. The daughter stated to her younger brother, who was still struggling with his feelings, that "You are where I was at two years ago. What he is saying is probably true. I know that now." Following that session, Richard's daughter, who had not spoken to him for two years, asked to go with him on vacation to Oxford, England. The two went off together and their trip was a great success. Eventually both children expressed a wish to see more of their father, after they realized that they had been brainwashed against him.

Not everyone can produce a videotape to disprove a false accusation or prejudice or to deprogram brainwashing, though we often wish we could. This does provide a clear, though unlikely, example of the use of reality to deprogram brainwashing and parental alienation syndrome. This very active reality confrontation would not have been as effective with children who were not as intelligent and high functioning. Also, it was crucial that Richard had 50 percent physical custody since their early childhoods, which helped to reinforce a real loving relationship on an unconscious level. Once the daughter reached almost 16, she felt more independent of her mother and more receptive to the reality confrontation and could use it constructively. Her brother also began to come around as well. This case illustrates that the Medea complex can continue for generations, in choice of love objects, ability to love maturely, and the treatment of children. As Richard told his children during a session, "This has been going on for several generations, and I'm going to do whatever it takes so that you won't have to go through it. Let it stop here."

REFERENCES

Biller, H. B. (1971). Fathering and female sexual development. *Medical Aspects of Human Sexuality* 5(11):126–138.

Dunne, J., and Hedrick, M. (1994). The parent alienation syndrome: an analysis of sixteen selected cases. *Journal of Divorce & Remarriage* 21(3–4):21–38.

Gardner, R. A. (1987). *The Parental Alienation Syndrome and the Differentiation between Fabricated and Genuine Child Sex Abuse.* Cresskill, NJ: Creative Therapeutics.

Hodges, W. F. (1991). The problem of parental access with very young children. In *Interventions for Children of Divorce*, 2nd ed. New York: Wiley.

Jacobs, J. W. (1988). Euripides' Medea: a psychodynamic model of severe divorce pathology. *American Journal of Psychotherapy* 42(2):308–319.

Juni, S., and Grimm, D. W. (1993). Sex-role similarities between adults and their parents. *Contemporary Family Therapy* 15(3):247–251.

Kelly, J. B. (1993). Current research on children's postdivorce adjustment: no simple answers. *Family & Conciliation Courts Review* 31(1):29–49.

Kramer, S (1995). Parents' hatred of their children: an understudied aspect of cross-generational aggression. In *The Birth of Hatred*, ed. S. Akhtar, S. Kramer, and H. Parens, pp. 3–14. Northvale, NJ: Jason Aronson.

Olver, R. R., Aries, E., and Batgos, J. (1989). Self–other differentiation and the mother–child relationship: the effects of sex and birth order. *Journal of Genetic Psychology* 150(3):311–322.

Otto, R. K., and Collins, R. (1995). Use of the MMPI-2/MMPI-A in child custody evaluations. In *Forensic Applications of the MMPI-2*, ed. Y. Ben-Porath, J. Graham, G. C. N. Hall, and M. Zaragoza, pp. 222–252. Newbury Park, CA: Sage.

Pine, F. (1995). On the origin and evolution of a species of hate: a clinical-literary excursion. In *The Birth of Hatred*, ed. S. Akhtar, S. Kramer, and H. Parens, pp. 105–132. Northvale, NJ: Jason Aronson.

Steele, B. F. (1970). Parental abuse of infants and small children. In *Parenthood*, ed. J. Anthony and T. Benedek, pp. 449–477. Boston: Little, Brown.

Troll, L. (1987). Mother–daughter relationship through the life span. *Applied Social Psychology Annual* 7:284–305.

Wallerstein, J. S., and Corbin, S. B. (1989). Daughters of divorce: report from a ten-year follow-up. *American Journal of Orthopsychiatry* 59(4):593–604.

11

The Impact of the Mother–Daughter Relationship on Women's Relationships with Men: The Two-Man Phenomenon

Dale Mendell

The mother–daughter tie is the most archaic, difficult, and in some ways the most important and lasting relationship in a woman's psychic life. Its influence permeates all dealings with subsequent objects, including adult love relationships; its imprint can be found on both oedipal and preoedipal intrapsychic fantasies and behaviors. In this chapter I discuss how early developmental issues with the maternal representation can lead to one particular form of adult object choice—the need to form stable relationships with two men at the same time. Following Goldberger (1988), I refer to this as "the two-man phenomenon."

The little girl's positive oedipal attachment to her father is generally considered to be the template for adult heterosexual object choice. However, unresolved developmental problems and fantasies stemming from mother–daughter difficulties can instead result in fixation on very early attachments to the mother. For example, unconscious pregenital longings for the mother and for being mothered may cloak themselves in the language and activity of adult genital sexuality. Dinora Pines (1987) cites the case of a girl who lost both her biological and her adoptive mother; as an adult she split off and denied her subsequent painful feelings of hurt and rage. Consciously she sought young men as adult sexual partners: "unconsciously she wanted to recover through foreplay all the primitive childhood bodily plea-sures as if in fantasy [he] were her mother again; . . . unconsciously her bodily experimentation contained a hopeless search for the lost [adoptive mother] she could not replace . . ." (p. 8). By substituting bodily sensations for feelings of hurt and rage there was an attempt to express love or hate toward the self or toward the other, to avoid depression, and to raise self-esteem. Yet this relationship with a man was unable to compensate for the earlier lack of internalization of a satisfied and satisfactory mother–child relationship, with the result that "each sexual partner was abandoned as cruelly and ruthlessly as she had felt abandoned by both her rejecting mothers" (p. 8). In this case the mother–daughter relationship was central in determining the shape of the patient's love life. Unconsciously she attempted to refind both the characteristics and functions of the lost childhood love object, including the provision of childhood bodily pleasures and self-esteem regulation, and when that failed under the burden of her needs, she translated the longing into an activation of bodily sensa-tions and defensively reversed the original mother–child trauma of abandonment.

Dynamics relating to the role of very early maternal representa-tions may be overlooked when a married woman maintains simulta-neous relationships with both her husband and a lover. A compulsion toward maintaining triangular relationships is frequently assumed to result from a pathological fixation on the original oedipal triangle, or to represent the splitting of the internalized paternal object.

For example, a woman who is frigid with her husband and sexually satisfied by her lover may experience a conscious sense of thrill and satisfaction that sustains the marriage, while unconsciously she enjoys her husband as a hated transference representative of her oedipal father. In the dual relationship, she experiences the satisfaction of an uncon-scious triumph over the father who had had both her mother and her under his control, whereas now she is the one who has two men under hers. The wish for the affair may also stem from unconscious guilt over experiencing her marital relationship as an oedipal triumph, while not daring to establish a total identification with the oedipal mother; thus the conflict between desire and guilt is acted out. . . . [Kernberg 1980, pp. 100–101]

However, upon analysis we discover that not all triangles are oedipal, even if they appear to be so on the surface, and that the paternal object is not always the major player in a woman's internal world. There are early, preoedipal triangular situations in which the little girl strives to defend her essentially dyadic relationship with her mother from encroachment by anyone, be it father, sibling, or friend. In addition, what may appear to be turning to the father out of oedipal object choice is frequently still in the service of the little girl's early attempts to separate from the mother, so that the father's function is that of a "counter-mother" or "other-than-mother." True oedipal triangulation requires three separately perceived people, with the third person having a significant relational meaning. The oedipal phase necessitates not only a change in major love object from mother to father, but also transformations in structure, internalization, and relationship modes. Intrapsychic developmental tasks include some resolution of the conflicting need for and fear of separating from the mother and a reasonably nonambivalent identification with the mother as a sexual woman.

Many factors may interfere along the path to this optimal development. Often the little girl's anger at her mother—which can result from struggles over control as anal-rapprochement conflicts arise or from the mother's attempts to interfere with masturbation as the girl begins to control her own genital body—will arouse anxieties over the loss of the mother and the loss of her love. "Should this anxiety become overwhelming, the girl's valuing of her femininity may be compromised . . . and instead an intense sadomasochistic relationship with the mother as central [can] ensue" (Tyson 1991, p. 588) and can impede the girl's ability to "make selective identifications with an ideally viewed mother" (p. 587). Such a scenario may inhibit the internalization of conflict, the development of a well-functioning superego, and even the wish to take the mother's place with the father.

As Horner (1985) states, oedipal issues are frequently assimilated into and transformed by preoedipal themes. Relationships then betray their preoedipal nature by the lack of internal differentiation between mother and father and by the essentially dyadic meaning of the seemingly triangular situation, or by object splitting. A case example of the permeation of the oedipal phase with unresolved conflicts around the preoedipal mother, resulting in the creation of triangular relationships in adult life, is found in Fuerstein's (1992) paper on women's ties to abusive men.

The patient, Dana, married a man who "seems to have embodied the qualities of the good maternal object in a male figure. . . . There was little passion found in the marital bed, and other men, who were sought out for affairs, were dangerous and sadistic and provided Dana with a lurid erotic life . . ." (p. 16). Dana perceived her mother as a cold disciplinarian, who called her daughter "disgusting" when the mother caught her masturbating; early feelings of pleasure in being the favorite of the father, a kindly, devoted man, were altered when a younger daughter was born. "Dana [felt] alone in a preoedipal sea of loss of self with the bad mother. The dilemma of needing this mother for sustenance while being driven toward separation from her was intensified due to the abandonment at the hands of her father" (p. 18).

Fuerstein views her patient as having made a "pseudo-change-of-object." Her early attempt to substitute father for mother as the source of nurturance and as the bridge leading away from an ambivalent tie to mother was hampered by her felt loss of him. "The girl's primitive idealization and attachment to the mother remains intact through a sadomasochistic relationship with the father/other man. A compromise solution is established, in which the rage at the mother is deeply repressed and is turned against the self in the masochistic position with the man. The woman remains powerfully tied to the mother and makes an unconscious pact with her: Through the 'beatings' from the father/other man, she remains tied to the mother through life and concomitantly is punished for her primitive aggressive strivings toward her. . . . Taking the father from the mother is not viewed just as an achievement of oedipal rivalry; rather, it is seen as a means of gratifying terrifying, aggressive wishes aimed at the maternal object, which will annihilate her" (p. 13). The origins for Dana's adult relationships to men were now delineated: the bad mother, desperately needed and just as powerfully hated, would be split off onto the sadistic, sexually exciting lovers; the good mother would be found in a husband.

Now I would like to examine the role that the early mother–daughter relationship plays in one particular form of triangular relationship, the "two-man phenomenon," in which a woman forms two simultaneous stable relationships, one with her husband and one with a long-term lover. It is more customary to think of men as being in two stable relationships over time; contemporary examples of the "two-woman phenomenon" include the film *The Captain's Paradise* and popular novels and television movies in which wife and long-term mistress confront each other over the man's hospital bed. A real-life example occurred at the recent funeral of François Mitterand, where his wife and their sons and his long-time mistress and *their* daughter stood next to each other at the grave site. However, the two-man phenomon also exists. Person (1988) cites a colleague as saying that all of her married professional women patients have had significant long-term affairs. While this is not true of the majority of my patients, I have also been impressed by the number of women in my practice who simultaneously have both husbands and serious long-term affairs and the even greater number who fantasize about having a continuing affair with a man of their acquaintance, although they do not enact the fantasy.

However, it is very possible that the frequency of long-term affairs is greater in men. And certainly the dynamics tend to be different, stemming from the difference in early psychosexual development between girls and boys. Many men create stable triangular relationships with two women in an attempt to reverse the defeat of the oedipal situation; possessing and satisfying two women is a protection against the possibility of reexperiencing the humiliating phallic-oedipal situation of competing with the father while being inadequate to satisfy the mother. According to Person (1988), such dynamics account for the prevalence of one gender-specific male fantasy—that of watching and/or participating in lesbian sex, which ". . . allows [a man] to control the source of his gratification by insuring that there are backup objects in the event that one vanishes" (p. 280).

Both girls and boys must grapple with the issue of separating from the mother, first in order to attain object constancy and its associated autonomy and then in the service of becoming separate, differentiated, genital sexual beings. Both men and women are prone to fears that erotic intimacy will reawaken symbiotic yearnings for the early mother–infant dyad and therefore need to believe that their romantic partner is quite different from the original maternal imago. However, as women's early psychosexual and object relational development follows a different path from men's, with a greater emphasis on fear of loss of the maternal object and of the object's love and greater difficulty in achieving separation and autonomy from the major identificatory figure, these issues prove more difficult for them. The lifelong themes of women's lives, expressed "differently and progressively more coherently throughout psychosexual development . . . include identifying with, separating from, and bonding with the mother" (Pines 1987) and the attendant differentiation between inside and outside, open and closed, as they relate to female genitalia. In particular, the little girl's earliest feelings of sameness between herself and her powerful, idealized mother, which are a primary source of her feelings of self-esteem, also promote the blurring of self and object boundaries, of lack of differentiation between outer and inner, and between self and mother. With early genital awareness, this feeling of diffusivity and lack of boundaries is reinforced by the unfocused, spreading nature of female genital sensations. The entrance to the female genital is an opening without a means of control; little girls, unlike little boys, need to turn back to their mothers for help with controlling fears and feelings, at the same time that they need to separate and become more autonomous (Bernstein 1990). One of my adult patients, who still both quarreled with and clung to her mother and went through a series of unsatisfactory affairs, complained: "I'm preoccupied with my vagina being wet and dirty and smelly—it's a place to cover up—I never know what's going on. I'd like to leave my diaphragm, or a penis, in permanently, to stuff it up." Adult difficulties in forming another intimate dyadic relationship, with a man, frequently stem from the anxieties associated with these issues.

Turning to the father, first as an ally assisting in separating from the mother, then to help with genital self-differentiation, and later as the chosen oedipal love object, has a number of hazards for the little girl. Fear of having lost her first love object because of her sexual desires makes those desires themselves seem dangerous. In addition, she fears that wishes for dependency and sustenance will not be met by the new object, that the offended mother, who does not want to relinquish her central role in either her husband or her daughter's life, will retaliate, and that, in identifying with the mother's genital sexuality, she will be drawn back into feelings of lack of differentiation between herself and her mother. Given these differing antecedent dynamics, it is understandable that many female erotic fantasies differ from those of men. One gender-specific female erotic fantasy is that of nursing a man back to health. Person (1988) interprets this fantasy as one of identification with the wounded man. I see this fantasy of caregiving, nurturing, and healing as a reassurance to women that needs for sustenance, tenderness, dependent gratifications, and advice—in short, the heart of the mother–baby dyad—will not be lost with genital sexuality and the change of object.

Given these differences in early development, it is understandable that a woman's unconscious motivation for maintaining two simultaneous significant relationships tends to differ from a man's. While such motivation can devolve from a number of developmental levels, for the women to be discussed, difficulties in the early mother–daughter relationship were central to their inability to integrate varying aspects of their requirements of a love object into a single love relationship. Goldberger (1988) describes three married patients who maintained two "monogomous" relationships over many years, in which "they are devoted to both partners, are intensely fearful of losing either one, and are tortured by guilt" (p. 230). Typically, these women married and had children at a young age. "When they married, they were largely defended against awareness of their unrequited longing for intimacy with their mothers. . . . With the nurturing of their own children . . . they experienced gratification of their earliest longings and became much more aware of them, only to lose this gratification again as the children grew older" (p. 232). At this point a second relationship was formed, of a closeness and intimacy unknown with the husband. "Their analyses revealed that their wish for intense closeness, their fear of re-engulfment, and their anxiety over separation and loss were connected with their conflicted early relationships with their mothers. The pleasure from the intimacy they achieved with their later lovers seems importantly derived from the large component of feminine identification in these men" (p. 232).

Goldberger's patients had followed one familiar female path.

They had defensively disengaged from intimacy with their mothers and, in large part, had married to escape from their conflicts with her. In their attempt to choose a romantic object quite different from her they picked men whom they perceived as nonmaternal. These women had temporarily protected themselves against becoming aware of their longings for the maternal dyad by fulfilling the need for mother–child closeness in the mothering of their own children. Only later did their yearning resurface, and they then found a lover who would fulfill their need for maternal bonding. However, they were able to enjoy the passion and excitement of the unconscious reunion with the mother provided through the relationship with the lover only with the counterbalance of their husband's clear-cut difference from them.

BETSY

An all-American beauty from a wealthy family, Betsy presented herself as cool, confident, and athletic. However, she felt herself to be a fraud, lacking interest, persistence, or the ability to acquire any real skill. Betsy was the daughter of a decisive, successful father, who was generally unavailable due to long hours of work and study, and a shy, approval-seeking mother, who was somewhat in awe of her socially successful daughter. Betsy attributed her difficulties to her ability since childhood to bully her mother and to the absence of firm directives. She felt that she was overidealized as her mother had been unable to have a child for many years prior to Betsy's birth. Feeling unable either to rely upon her mother as a role model or to live up to her mother's admiration, she felt fradulent. Yet she was blocked from identifying with her father or his ambition, in part because he was not available as a reliable support and in part because it seemed disloyal to disidentify with her mother's passivity and lack of control.

Betsy was impatient with her mother's daily telephone calls, feeling that there was a silent demand to share the very fabric of her life. "I can't stand my mother trying to get into my life; why doesn't she have her own life?—yet I feel I owe her my life because I was *her* whole life, and I'm guilty that I don't want to give it," said she. Oedipal-stage interpretations around competition and envy were dismissed; "No, it's as if she 'made' me like a piece of sculpture, and she's trying to chip away fingers and toes to create her own image. Sometimes I feel I don't know where she begins and I end. *That's* why I don't want to tell her anything—she'll take it away." Betsy feared the resurrection of early diffusivity and blurring of boundaries unless she avoided her mother's attempts to overidentify with her.

Betsy's marriage to an attractive, attentive young man was initially happy. She felt that her husband supported her attempts to become more autonomous while at the same time he nurtured her. He served as a buffer between Betsy and her mother, absorbing a portion of the older woman's attention, so that Betsy was able to relax her vigilance about feeling invaded by her mother's interest in her life. However, when her attempts to become pregnant were unsuccessful and she had to undergo a painful and frightening fertility procedure, she was not able to maintain her equilibrium. "I feel like I'm slipping out of control—with eating and everything else—since that test—I can still feel it, that instrument grabbing me inside and not letting go—so intrusive, like a rape—feels like violent sex. It's linked with my mother's saying that sex is bad." Offered another oedipal-level intervention: Like a punishment? Betsy again dismissed it: "No— more like: that's the way it *is*—so control isn't what I have. That new feeling of not wanting to be touched by John [husband] is like not wanting to be touched by my mother." Early fears of lack of genital control and penetration anxiety had resurfaced.

For Betsy, having to utilize infertility procedures meant that she was no longer able to stave off early identifications with a mother who seemed unable to control her own body or to help her daughter control hers. "The . . . issue of psychic boundaries flowed from the anxiety about body boundaries" (Bernstein 1990, pp. 159–160). As Betsy felt that her husband had also proved unable to help her control her genital body, he became for her a representation of her mother, a powerless, repudiated figure to whom she, however, remained tied. Her "solution" was to immerse herself in diet and exercise, and to begin a long-term affair with a body builder. Unconsciously, she sought a second male figure to help her as neither her mother nor her husband (or incidentally, her female therapist) had been able to.

ADELE

Adele is the middle of three daughters of an impoverished Eastern European immigrant family. When Adele was 3, her father brought her and her older sister to this country, leaving the mother and a 2-year-old daughter to follow. Reluctant to leave her home and parents, Adele's young mother delayed her own immigration by some months, leading the father to outbursts of: Your mother doesn't love us! Overwhelmed by the strangeness of language and place and the descent of a bevy of noisy, "take-over" American relatives, but most of all by the absence of her mother, Adele remembers spending her time either curled up in bed or staring blankly at an old black and white television set while sucking her thumb.

When the mother returned to the family, Adele rarely left her side. She tried to comfort her mother as she herself had needed comforting and to help the mother negotiate a new world that was threatening to the mother as well as to Adele. Ferociously jealous of her siblings, Adele tried to interpose herself between her mother and sisters, disciplining them and making sure they cleaned up and didn't burden the mother. She was the child mother would take into bed to be her ally in keeping a drunken father from entering the room. Oedipal development was hampered by the father's clear favoritism for the other sisters, as well as by Adele's external separation from her mother, reinforcing difficulties in intrapsychic separation.

As a young woman, Adele sought men of different cultural backgrounds to whom she would complain about her mother and through whose interest and consolation she attempted to heal old wounds. Eventually she married such a man, while still jealously attached to her mother and vigilantly scanning the mother's preferences. Ultimately, her husband's presence was not sufficient to ensure against depressive affect and her complaints about his occasional disinterest and "absence" repeated her initial complaints about her mother. Angry with, but deeply connected to, her husband, Adele began an ongoing affair with an unavailable Russian emigré, whose passion and warmth, as well as the realistic threat due to the political climate of the time of his being taken away without notice, re-created her fantasies of the mother before the actual separation. She felt particularly blissful when, held in his arms, he sang her to sleep with Russian love songs.

In Adele's case, early maternal absence, combined with the internalization of father's edict (Your mother doesn't love us!), resulted in childhood depression and fierce jealousy. Under the stress of the mother's prolonged absence at a point when object constancy had only recently been attained, internalization of a mental representation of a good, loving mother never became stable. Thus Adele's only security resided in being mother's favorite and therefore constantly in her thoughts. While she sought to embody her fantasy of a loving mother who would never leave in her choice of a husband, each time Adele felt she was not the very center of his life, the original trauma was revived and her husband was perceived as the abandoning bad mother. Her solution was to find a lover who fit the fantasy of the longed-for, unavailable, but passionately loved good mother while still remaining tied to her husband as the loved and hated abandoning object.

CATHY

Unlike Adele and Betsy, but reminiscent of Fuerstein's patient Dana, Cathy was the daughter of an extremely controlling and manipulative mother who perpetuated a matriarchy in which one daughter was picked to cater to the mother to the exclusion of her own needs or to the needs of her husband and children. From an early age Cathy was the daughter designated to serve her mother. As a child, Cathy idealized her mother, who always seemed to know the right thing to think and do, and became anxious and depressed when separated from her. Sleepovers and summer camp proved to be impossible situations; even schooldays were dreaded, almost to the point of school phobia. Separation produced massive anxiety as unconscious rage at the critical, overcontrolling mother was experienced as dangerous to the mother, whom Cathy also loved and needed.

In many ways Cathy sympathized and identified with her father, also helpless in face of the mother's demands. While she could not stand up for herself, feeling that her mother was, after all, probably right, she *did* attempt to stand up for her father. In so doing she attempted, with little success, to help him throw off the mother's domination and therefore be availible to help Cathy.

Cathy's mother's feeling of ownership of her daughter increased incrementally at the start of adolescence, increasing Cathy's desire to have her own life and sexuality and her guilt over her hatred of her mother. Striving to liberate herself from her thrall to her mother, Cathy began to date, but had a pregnancy scare after her first sexual experience. It turned out to be a false alarm, but by the time that was discovered, Cathy's mother, appalled by this evidence of her daughter's insubordination, had rushed her into marriage. Cathy felt that her husband, of whom the mother approved, was in many ways an extension of her mother—a family member to whom she owed loyalty but whom she resented and secretly rebelled against.

Cathy began an affair with an unconventional and somewhat sadistic man who encouraged her to be adventuresome, to take risks that shocked and titillated her, but also to be at his beck and call. The power and intensity of the relationship stemmed from a compromise solution in which Cathy remained tied to her mother through her primitive idealization and masochistic submission to her lover at the same time that he represented an opportunity for wild rebellion against the controlling mother.

For Cathy, her husband represented one part of her tie to her mother in which she remained a dutiful daughter and gave up her strivings toward autonomy and adult sexuality out of guilt and fear of punishment for her aggression toward the mother. Cathy felt that the marriage belonged to her mother, toward whom she felt a sense of masochistic surrender. On the other hand, she prized her lover as an externalization of the wild anger and contempt she'd been unable to express by herself and as someone who gave her permission to mock the mother. Until she entered treatment, however, she was unable to own any of these feelings, and had to punish herself through subordination to an unruly and essentially destructive man.

Each of the women discussed in this chapter was unable to achieve an integrated and sublimated love with one object, due mainly to the lack of resolution of the conflict between achieving intrapsychic separation and autonomy from the mother and still retaining the needed sustenance, identification, and bonding with her. While each woman has a different and particular set of dynamics, they all attempted to solve this dilemma by having two men in their lives, each of whom provided different internal representations of varying aspects of the mother, or defenses against such aspects. Fuerstein's patient, Dana (who, unlike the rest of these cases, had a series of short-term affairs), preserved the positive aspect of her maternal representation by investing it in the person of her husband and retained the sadomasochistic relationship with the mother by forming relationships with sadistic, sexually exciting lovers. Goldberger's patients, threatened by the fear of regression and the loss of autonomy implicit in surrendering to their yearning for maternal closeness, protected themselves by isolating each portion of their conflict in relationships with two men, one of whom provided maternal intimacy while the other represented autonomy and strong boundaries. Betsy's husband was perceived as the passive and helpless mother who could not help her master her need to feel in control of her own body; assailed by the threat of regression and the loss of control, she turned to a second man. Adele's infantile expectations, fueled by early abandonment, were disappointed by her husband, who appeared to her to be the abandoning, never-good-enough maternal object to whom she was nevertheless tied, and she sought the good mother again in the person of her lover. In an attempt to escape from maternal entrapment and to gain personal and sexual autonomy, Cathy chose a wild and rebellious lover, by whom she felt alternately liberated and restricted, but felt too angry and guilty to leave her husband, whom she perceived as a substitute for the entrapping mother.

In these women the lifelong themes of identifying with, separating from, and bonding with the mother remained fixated at early stages of development, such that oedipal issues became dominated and distorted by unresolved preoedipal conflicts. As a result, adult relationships with men remained in the service of attempts to solve problems relating to early issues of separation, autonomy, and feminine identifications.

REFERENCES

Bernstein, D. (1990). Female genital anxieties, conflicts and typical mastery modes. *International Journal of Psycho-Analysis* 71:151–165.

Fuerstein, L. A. (1992). Females in bondage: the early role of mother and father in the woman's tie to abusive men. In *Psychoanalytic Perspectives on Women*, ed. E. V. Siegel, pp. 9–24. New York: Brunner/Mazel.

Goldberger, M. (1988). The two-man phenomenon. *Psychoanalytic Quarterly* 57:229–233.

Horner, A. J. (1985). The Oedipus complex. In *Treating the Oedipal Patient in Brief Psychotherapy*, ed. A. J. Horner, pp. 25–54. New York: Jason Aronson.

Kernberg, O. F. (1980). Love, the couple, and the group: a psychoanalytic frame. *Psychoanalytic Quarterly* 49:78–108.

Person, E. S. (1988). *Dreams of Love and Fateful Encounters: The Power of Romantic Passion*. New York: Norton.

Pines, D. (1987). *A woman's unconscious use of her body: a psycho-analytical perspective*. Paper presented at the Second Carole Dilling Memorial Lecture, New York, January 10.

Tyson, P. (1991). Some nuclear conflicts of the infantile neurosis in female development. *Psychoanalytic Inquiry* 11:582–601.

PART IV

CLINICAL
CONSIDERATIONS

While we have traced the development of the mother–daughter dyad with both its benign and pathological consequences, we need to examine the clinical session material to test whether the quality and nature of such development is also manifested in the present. In other words, does transference recapitulate developmental history?

Psychoanalytic theory holds that affects that were mobilized toward significant childhood figures are transferred to other people in the present and the analyst in particular. If the theory is valid, then transferences ought to recapitulate the history of individual development, specifically as it relates to intimate relationships in a dyadic context. Jill Morris utilizes dreams and fantasies like a television screen that accurately reflects transferential feelings and developmental difficulties. Both Ronald Katz and Agnieszka Leznicka-Los study the dimension of countertransference and what it can tell us about the patient–analyst interaction. Katz illustrates how basic forms of attachment are formed early in life and endure because of their survival value. He views such historic identifications as psychobiological channels that transmit intergenerational wisdom. Leznicka-Los demonstrates the complexities inherent in the therapeutic dyad when the female therapist is younger than the female patient. She suggests, based on her observations, that the therapist will at times be the mother to the patient and at other times fill the role of the patient's child.

How transference and conflict are mirrored in dreams is reported by Morris. One important affect leading to conflict is illustrated by Marilyn Meyers, who suggests that mothers may envy their daughters when they feel that they are unable to compete with them. On the other hand, the benign oedipal mother, says Roberta Ann Shechter, may have a powerful effect on a patient, leading to a transference-cure. Patients at an oedipal level of development may benefit from the curative aspects of transference, which may lead to structural change. Such ego repair is brought about by identification with the analyst's analytic skills and the corrective transference experience.

12

Mothers and Daughters— The Tie that Binds: Early Identification and the Psychotherapy of Women

Ronald Katz

> By the time a girl developmentally turns to the father, she has normally learned the nature of an object relationship once and for all from her mother.
>
> —ERIKSON 1968

The human infant is the product of a relationship between two separate organisms—it grows in connection to another and its survival and existence after birth is dependent upon its relationship to another. The human infant is relationship dependent and relationship-oriented. In utero this relationship is automatic—all needs are met with minimum expenditure of effort. All energy is consumed by the growth process, which proceeds at an enormous pace. With the advent of birth, the relationship and the fullfillment of needs ceases to be automatic. Energy is diverted from growth to the procedures for need gratification as the conscious mother meets the increasingly conscious child. (By *conscious* I mean the deliberate awareness that the child has unfulfilled needs that the mother has to satisfy by appraising the situation and making efforts at implementing problem-solving behavior. It is generally accepted that these "conscious" appraisals and behavioral attempts at amelioration are influenced by unconscious factors.) To the extent that the mothering relationship is adept at meeting the infant's needs, energy diverted to the process of need fulfillment is restored to power the processes of maturation. The quality of ego development is reflective of the adequacy of this relationship (Hartmann 1952). The child's innate "equipment" is turned on and fine-tuned by the mother's ministrations (Kestenberg 1995). It is assumed (Rubinfine 1962) that the infant is born with an inherent mental organization ready to make this relationship possible—a *schema* in Piagetian terms—which becomes specifically molded by the infant's experiences with the mother to make attachment possible. An extero-uterine psychobehavioral umbilical cord, if you will. The infant incorporates experience into this schema and the schema is thus modified and altered to facilitate the child's accommodation to the mother. "Thus, the earliest frustration–gratification experiences leave the imprint of their characteristics on the process by which psychic representations of the object are formed, and on their content. The firm establishment of these object representations play an essential part in the process of identification" (Ritvo and Solnit 1958, p. 80). The mother molds the relationship and it reflects her state of object relationship and her own, internalized, maternal ideal. The outward manifestations of the attachment process is the child's active imitation of the mother's behavior in relation to the child specifically and in relation to the world in general. Early experiences outside or foreign to the schema are thought to be ignored (Wolff 1960). Experiences of too intense stimulation (frustration or gratification) are denied so that the child can assimilate the experience and thus accommodate to the mothering situation. In other words, the psychic apparatus functions to maintain the essential relationship to the mothering one and defenses are utilized in that service. The relationship with the mothering object is the essential element for life and object loss the greatest threat. These internal mechanisms of adaptation are mobilized and "charged" by the interaction of the relationship [through the interplay of tension resulting from internal or external pressure/need and external/maternal gratification]. Need tension resulting from internal or external need/stimulation promotes object seeking and object awareness [attempts to assimiliate]; need gratification results in a state of accommodation or adaption. Energy is diverted from growth and maturation to need-reducing activity and is restored to maturational activity once tension is relieved and homeostasis restored. The relationship pattern of need tension/need gratification with its concomitant behavioral and emotional correlates becomes a permanent aspect of the schema—the child accommodates to the particular relationship internally and externally. "In the interaction of mother and infant, the mother serves as regulator of the child's instinctual needs. How she influences the balance between discharge and maintenance of tension may be crucial for the child's ability to substitute ego aims for instinctual aims" (Ritvo and Solnit 1958, p. 83).

Rudimentary as our instruments of measurement may be, it is clearly discernible that by 2 weeks of age, the infant can differentiate the mother from others, by 6 months of age can imitate the mother's behavior in relation to the child, and by 8 months a firm attachment to the mother is observable (Spitz 1959). Certainly by 18 months of age the child has a permanent memory of the mother and of the relationship with the mother, which persists regardless of her presence (Werner 1957). By the age of 3, with the development of representation thought and the ability for symbolization, the child establishes an identification with the mother and with her gender. Observation has shown that through identification the child is capable of imitating the mother's attitude, behavior, feelings, defenses, prohibitions, rules of conduct, and expectations (McDevitt 1996). This external attachment with its internal psychophysiological correlates manifests itself by the age of 3 as a permanent identification in which the child can play both roles irrespective of the presence of the mother. The nature of this bond is not a "general attachment" but very specific to the mother and reflects the idiosyncrasies of the particular parent–child relationship. This identificatory bond is enduring and strong and will persist for life regardless of satisfaction or frustration (Solnit and Neubauer 1986).

Freud (1912) wrote of this schema, but referred to it as a cliché, stereotype, or prototype in the person, which perpetually repeats and reproduces itself and into which new people and relationships are woven. In referring to the basis of the schema—the mother–child relationship—he writes:

> Let us bear clearly in mind that every human being has acquired, by the combined operation of inherent disposition and of external influences in childhood, a special individuality in the exercise of his capacity to love—that is, in the conditions he sets up for loving, in the impulses he gratifies by it, and in the aims he sets out to achieve in it. [p. 312]

Videotape recordings of children's relationships with their mother from 18 months to 72 months have been shown to remain essentially the same over time and to be duplicated with other "substitute" mother figures (Rubin 1995). A child who has a warm, affectionate relationship with the mother will relate to others in a warm, affectionate manner, whereas a child with a guarded, distant relationship will relate to others in a guarded, distant manner. Mary, an 8-year-old girl diagnosed as ADD was brought to my office after being described as an uncontrollable behavioral problem both at home and in school. Only with massive amounts of Ritalin could she be controlled. She was thought to be severely learning disabled, perhaps retarded. During her initial session she frenetically picked up everything in my office, looked in every drawer, jumped on every piece of furniture while constantly but discreetly looking at me as if waiting to be yelled at. She asked for food, to watch TV, and to look at comic books. She refused to acknowledge my questions or presence except when asking for food or comics or TV. Mary was clearly in a state of tension and engaged in object-seeking, tension-reducing activity. Her schema or internalized mother–daughter object relationship incorporated the expectation of punishment. She was able to accommodate to the "relationship objects" and reduce her tension only in extremely limited ways. Accommodation was possible only by denial of the feared aspects of the object. An enormous amount of her energy was spent on tension-reducing activity and defensive operations. She asked for the only forms of gratification obtained from the mother and it was only within those limits of her internalized mother relationship [schema] that she could relate to me. For one year in my office I fed Mary when she asked to be fed (cereal after school when she was very hungry), gave her comics when she requested, and watched TV with her when also requested. She would increasingly look at me out of the corner of her eye during the sessions to see if I was angry. When reassured by my friendly, benign, attentive gaze that the relation was intact, she would relax and return to reading or TV watching. Tension was reduced, accommodation was achieved within the scope of her schema, and her energy could once more be freed for maturational growth. As this pattern became established, her hyperactive, tension-reducing activity decreased markedly. After a year, Mary started to talk to me. She no longer wanted to watch TV and the requests to eat became sporadic. She started involving me in activities and could allow me to talk (although I had a very prescribed role and lines of dialogue during the play). Her classroom teachers reported that she was much improved in school and that more time was spent in educational activities and less in behavior control. This was reflected at home as well. Her mother reported that instead of yelling at and trying to hit her baby brother, Mary now tolerated him without upset and occasionally played with him. Her Ritalin intake was modified accordingly. Mary's schema [internalized mother relationship] was reflected in the particular type of relationship that she reproduced with me. I became the potentially threatening quasi-libidinally satis-fying object to whom she related in a characteristic manner. By operating within the scope and limitations of her schema, I was able to modify her schema, thus altering her other relationships accord-ingly.

The child exists independently, but only because of and in relation to its mother. This life-preserving relationship becomes permanently installed within the child so that by the time the child can become physically separate and relatively autonomous it can still "take the mother along," thus lessening the danger inherent in object loss. The child is capable of being the mother in relation to herself as well as herself in relation to the mother. This capacity manifests as an identification and self concept—an imprinted blueprint that becomes the frame of reference for forming new relationships. Identification is one of the main pathways by which the child becomes the organizer and initiator of independent activities (Ritvo and Solnit 1958) and through it energy formally directed to the mother becomes available for other activities and functions (Freud 1923).

Ms. M, a 40-year-old woman patient and a second-born child,

revealed that she felt that she did not exist; she couldn't think of anything worthwhile about herself. Despite years of recognition and acclaim in her field of endeavor and as a mother, she felt unlovable and worthless. All of her successes were merely a superstructure built on an empty core. Analysis revealed that Ms. M's primary schema was molded by a deeply narcissistic, neglectful mother who responded to Ms. M's physical needs while psychologically relating to her as if she didn't exist. Ms. M's mother, also a second-born child of a narcissistic and psychologically neglectful mother, felt that Ms. M was just like her and related to her maternally as she had been related to. In group therapy Ms. M did not want to reveal herself and was convinced that no one would be interested or would respond. People were encouraged to ignore her. In her individual analysis she expressed the view that when she couldn't physically be seen she was forgotten. Ms. M's "self concept" and sense of identification reflected her mother's dynamics and behavior rather than her own personality and attributes. The internalized mother–daughter relationship was the channel through which these new relationships were forced to pass.

Since Hartmann's introduction of the term *object constancy*, and Anna Freud and Spitz's work further defining its dimensions in the 1960s, this schema or stereotype has been referred to as the constant object and as an introject. It is probably more accurate to speak of the constant object relationship since the schema develops from the mother–child relationship. After the concept of a constant object was established, Mahler (1965) focused on the quality of the constant object. In her studies of the separation-individuation process she found that an experience with and internalization of a positive libidinal maternal relationship was a necessary ingredient to helping the child traverse the rapprochement subphase and thus achieve greater demarcation of self and object representations [greater internal separation]. Having a positive, loving mother internalized not only helped the child to separate but provided the child with a lasting source of sustenance, comfort, and love when he or she was away from the mother (Mahler and Furer 1968). The child was able to evoke the memory of the loving mother in her absence, thus enabling the child to have a greater degree of security, which facilitated the maintenance of the separation. Ms. Q, after working in psychotherapy, began experiencing her therapist as an "internalized constant object" and described this awareness, which occurred during a visit to her parent's house when they began to fight. "I was getting very upset and felt myself being drawn into it once again and suddenly it felt like your face appeared and I felt calm and cared about and my parents weren't able to get to me as they usually do."

With a positive libidinal or "good enough" mother relationship, gratification of need tensions is sufficient enough that not too much energy has to be permanently diverted to object-seeking, tension-reducing, and defensive activities in order to make assimilation and accommodation possible. Thus the relationship with the mother is preserved while providing the child with sufficient energy for growth and development. Unrelieved tensions could be increasingly tolerated and unrelieved frustrations dealt with without threatening the essential security of the relationship to the mother or the child's growth potential. The child is able to tolerate ambivalent feelings and negativity can be neutralized. The internalized constant object relationship then provides the child with an active orientation to basically successful relationships and a positive self-concept. "Imitative behavior that proceeds mainly on the basis of a predominantly positive libidinal tie is likely to become a partial identification that is useful for adaptation" (Ritvo and Solnit 1958, p. 81). Tyson (1996) has proposed that a criterion for judging the presence of this positive libidinal relationship is the capacity for affective regulation, an important capability necessary for independent functioning. She sees this as the ability to use affect as a signal to mobilize defenses and activate behavior to avoid disruption of functioning and disorganization of thinking. A "good enough mother" functions as a soother, comforter, and regulator of affects during intense affective states. The mother responds in a way to help the child regain control and equilibrium. The child internalizes this ability and in identification with the mother is able to perform this function for herself. Ms. R's mother was not this way at all. She couldn't help the child during intense emotional states and inevitably "lost patience" with her, got angry, or sent her away. In the transference with me, Ms. R was terrified of having strong feelings aroused in her. She was convinced that I would hate her and get rid of her. At the very least, she'd become overwhelmed and disorganized and I wouldn't know what to say to her and she'd feel humiliated and uncared for. She expended a great deal of time protecting herself from becoming emotionally stimulated.

When the introject is not "good enough," excessive energy is spent in object-seeking, tension-reducing activities and deployed in defenses designed to facilitate adaptation to the insufficiently satisfying mother. Under these conditions, overly frustrated needs leading to aggressive feelings outweigh the neutralizing force of the libidinal reservoir; the memory of the mother becomes a source of insecurity and persecution and fails to sustain the child in the mother's absence (McDevitt 1996). These experiences of "too much" frustration and the resultant internal loss of object love can also lead to regression to a need-satisfying level in relationships in which the other person is seen increasingly in terms of the person's needs rather than as an individual in her own right (Edgcumbe and Burgner 1972). This can happen temporarily when there is an internalized positive libidinal mother or chronically when there is an internalized "not good enough" mother. On a behavioral level, having too much unbound aggression can become a direct threat to the essential relationship with the mother and has to be defended against. (By "frustration" it is implied that certain impulses or desires, whether conscious or unconscious, emotional or physiological, are being blocked from gratification. This frustration can also stem from innate differences in temperament between parent and child which may prevent them from becoming an effective "team.") In some situations one can come to view their own needs, desires, and impulses as bad and as a threat to the relationship when their attempts to seek gratification or relief of tension bring them into dangerous conflict with the mother. Ms. R didn't want to acknowledge that she wanted something from me: "It was stupid . . . I shouldn't want it. . . . I'm crazy for even thinking this way. . . ." Another woman, whose mother reacted to any expression of wants on her part with rage, reported on starting therapy that she had no idea of what she either wanted or needed. How the patient handles the mounting frustration-aggression often depends on what was the maternal model that had been internalized and identified with. The patient also maintains her own behavioral patterns that had been developed as part of her accommodation process to the mother. Whenever Mrs. L's mother got angry, she flew into a dangerous, psychotic rage. Mrs. L learned to run away and hide at those times.

Now, as an adult, she will alternate between exploding in barely controllable rages or getting into her car and driving off for a few days. One patient may avoid the therapist to protect the relationship from her aggression whenever it flares up; another, raised by a continuously threatening parent, learned to keep her distance all the time. Another may keep her distance psychologically by becoming silent. Patty refused to talk to me. In response to my questions I learned that she was angry with me, and could think of nothing else. She didn't want to leave me and she was convinced that letting it out would also destroy the relationship. She remained silent in her sessions for three weeks until her anger subsided. Miss C 's mother yelled and ridiculed her whenever her activities didn't reflect the mother's interests and values. Miss C learned to use identification with the mother and depression as her two major defenses against her aggression. Eventually these defenses became a permanent aspect of her internalized schema and "greeted" all new relationships.

Internalizing a "not good enough" relationship further drives the individual to form "not good enough" relationships with others, constitutes the basis for a poor self-concept, and provides lasting expectations of frustration. Miss Z, born 10 months after her sister, never "got enough" and felt perpetually frustrated. Her object-seeking, tension-reducing activity took the form of excessive crying. Her mother's ministrations to her needs combined attempts at controlling her expressions of frustration by physical restraints and threats with belated gratification. Miss Z came to therapy wanting help in overcoming her attraction to sadistic men who tied her up, humiliated her, and eventually gratified her. After two years of treatment, Miss Z's primary schema had been modified enough so that she was able to form an attachment to a nonsadistic man, whom she married; she subsequently left treatment. Miss Z returned two and a half years later for help with her child who, she complained, was torturing her with constant crying, complaining, and demanding. In addition, she felt consumed by fantasies of men in her past who humiliated and tortured her while feeling sexually frustrated with her nonsadistic husband. The primary mother–daughter schema that had only partially been modified was still a source of relationship frustrations and had become the main blueprint by which the newly created relationship with her own child was structured.

Meyers (Berberich et al. 1996) has written how the constant object, and the capacity to develop a constant object, once established does not disappear. The constant of the internal relationship to that object remains even though the object itself may not be present or be a source of need satisfaction.

Ms. P was born a very sickly and frail child and reported that during the first year of her life she hovered between life and death. Her mother was very attentive to her and nursed her back to health. When Ms. P was almost 4 years of age, her mother left her in the care of her father with whom she stayed until she was 15. She did not see her mother during those intervening years. The father was sexually and physically abusive to Ms. P. She was forced to develop a relationship with him for her very survival. By the time Ms. P was reunited with her mother, her secondarily developed schema, based on her relationship with her father, was the dominating lens through which her experience of the world was filtered. She had become sexually promiscuous with sexually and physically abusive men and in turn had become sexually abusive as well. Relationships were viewed as experiences of conquest and control through sexuality. The early primary relationship with the mother had been supplanted by a totally different one with the father. The primary relationship was dormant, however, not destroyed, waiting to spring back to life just as a desert will bloom after a great rain. In the aftermath of her reunion with the mother, Ms. P made a suicide attempt and was hospitalized. Thereafter, the primary relationship resumed with Ms. P hovering between life and death under the constant threat of suicide and her mother trying to maintain her life and restore her to healthy functioning. Therapy began at this point. Ms. P lived with her mother, re-creating their primary relationship, while in the transference Ms. P played out both father and daughter roles of her secondary schema with the analyst. She became both the sexual provocateur and seducer [father/self] of the analyst [child/self] and in turn the terrified potential victim [child] of the hurtful and sexually preoccupied therapist [father]. This transference relationship developed and was worked through and modified. Outside of therapy, this work was reflected by a marked decrease of sexual promiscuity and abuse. As the working through of the secondary schema proceeded, in its place arose the mother–daughter relationship transference, with Ms. P alternatingly playing the child and mother roles while placing the analyst in the complementary position. Ms. P was either in the position of being in danger of dying through suicide or severe life-threatening illness [with the analyst being the rescuing, life-sustaining mother] or she was the caregiving, health-preserving, life-producing mother who nurtured and sustained others, including the "needy" analyst [child self]. The primary mother–daughter schema was recharged in the transference relationship, worked on, and modified. Paralleling this work outside the therapeutic setting, we saw a marked decrease in suicidally threatening and self-destructive behaviors. Her motherly reenactments matured from someone who recklessly got pregnant to someone who bred and nursed sick animals; playing active roles in disaster relief operations and educating and caring for the children in her living environment. Her energy, rather than being totally consumed in replaying her schematic relationships, was freed to power the growth of her personality in new endeavors and directions. Her defensive operations decreased as did her level of relationship-threatening anger.

When the mother cannot tolerate the child's being a separate person with her own personality and needs, and demands instead that the child mirror her, separation becomes heavily tinged with basic terror for the child. The mother's intolerance or "demand" can take different forms, with the two basic ones being that the mother will neglect or avoid the child when she is not mirroring or else be physically or verbally punitive. Either approach cuts the child off from the needed life-sustaining relationship. The child has to meet the mother's needs for care in order to have its own needs met. If the child needs to expend "too much" energy to maintain the relationship, there remains "too little" for personal growth and maturation. The child's personality needs are undernourished—she does not feel like a whole or real person in her own right. Those aspects of her own personality that reflected the mother's personality needs exist conflict free, but the rest of the personality becomes like the dark side of the moon—hidden, dangerous, and removed from needed energy for actualization.

Ms. K's mother needed her to hold the family together. The advent of her birth kept the father from leaving the mother and the family stayed intact. She received her mother's love and interest for her efforts at keeping the family together. Apart from this, Ms. K did not exist for her mother. Her "independent" views, needs, and feelings were unsolicited, unwanted, and a stimulus for both anger and threats of abandonment. As an adult, Ms. K worked as a professional facilitator, helping the corporate family stay together. In her private life she became a mother with her own family, which she struggled to keep together. Apart from these roles she felt that she was nothing and did not exist as a person. She didn't feel loved because one can't love something that doesn't exist. In treatment she was fearful of lying on the couch because if I didn't see her in front of me then I would forget that she existed. When away from the office she was convinced that I didn't exist and that she didn't exist for me. In group therapy she would participate to facilitate the group's working harmoniously, but would avoid personally revealing her self.

Miss W also existed to reflect her mother's needs, but those needs were different from those of Ms. K's mother. Miss W's mother needed mirroring and required her daughter to be just like herself—to talk the way she talked, to think the way she thought, to have the interests that she had, and to behave the way she behaved. When Miss W's own personality manifested itself, she was ridiculed, threatened, attacked, and ultimately abandoned. Those needs of Miss W's that couldn't be repressed to avoid conflict with the mother were suppressed from view but aired in the private darkness of her fantasy life and solitary playroom. To survive, Miss W needed to become a clone of her mother. In therapy Miss W was terrified to say anything that she thought I would not like and approve of. She was emotionally convinced that I would attack her both verbally and physically, and if not that, totally abandon her at the very least. In therapy she expressed very well both her need for her mother and her problem with it as it related to the transference: "If you're not exactly like my mother, then I feel you don't care about me and I can't tolerate that, but if you're exactly like my mother, then I couldn't stand that either." When faced with the opportunity to express her true but previously suppressed and hidden self, Miss W manifested the transference of the entire mother–daughter relationship to the analyst: "If I tell you what I really think, I'm afraid that you will get angry and attack me or else throw me out or say nothing but psychologically withdraw and no longer be there for me. But even if you assured me that none of that would happen, I still couldn't tolerate it if you didn't respond exactly as I want, to say just what I want you to say the way I need you to say it." In the transference she was both the frightened child and the demanding mother who insisted on the "other" being a clone reflecting her needs.

Freud pointed out that one of the values of the transference is that it provides a real opportunity—if not the only opportunity—to resolve the basic complexes that are manifestations of these primary mother–child relationship problems. The transference brings the problems to life in the office for you can't "kill someone in effigy." The analyst has to facilitate and accept the development and unfolding of the primary schema. The analyst has to fit into it in order to get into it. Like a computer program, the schema seems to be modifiable once you've gotten inside it. And to carry the analogy to a computer further, you can always add new, additional programs and work around and not modify the original, primary program, but it may still drain memory capacity and energy. The degree to which the original program—the primary schema—is a source of pathology and needs to be modified needs to be understood and evaluated. Miss E came to therapy to help her separate from her current husband and find someone more suitable. She described her relationship to her mother as "great"— warm, supportive, loving, and so on, and this was reflected in the developing transference relationship. I was either seen as the warm, supportive, concerned mother or the connected, loved, controlled child. In her outside life Miss E had numerous friends, good relationships, and was successful at work. Her mother unfortunately had died of cancer when Miss E was 12 after several years of decline and Miss E hadn't evolved fully in her dependence–independence continuum. Her father remarried and it was the stepmother's influence on this still dependent young woman that greatly influenced her choice of mate against her own instinctual feelings. In therapy Miss E didn't need any modification in her basic schema, but rather support and guidance in developing her own personality. Searles (1973) relates to this issue: "Whether any one patient needs to run that whole course [phases of ego development] will depend upon the level of ego development he has already attained at the beginning" (p. 247).

The concept of "object constancy" has evolved and expanded to include the quality of the mothering object. In this expanded version the identified-with mother has to be a source of positive libidinal satisfaction in which gratification outweighs frustration, positive stimulation exceeds negative stimulation. When this occurs, the capacity for constant relationships becomes a crucial switch point without which subsequent development in drives, affect, and ego will be severely distorted (Edgcumbe and Burgner 1972). This concept, also referred to as the capacity for "total object relationships" (Kernberg 1975), is seen as essential for the capacity to tolerate ambivalent reactions, to shift from a need-satisfying to an object-relations orientation and to neutralize aggression. Meyers (Berberich et al. 1996) sees those with borderline pathogy as not having had a "good" mother to identify with and so weren't able to internalize a need-fulfilling object.

The implication of this for psychotherapy is that in those cases in which the identified-with mother wasn't "good enough," the primary mother–child schema has to be modified for psychological growth to take place and for separation-individuation to proceed. In essence, the therapist has to enter into the schema and be perceived by the patient to be like the mother but then to change and become "a positive libidinal object." The feasibility of this was demonstrated by Meyers (1996), who described the case of a female patient who was convinced that Dr. Meyers would get sick of her and hurt her like everyone else but who developed object constancy as a consequence of Dr. Meyers's maintaining a constant analytic relationship, the ingredients of which included listening steadfastly, not coming too close, but remaining reliable and dependable. Bergman (Berberich et al. 1996), in treating deprived and disturbed children, found that "important aspects of the separation-individuation process are experienced in the therapy situation. Beginning identification with the therapist is often a significant sign that a change has been made and a developmental process has been set in motion" (p. 248). Searles (1973), in reporting on a case, writes, "The patient has needed to come to experience the analyst as being equivalent to the early mother who comprises the whole world of which the infant is inextricably a part" (p. 248). The clinical material presented in this chapter by the author consists entirely of female patients working with a male psychotherapist, thus suggesting that the analyst can come to be experienced as the early mother regardless of gender.

The outline of the patient's schema reveals itself in two ways: in the "material" recounted [from the past and present and dreams] and in the here-and-now functioning in the office. The former helps the therapist to understand the schema while the latter also supplies the opportunity to enter into it. Mrs. T recalled in a series of sessions how she would be totally ignored by her depressed, self-absorbed mother, who most often sat on the couch staring into space or else falling asleep. Her mother would get angry and attack Mrs. T if she disturbed her. Mrs. T could maintain this essential primary connection by following the dictum "silence is golden." She lived in fear lest she inadvertently disrupt this equilibrium. As Mrs. T spoke, the analyst experienced an enveloping sense of tiredness and self-absorption that began with the session and evaporated on its cessation. When Mrs. T eventually braved asking the therapist's opinion of what she had been talking about she was relieved not to be yelled at and pleased that she had been listened to. Just as the original mother–daughter relationship was constructed on the interactions initiated by the child's frustration and subsequent object-seeking behavior, so too does it get reconstructed in the office. The patient's schema will naturally tend to channel the therapeutic relationship through its idiosyncratic confines. The therapist calibrates the response to meet with the patient's verbal or nonverbal initiation of contact for need fulfillment. The therapeutic response to the patient's contact is the channel through which the analyst moves to modify the primary schema. As the analyst comes to be increasingly more "in the schema," the analytic relationship becomes charged with the transferred relationship. This is manifested both in the patient's thoughts, feelings, and behavior as well as in the analyst's. As the analyst allows herself/himself to be drawn into the patient's psychological orbit, he or she will experience the gravitational pull on his or her being. This is the induced countertransference. If unexpected, unrecognized, or misunderstood, the induced countertransference can startle and disturb the analyst. A therapist reported to me that she was a terrible failure because she felt cold, distant, and angry with her new patient, who was obviously in great need of loving care. It was only after she understood that she was experiencing the introjected "mother" of the primary schema that she realized the treatment was progressing well and that she was emotionally receiving significant "material" about the patient's past.

Another therapist lamented to me that she had defective empathy. Her patient had been describing scenes from her childhood in which she had been physically abused by both her mother and her father. Far from feeling sympathy for the patient, the therapist felt detached and numb and, if anything, frustrated with the patient. The therapist had reported on the case to her supervisor, who implied that she had defective empathy that was related to her own childhood. This depressed the therapist and didn't foster any understanding of the case. Upon exploration with the therapist it became clear that she was very empathic with the patient and it helped shed light on the early parent–child relationship. As a child, the patient had to suppress her reaction to the physical abuse by both parents. She had no ally or support and had to accommodate to the abusive parent for survival. She repressed her anger, and felt numb and detached while maintaining the primary relationship. Her unrelieved frustrations were suppressed and sublimated in intellectual pursuits. The therapist's induced countertransference helped her to understand the patient emotionally as well as intellectually once the countertransference was recognized as a source of emotional communication from the patient. Since the patient has internalized and identified with the entire early mother–child relationship, the analyst, through the countertransference, is helped to "know" about that experience. Just as the patient is often unconscious of the transference, the analyst is often unconscious of the countertransference.

Ms. B was lying on the couch, barely saying a word. During one of the long silences the analyst started to get chest pains and thought that a heart attack was imminent . . . after it persisted the analyst grew fearful and asked the silent patient if she had a fear of having a heart attack. In a burst of relief the patient blurted out, "How did you know? I was lying here terrified that I was about to have a heart attack." The analyst's chest pains evaporated.

Freud cautioned analysts against "acting " on the countertransference for self-gratification but he did not preclude analysts from understanding and utilizing it to facilitate the analysis. The primary schema, formed during the preverbal period of life, can only be communicated emotionally and behaviorally and so is received emotionally by the analyst. Just as the patient is often unconscious of the transference, the analyst is often unconscious of the countertransference. The analyst must recognize, tolerate and accept, and finally understand the induced feelings and behavior in order to decipher the communication and ultimately utilize that information to modify the primary schema of the patient. The therapist needs to struggle through the resistances to recognizing and understanding the induced countertransference as well as through the patient's resistances to understanding the transference. Tyson's description (1996) of the ideal caregiver can be applied to the analyst as well: "The caregiver must be able to convey that a sense of continuing safety prevails in spite of the child's affective storm . . . the mother must reassure the child that his angry, murderous thoughts will not frighten, infuriate, hurt or kill her" (p. 103). As the schema reproduces and envelops, the analyst, from within, can help the patient to see its dimensions, rhythms, and patterns and begin the process of change.

In conclusion, the primary relationship with our significant caregivers is introjected and resides within us as a lifetime-lasting beacon to aid with the guidance of our life's journey. It is a psychobiological channel that transmits the acquired wisdom of the generations. It manifests its presence in our basic identifications. It is enduring yet capable of modification. Formed during the preverbal period of life, it remains to a great extent unconscious and automatic. When the internalized adaptations necessary for survival and growth in the primary environment ill-serve to facilitate successful adaptation to the world at large, psychotherapy can be a useful instrument in making the necessary course corrections. The clinical examples presented in this paper to illustrate the active presence of the internalized primary relationship were all of female patients working with a male analyst. The work demonstrates that it may be possible to modify the basic internalized patterns of interpersonal relationships forged in the crucible of the mother–daughter dyad regardless of the sex of the analyst.

REFERENCES

Berberich, E., Bergman, A., Janssen, P. L., and Meyers, H. C. (1996). Mapping out the internal world. In *The Internal Mother*, ed. S. Akhtar, S. Kramer, and H. Parens, pp. 47–91. Northvale, NJ: Jason Aronson.

Edgcumbe, R., and Burgner, M. (1972). Some problems in the conceptualization of early object relationships. Part 1. The concepts of need satisfaction and need satisfying relationships. *Psychoanalytic Study of the Child* 27:315–334. New York: Quadrangle.

Freud, S. (1912). The dynamics of the transference. In *Collected Papers*, vol. 2, pp. 312–322. New York: Basic Books.

———— (1923). *The Ego and the Id*. London: Hogarth.

Hartmann, H. (1952). The mutual influences in the development of ego and id. In *Essays on Ego Psychology*, pp. 155–182. New York: International Universities Press.

Kernberg, O. (1975). *Borderline Conditions and Pathological Narcissism*. New York: Jason Aronson.

Kestenberg, J. (1995). Panel Discussion. Washington Square Institute Annual Conference, New York City.

Mahler, M. S. (1965). On the significance of the normal separation-individuation phrase with reference to research in symbiotic child psychosis. In *Drives, Affects, Behavior*, vol. 2, ed. M. Ichur, pp. 161–169. New York: International Universities Press.

Mahler, M. S., and Furer, M. (1968). *On Human Symbiosis and the Vicissitudes of Individuation*. Vol. 1. *Infantile Psychosis*. New York: International Universities Press.

McDevitt, J. B. (1996). The concept of object constancy and its clinical application. In *The Internal Mother*, ed. S. Akhtar, S. Kramer, and H. Parens, pp. 15–46. Northvale, NJ: Jason Aronson.

Ritvo, S., and Solnit, A. J. (1958). Influences of early mother–child interaction on identification processes. *Psychoanalytic Study of the Child* 13:64–91. New York: International Universities Press.

Rubin, B. (1995). *Parent–Child Research Videos*. Presented at International Federation Conference of Psychoanalytic Education, Denver, CO.

Rubinfine, D. L. (1962). Maternal stimulation, psychic structure and early object relations. *Psychoanalytic Study of the Child* 17:265–282. New York: International Universities Press.

Searles, H. F. (1973). Concerning therapeutic symbiosis. *Annual of Psychoanalysis* 1:247–262.

Solnit, A. J., and Neubauer, P. (1986). Object constancy and early triadic relationships. *American Academy of Child Psychiatry* 25:23–29.

Spitz, R. A. (1959). *A Genetic Field Theory of Ego Formation: Its Implications for Pathology*. New York: International Universities Press.

Tyson, P. (1996). The development of object constancy and its deviations. In *The Internal Mother*, ed. A. Akhtar, S. Kramer, and H. Parens, pp. 93–113. Northvale, NJ: Jason Aronson.

Werner, H. (1957). *Comparative Psychology of Mental Development.* New York: International Universities Press.

Wolff, P. H. (1960). The developmental psychologies of Jean Piaget and psychoanalysis. *Psychological Issues,* Monograph 5. New York: International Universities Press.

13

"Will You Be Able to Hear Me?" Some Aspects of the Transference and Countertransference within the Dyad of a Young Female Therapist and an Older Female Patient

Agnieszka Leznicka-Los

INTRODUCTION

This chapter discusses the dyad of a young female therapist working with a patient old enough to be her mother. It will focus on the dynamic of this particular constellation and its impact on the course of treatment. I will present theoretical findings about the role a therapist's gender and age play in treatment, as well as a brief review of the transference–countertransference phenomena relevant to this dyad. Using case examples I will explore the influence of the age and gender of the therapist and the patient on the dynamics of treatment.

In recent years there seems to be an increase in the number of young professional women entering the field of analysis and psycho-analytic psychotherapy. We also notice the growing number of older/middle-aged women looking for professional help. This phenom-enon presents a generation gap between the two. This is a reversal of roles (at least on the manifest level): the therapist who by age would be a daughter plays the role of a preoedipal or oedipal mother to the patient. What role does the age of the therapist play in this particular constellation? How does this particular dynamic evolve and change, starting in the first session with the patient's question: "How could you possibly understand me? You are young enough to be my daughter!" What is the unconscious meaning of this comment? Is this question significant or does it serve only as a resistance?

I will postulate that the unique nature of this dyad plays an important role and has a profound impact on treatment. I started to explore this phenomenon when I began working with female patients resembling my mother in age. Never before had I given so much thought to the age difference between me and my patient.

THEORETICAL FRAMEWORK

The importance of the mother–daughter bond has long been recognized in classical psychoanalytic literature. In 1931 Freud wrote about the intensity of the preoedipal attachment of the little girl to her mother. In 1944 Deutsch, in her book *The Psychology of Women*, wrote as follows: ". . . full of hatred and rage, she wants to rear herself away from her mother's influence, although at the same time she frequently betrays an intensified, anxious urge to remain under the maternal protection. A corresponding process takes place in the mother: . . . she wants to keep the child under her protection and yet she knows that she must lessen and in the end desist from this protection" (p. 20).

According to Bernstein (1993), the analytic female–female dyad may be particularly vulnerable because the gender of both repeats the original dyad, which leads to the most archaic, dangerous, and at the same time potentially most healing conflicts. She also pointed out feelings of comparison and competition aroused in this particular dyad.

Clover (1991) describes that every little girl has to mourn the special closeness to her mother as maturation pushes her into separation. The girl child is a restitution for the mother in undoing the loss of her own mother in separation. Allowing a girl to pull away may be felt as giving up her mother again. This conflictual experience is reenacted in women's relationships with other women. It emerges in the transference–countertransference. Every woman repeats the conflicts inherent in the unique relationship with a mother in every normal developmental crisis of the life span.

During the last twenty years psychoanalytic writers started to focus on the question of how gender of the analyst or therapist may affect the transference in psychoanalysis and psychoanalytic psychotherapy. There are a number of articles on the impact of the analyst's gender on the transference. The classical analytical position stresses that in good analysis the gender does not make a difference, that all significant objects are reexperienced in the transference if the analyst permits and facilitates their emergence (Bernstein 1993, Blum 1981).

Freud himself described transference as a fixed disposition within the individual to repeat his or her infantile conflicts with the person of the analyst (1912, 1915). Later writers such as Sandler (1976) view transference as less fixed and more possibly influenced by present realities within the analytic situation, including the gender of the analyst. "Transference elements enter to a varying degree onto all relationships, and these are often determined by some characteristics of the other person who (consciously or unconsciously) represents some attribute of an important figure of the past" (p. 44). Following Sandler's comments, the age of the therapist may be considered as such a specific attribute. Meyers (cited in Kalinish 1981) stressed that early in treatment initial transference reactions are certainly affected by whether the analyst is a man or a woman. Ticho (cited in Kalinish 1981) pointed out the wish for a mother in the initial statement of a patient seeking a female therapist. Both of them agree that the gender of the analyst may create special problems. According to Kulish (1986), transference does take as its starting point unconscious, genetically and internally based disposition, which is influenced by and influences the interpersonal process of which it becomes a dynamic part. This issue of gender touches upon the role of the reality in the unfolding of transference. In the same article Kulish pointed out the general agreement on several points: the gender of the therapist can contribute to major resistances within the transference, especially early in treatment; gender shapes and colors the content of the clinical material, and gender may determine the order in which the material emerges. "It is my feeling that gender can be a major organizing factor both for the patient and for the analyst. . . . Our manifest sex is often one of the few things our patients know about us, and fantasies, curiosities and feelings revolve around it" (p. 402).

I would like to attribute the above thought to the issue of the age of a therapist as well, since the age is another obvious factor patients know about us. In my opinion, the age of the therapist may stir up resistances, fantasies, and feelings that may be detected through dreams, fantasies, and the dynamic of transference and countertransference.

Heinmann (1950) refers to countertransference as the tool for understanding the patient. The analyst's emotional response to the patient can be used as a basis for understanding the patient's material. According to Racker (1968), countertransference reactions of great intensity, even pathological ones, could also serve as tools. They represent the expression of the internal objects of the patient via the process of the analyst's identification with them. The repression of the countertransference leads to deficiencies in the analysis of the transference. He looks at the analysis as the interaction between two personalities

. . . in both of which the ego is under pressure from the id, the superego, and the external world; each personality has its internal and external world; each personality has its internal and external dependencies, anxieties and pathological defenses; each is also the child with his internal parents; and each of these whole personalities—that of the analysand and that of the analyst—responds to every event of the analytic situation. [p. 132]

Sandler (1976) supports Heinmann's and Racker's point of view by pointing out the meaning and importance of such a skill as free-floating attention: the capacity to allow all sorts of thoughts and associations to enter an analyst's mind while listening to the patient. Sandler suggests that the irrational response of the analyst, which he sees as a blind spot of his own (think age!), may be also regarded as a compromise formation between his own tendencies and the role that the patient is forcing him into. Blum (cited in Kalinish 1981) refers to countertransference as a ubiquitous phenomenon and source of data itself. Kulish (1986) in her article stresses the gender issue and its impact on the countertransference.

> As the confusing array of material emerges in the course of the treatment, we process it through the filter of our own feelings, past and present experiences and our theoretical expectations which are partially determined by our gender. Thus gender carries inevitable blind spots, biases and countertransferences as well as special sensitivities, capacities, and understanding. [p. 402]

I would like to add the age factor to this list and stress its importance. I will look at the clinical material, taking into consideration this unique combination of gender and age and the effect it has on both the patient and the therapist.

CLINICAL MATERIAL

The focus of the clinical material will be on the transference and countertransference phenomena. In addition to my own case I present two other cases drawn from my interviews with two female therapists. I asked them about their subjective emotional experience when working with female patients resembling their mothers in age. Interviews were taped and then transcribed. They were informal and relatively unstructured. These two female therapists share my interest in psychoanalytic psychotherapy utilizing a psychoanalytic model with an emphasis on the concept of transference, countertransference, unconscious conflict: impulse, defense, and compromise formation. The three of us were 33 years old when working with these particular patients and we all had at least six years of clinical experience. Material presented below is verbatim and edited for purposes of this chapter and anonymity.

Therapist 1: Case of Ms. A

Ms. A is a 56-year-old woman. She came to treatment after having a mastectomy. She was depressed and complained of not having motivation or zest for life. She was transferred to me after about a year of treatment. (Her previous therapist left a clinic on a maternity leave!) They worked on a twice-a-week basis. She has been in treatment with me for two years, at first twice a week and later on once a week. After a year of twice-a-week visits she decided to reduce her sessions to once a week, saying that she does not find me helpful. She decided to continue on a weekly basis, adding that she does not have anything better to do with her time.

Ms. A. is an attractive blond woman who looks younger than her stated age. She is very intelligent with a sarcastic sense of humor. She comes from a lower-middle-class background. She has a sister twelve years her junior and a brother fourteen years younger. She was brought up in an abusive environment: "My stepfather was very verbally abusive, my mother too, she did not give a shit what I was doing. To her I was a stupid little brat. My stepfather wanted me out of his house." Her present relationship with her mother is filled with anger and jealousy over her younger brother and sister who are her mother's favorites. She sees them a few times a year.

Ms. A has never married and lives on her own. The only person she is relatively close to is her boyfriend, with whom she is not physically intimate (according to her, he does not want to have a sexual relationship with her). This causes a constant frustration. Ms. A says, "Now it would be impossible to have sex with me because who wants a woman without a breast!" This boyfriend is the love of her life—at least he used to be. She met him when she was in her twenties. They stayed together for ten years and broke up. She moved to a different state, had a number of short-term relationships. "I loved sex, now I cannot even have it. I feel so dry inside, after so many years of not having sex. Rob, my boyfriend, never liked it or at least he did not like it with me. I had to use a lot of tricks, so that we could have sex once a week." I asked her if she ever considered having a long-term relationship with someone else. She said that she never met someone that she loved as much as Rob. She was in her forties when they started seeing each other again as friends. They go on vacation together, and at times he contributes generously to her finances.

Our first sessions started off by bringing food to my office. During our sessions she would eat and brush her hair. She used to put her food on my desk. Whenever I tried to analyze her behavior, she got offended and refused to cooperate. I was left helpless. I wanted to regain my control. At some point I said that the session is not a place for eating but for talking and asked her thoughts about it. In the very next session she said that she was thinking about changing to another therapist. She stated that her previous therapist was much better and more understanding. After learning that she also brought food to her sessions with her previous therapist, I explored the possibility of how much she missed her. I also pointed out how angry she may be at her previous therapist for leaving her. "No way," she said; she was not angry. Her previous therapist was very nice and soft-spoken, and it was perfectly understandable to her that she left because she wanted to have a child. I asked her if she ever wanted to have children herself. She said No, because she felt too "screwed up." She then added that later, when she started to think about having a child, it was almost too late and she did not have anybody with whom she could have a child. This was said in a very matter of fact voice with no emotion.

Almost from the first session I tried to bring to focus and analyze the negative transference to me in relation to her previous treatment. She devaluated me a lot, a sort of brushing me off. From her point of view, I was too young, and too inexperienced with life. If I interpreted things, she refused whatever I said. I was a horrible Freudian-oriented therapist who wanted to analyze and put meaning to everything. If I just listened, then she said that nothing was happening in treatment. When I pointed out this dynamic, she commented that I wasn't a good therapist for her, that I was too young and did not know anything about having cancer, getting older, going through menopause, and living with one breast. She complained about hot flashes and used to bring a little fan with her; while fanning herself she commented, "You will go through the same shit when you become menopausal."

I listened to her reproaches. I tried to use them as a vehicle to explore her feelings about all the above-mentioned subjects. She made a few comments, but material never deepened. I listened to her associations and picked them up as a starting point, but it rarely went deeper. Her accusations of me not helping her were relentless, but she always came to sessions with a smile on her face and looking like a person who accepted life's disappointments. At times she greeted me at my office with a smile and salutation of "Hello, kiddo."

At the same time a lot of thoughts and feelings were going on in me. I felt terrified. I pictured myself being old, sick, and lonely, and having a miserable life. I overidentified with her. After some sessions I felt sick physically and emotionally. My life did not make sense anymore. For some mysterious reason I will be punished like she was. In my countertransference I hated her life. I was afraid that I would end up the way she did. She left the sessions and I felt poisoned. I was convinced I had undiagnosed cancer. Although she expressed her fears and worries that her cancer might recur, she did so in a very matter of fact and accepting way. She became everything I feared and did not want to be. Her lonely life scared me to death. She did not do anything with her life, did not achieve anything, did not have a family. She ended up on disability and bankrupt.

I dragged myself to her sessions. I never knew if she would be nice and friendly or if she would start to torment me about my age and lack of experience and how pointless it was to sit with me in one room but she would do it because it was a way of killing time. Now, in retrospect, I see that she had to feel tormented and scared to death, and hated her life at least as much as I hated it.

I was never able to use this material, to use my feelings and thoughts and give them back to her as her own. Most of the time with other patients I don't have this difficulty. With her, I never allowed myself to make comments based on my extremely strong countertransference, except for pointing out how much she devalued me and how angry she seemed to be at me. I think I could not use my countertransference because I was afraid that it would be like opening a Pandora's box, all these horrible things would be out in the open. Of course, all of this was unconscious on my part. It was like having a mother who was going through a terrible time, and her daughter does not want to face it, it is too threatening and too overwhelming. You want your mother to be intact, not sick and miserable with an enormous amount of aggression. This also, as I understood later, evoked a lot of fear about my own mother's health and a terror of her becoming ill as well as my own frailties.

My age, 33, played a very important role in Ms. A's treatment. It was the catalyst that brought up the material about Ms. A's failing health and lost youth. It also brought up her regrets that she did not live her life to its full potential; her envy and anger that she would not feel fulfilled anymore as a woman. This material was never worked through because of my own

conflicts and inability to effectively use my countertransference as well as her
extremely strong resistance to work on any of these issues.

I just tried to run away from it. It felt too frightening for me to use the feelings and thoughts she brought out in me. I did not want to torment her and myself. I was afraid that I was not strong enough to carry this weight on my shoulders. Maybe in her transference I became her neglectful young mother who was unable to soothe the suffering and deprived little girl.

I also became an aspect of her, the part of her who wanted to achieve and never became, and for this reason this part had to be buried, rejected, and devaluated. It was exactly the way I felt with her: ignored, rejected, devaluated, and useless.

Lately she's started to talk about changing therapists. I again try to explore why she does not want to work with me. She says that nothing happens and that I take things too personally. She says that I am a nice person but treatment with me is useless. Recently, almost screaming on the phone, she said, "I have no guts to tell you that I am leaving you, because you take it too personally and you will feel hurt." This happened about a week after she came out of the hospital with a diagnosis of a recurrence of her cancer. *I think that part of this particular transference and countertransference dynamic is based on her splitting. I became her hateful, youthful part, which she craved to regain but could not and she is left with sickness and the fear of dying.* I am not convinced that by showing her this dynamic she will remain in treatment. Her eventful departure is so much linked to my age and her rage and envy of the time of her life that is lost to her forever.

Discussion

In this particular case, as the therapist pointed out, the unique combination of gender and age served as a catalyst that brought up denied and split-off unconscious material about the patient's lost youth, femininity, health, and mortality. This material was acted out in form of hostile devaluation and rejection of the therapist. The particular makeup of this patient, including her age and her physical illness, touching on the core of her femininity, initiated a very strong feared identification on the therapist's side. The therapist feared an identification with an older, sick, and extremely angry and unhappy woman. This feared identification was repressed and acted out by means of avoidance. Following Racker and Sandler, these strong reactions could have been used in the treatment to understand the internal struggles of the patient and the role in the patient was forcing on the therapist.

In her countertransference the therapist became the fearful daughter who sees in her mother-patient the unhappiness and terror that will be her future. This feared and hated identification with the mother-patient could be motivated by the therapist's wish for closeness. This wish for closeness conflicts with the therapist's struggle for her own identity. Only to the extent the therapist has established her own identity would she be less fearful of identifying and interpreting the patient's struggle (see Deutch 1944, p. 2).

The four major issues were physical appearance, menopause, aging, and illness. One can only speculate whether the above-described dynamic would occur with such a dramatic intensity if the therapist's obvious attributes of being a young female were different.

Therapist 2: Case of Ms. B

She was a woman of about 56 when she was assigned to me, diagnosed with a bipolar disorder. Her daughter persuaded her to come to treatment. She was deteriorating. She did not take her medication regularly, and was getting a little "psychotic around the edges." She was on lithium, and had a few psychiatric hospitalizations in the past. She had divorced long ago and had raised a daughter alone.

After about two psychotherapy sessions, she was hospitalized for physical reasons for about five months. She has emphysema and heart problems and almost died. The last thing she should probably do is smoke and she was a very heavy smoker. We worked together for about a year. She was a very smart woman, with a Ph.D. in psychology, who was never able to work because of her psychiatric illness. She wanted someone to talk to. I realized that part of the transference was her letting me know that I was only a social worker and she was a Ph.D. This was brought up a lot. She also mentioned that she preferred working with men. She was extremely competitive, reminding me about her Ph.D. She put me down a lot, here and there. She had a lot to say about her previous psychiatrists, who they were, and how important she was to them. I struggled with her being competitive for a long time. I felt very angry, and it was harder than with other patients to put it aside. I felt defensive, angry, and hostile. I felt that I had to defend myself. I felt very criticized. I felt diminished. I hated the feeling that I felt that I had to fight for acknowledgment. I felt I had to prove myself. I had to struggle, to understand it. I did not want this to interfere with my work with her. There were moments when I got all caught up with this. By realizing how intensely I felt, I also realized how intensely she felt. We were in competition, it was not just me, or just her, we were competing. At some point I realized how threatened in fact she felt.

I also found myself in competition with her daughter. Her daughter worked in television and received a high salary. I felt she was also competing with me through her daughter. Her daughter was an extension of herself. I found myself thinking that I wanted her to think about me as smart, as capable and as successful as her daughter. I remember the sense of inner pride when she told me a few times, "You know, you are really good, you made me think about something." I realized at times that I felt insecure around her. She insisted on me calling her a doctor. I had a hard time with this, and she knew it. *There was a lot of competition on both sides and I think this is very redolent of my relationship with my mother. This competition was stronger because of her being my mother's age.*

The other thing that was very significant was that she was my patient throughout my pregnancy. She mentioned that I was her daughter's age. She was dying for her daughter to have a child. We spoke a lot about my pregnancy and why her daughter was not getting pregnant.

When she got out of the hospital I was already pregnant. When she came back she was very much altered: her hair was more gray, and she lost all her teeth. She was very embarrassed about it, and very self-conscious about her looks. She lost a lot of weight. She came back almost dying herself and here I was going to have a baby. Seeing her so sick reminded me of my mother's age. I remember, Mrs. B would arrive with long dresses, not wearing a bra. I can remember noticing how low her breast hung. How vulnerable it looked; how vulnerable she looked. This was painful to see. At this same time I was getting bigger and bigger. As she talked she looked at my stomach and it was sort of disconcerting. I was uncomfortable. I knew I was leaving. I felt very guilty about it. I felt guilty about my pregnancy. I worried about the jealousy that it evoked. Here was a woman who faced death, and we spoke of how much she loved sex, and loved having love affairs. We would talk about it but always sort of finished by saying that it will not be a part of her life anymore. She was a woman who was beginning to face the fact that she was past menopause, that she was not going to have another child. *Her envies were one of the most prominent things, envies of youth, fantasies of a middle-life sexuality, and fertility. Here, right in her face, was a young and pregnant therapist.* The hard part for me, working with a woman this age, was my fantasy of what must have been going through her mind. I also wondered what would go through my mind at that age, I wasn't going to bear more children or maybe I never had and now it was not even an option. I reminded her of the life she did not have, because she was so sick.

In my countertransference she was my mother. It evoked conflicts I had about surpassing my parents. I realized I was coming to the peak of my life. Just looking at her and watching her frailty was very scary to me and very troubling. Just this thing with breasts, my breast filling up, getting bigger. And I see her breast, like my mother's breast, sagging and smaller and vulnerable. I felt very protective, her vulnerability was unbelievable to me. This was very moving. I just remember being struck by it. She would pick up her dress and show me, she had eczema. It was horrendous. I did not particularly want to see all that much. She would show me these spots of flaky skin, on her hands and legs. I thought with horror of this happening to my mother. That she will look so vulnerable and sick. It terrifies me that someday my mother will look so frail.

I was quite weak on trying to explore her mourning, and the loss of her youthful femininity, because of my fear of her envy of me. I was very much aware how it must feel. At times the tension and hatred between us was incredible. Toward the end when she could talk about it we were a lot closer.

In some says the age difference advanced the work. It was very palpable from the very beginning. In a year we got through quite a lot. I must say by the end she stopped smoking. She had smoked two, three packs a day. By the end I was very much able to be maternal to her, in a way that was not a put-down. I think she was very much able to accept it. She helped me to do it. We were able to accomplish this together. I was able to somehow convey to her that I truly respected her, her knowledge, and how much she was able to accomplish. This is how we repaired the relationship. I finally was able to understand her hostility, as well as my defensiveness, and was able to talk about how much she had done. Despite her illness, she managed on her own, received her Ph.D., and produced a child who was healthy and successful. *It was a constant shift from being a mother to being a daughter on both sides.* At the end I became her mother, but at some point I was her daughter in my countertransference. I can say that the age and gender and my pregnancy was a focal point of treatment. Part of our relationship was competition between a mother and a daughter. *What is so poignant about this dyad is that you are not talking just about the lack of experience, you are too young to know, but there is this physical side: your youth, your figure, what is ahead of you in your life, lovers, and children. That I think really heightens up what is absent. Brings these things into the fore.*

I realized how this woman was like me. She was a 33-year-old woman in an almost 60-year-old body. She had the same longings, the same sense of competition, wanting companionship, wanting to be acknowledged. This really came through to me, this sense of being trapped, the fierceness of her longings. I hadn't had this experience yet of feeling at odds with my body. This is what comes up in this situation, the older person being envious of the younger person. This was clear with this woman, we were able to work through part of it.

Discussion

In the above case the outstanding issues were competition, rivalry, and comparison with a mother-patient. Bernstein (1993) also wrote about feelings of competition and comparison being evoked in the female–female dyad. Mrs. B competed with the therapist through her daughter, who represented an extension of herself. The patient's envy of good health, youth, and femininity was manifest in her devaluation and competition with the therapist. For the therapist this was an enactment of an oedipal fantasy. The therapist's unconscious wish for the mother to die almost comes true. The mother-patient goes to the hospital, her life being threatened; the therapist gets pregnant and her life is in bloom. The therapist's fear of punishment for being an oedipal winner was manifest in fear of the patient's anger and envy. Also present was a sibling rivalry for a mother's love. Additionally, there was guilt over leaving a mother and having a more successful and fulfilling life.

Fear of illness, aging, loss of femininity were issues common to both described cases. The therapists feared an identification with their sick, bitter, and unhappy female patients. They had difficulty in exploring material that touched on the core of their femininity. They also feared the patients' envy for having attributes and opportunities that were lost forever to these older patients.

Therapist 3: Case of Ms. C

This is a woman who is about 60 years old (my mother is in her late fifties). The patient is a mother of two; one of her sons committed suicide. She was diagnosed with borderline personality disorder and dysthymia. She had a prolonged grief reaction to her son's death, which occurred about eight years ago. She has been in treatment once a week, at times twice a week, for three years. At the very beginning of treatment she had doubts if I would be able to help her because I was so young, but very quickly she became attached. It feels to me as if she is the child and I am the mother. Yet she will respond to me very often in ways that are very motherly: "You haven't cut your hair lately . . . you look tired . . . are you getting enough rest?" She is a patient I like very much, but at times I want to strangle her. She evokes a certain level of anger in me. When she gets physically ill she becomes nonfunctional, although it may be a minor illness like a cold. She gets panicky and extremely needy. During these times she would call me, five times in one day. I try to set boundaries with her. She becomes much more dependent when she is feeling physically vulnerable. This was a dynamic for me with my mother, who was a mother, but I was a parent. My mother was not very mature and she was someone who depended on me a lot for adult advice and support. She would come to me particularly in a crisis and lean on me. This situation put me in the role of the mother. I of course resented it. I wanted to be a child who leaned on her. So when this patient cannot get enough of me, I want to pull away. I get angry at her. At times I feel that I don't want to help her, because she is so needy. I think that this is a combination of her being motherly, my mother's age, and my age. I try not to act it out by pushing her away, but instead show her patterns of relating.

This bond is different from that with other patients. I cannot really describe it. Sometimes it helps treatment, sometimes it hurts treatment. It hurts treatment, because her particular dynamic is so similar to what I experienced. I actually tend to be more gratifying that I should be. I am more gratifying with her than with other patients. In her transference I am the mother and the daughter she did not have. I play both. I am struggling to tolerate and contain her anger and her fears. She is very fearful. She regresses to this childlike person who then falls apart. This was a kind of similar situation I had in my life. So in a way, I protect her from my limit setting.

She responds to her children wanting her to mother her. In that regard I am one of her kids also mothering her. It is a daughter transference of being mothering.

I am aware that she is looking back at her life with tremendous regret, questioning her parenting, her marriage, and her early life. I am sure that she sees me as being in a completely different stage of life. She will occasionally ask things like, "When are you going to have a baby?" As if she would then become a grandmother. In treatment she speaks of her fear of her son's never getting married and having kids. She is the kind of patient who would be very jealous if I got pregnant, but on the other hand she would fancy herself to be the grandmother. She said that she would like me to get pregnant. It makes me wonder if there is a jealousy and envy of me having these things ahead of me.

She sees me as very special and very helpful. There is a negative side to that which is me not being able to set limits and helping her to tolerate frustration. I also have difficulty tolerating her anger. She comes in and unlike other patients it almost feels like she comes for a visit versus coming to the session. *Something about her age and my age makes me less inclined to confront it. If it were someone contemporary it would be a lot easier for me to set boundaries. It is like this mother–daughter thing again. I would be rejecting her and she would get angry and reject me.*

I think I protect her but actually I am protecting myself, from her rage. It is sort of keeping things at bay. My fantasy is that her rage will kill me, or that she will kill herself. This reminds me a lot of my mother. I was terrified, but with this patient I get angry. I feel that I try really hard and nothing is enough. It is what I probably felt when I was young.

Her son got involved in her treatment. He brings her to sessions and he picks her up. He is in contact with me, with her permission. He communicated to me in a way which is: "We got to get mom going here." He is in his thirties, and relates to me as if we are siblings and she is our mother. It feels this way.

She had a picture of her son who killed himself and talked to him every night before she went to bed. After this summer she put the picture of her dead son away and does not talk to him anymore. I am curious what it means. Did I replace him in her transference? She used to say: "I talk to him." This is what she does with me, she talks to me. She lost a child and gained one.

I find myself looking at her and thinking about aging, late menopause, the wrinkles, and gaining weight. It is almost like being a daughter hearing about her mother going through these changes. I keep thinking what is going on with my mother when I look at my patient. It makes me feel sad. I feel for her struggling with time. It makes me think that bodies do change, we age and how it is going to be for me. I tend to have these thoughts with all my women patients who are in their fifties.

I have been more nurturing to this patient despite all other feelings. I have more maternal feelings for her, but I also feel that she has maternal feelings toward me. I am more protective of her. I have been very involved with her treatment. I also experienced more anger at her than at most of my patients, and more frustration. I also feel proud of the work I do with her, despite the ups and downs. In a way it is a different kind of investment. When I started working with her or my other older female patients I had thoughts that age may be an issue. I was afraid that they would say that I was not experienced enough, that I would not be able to understand them. I am comfortable being a daughter taking care. On some level I don't want her to be mad at me. I don't want to disappoint her. It's about mother–daughter stuff. In my countertransference she is a mother and I am her daughter. Gender and age are very much in the room. You cannot avoid it or change it, and associations eventually lead there.

Discussion

What seems to come forward in the case of Ms. C is a conflict about separation. This case is a good illustration of Clover's (1991) remarks that a girl has to mourn the special closeness to her mother as maturation pushes her into separation and that a girl child can compensate for the loss of one's own mother. Difficulty in setting boundaries, the need to gratify the patient, can be understood as the therapist's unconscious fantasy, that separation from mother may kill both of them. This may also represent the therapist's warding off her aggression by taking care of an extremely needy and demanding mother. This can be the therapist's own struggle for closeness and separation as well as the role the patient forces on the therapist, as Sandler (1976) pointed out. The result is a compromise formation between the therapist's own conflict and the role the patient forces upon her. Again, as in the two previous cases, the theme of aging and femininity comes up, in addition to issues on separation.

CONCLUSION

The mother–daughter dynamic was very much present in the patients' and therapists' conscious and unconscious thoughts, feelings, and fantasies. It seemed to determine the clinical material. The specific circumstances were three older women patients, severely disturbed, very conflicted, depressed, angry, and bitter. On the other side three young female therapists, struggling with their own conflicts and issues about their identity. Both therapists and patients struggled with this generation gap.

The patients' issues were envy and anger for their lost youth, motherhood, and femininity, which were heightened by the present attributes of the therapists. For the therapists this dyad brought up fears of aging, fears of their own mothers' mortality as well as their own, which were heightened by their patients' age and illnesses. Also feared was identification with older, sick, and unhappy women. Working with these three older and sick patients stirred up guilt and conflicts about surpassing their own mothers and the struggle for their own identity. In the three cases some aspects of countertransference were acted out. They were related to this unique dynamic of the mother and daughter and age difference. In the case of Ms. A, fear of identification with the sick, angry older woman. In the case of Ms. B, fear and guilt over fertility, femininity, and fulfillment, which meant surpassing mother. In the case of Ms. C, a wish for closeness and struggle for separation. The conflict about separating from one's mother was present in all of these cases. This particular combination of age and gender for both the therapist and the patient served as both a resistance and as a vehicle to unconscious fantasies. It prevented these three therapists from exploring material connected to the mourning process of their patient's declining health and femininity. It meant identifying with their own mothers' struggles and brought up fears of regression, loss of boundaries, loss of identity. At the same time it produced guilt and fear over separation and identity.

As Heinmann (1950) stressed: to understand one's own counter-transference helps one to understand a patient. In these three cases it meant taking a long journey back to one's unconscious girlhood fantasies, wishes, and conflicts about being with, being like, and separating from a mother. Because of this unique dyad, the wish to be heard was a prominent concern to both patient and therapist. They were asking each other: Will you be able to hear me?

REFERENCES

Bernstein, D. (1993). *Female Identity Conflict in Clinical Practice*. Northvale, NJ: Jason Aronson.

Clover, V. (1991). The acquisition of mature femininity. In *Women and Men, New Perspectives on Gender Differences*, ed. J. D. Blum, pp. 75–88. Washington, DC/London: American Psychiatric Press.

Deutch, H. (1944). *The Psychology of Women*. Vol. 1. London/New York/Toronto: Bantam, 1973.

Freud, S. (1912). The dynamics of transference. *Standard Edition* 12:99–108.

——— (1915). Observations of transference love. *Standard Edition* 12:157–171.

——— (1931). Female sexuality. *Standard Edition* 21:223–243.

Heinmann, P. (1950). On countertransference. *International Journal of Psycho-Analysis* 31:81–84.

Kalinish, L. J. (1981). Transference and countertransference in analytic work by and with women. *Bulletin of the Association for Psychoanalytic Medicine* 21:19–30.

Kulish, N. M. (1986). Gender and transference: the screen of the phallic mother. *International Review of Psycho-Analysis* 13:393–404.

Racker, H. (1968). *Transference and Countertransference*. New York: International Universities Press.

Sandler, J. (1976). Countertransference and role-responsiveness. *International Review of Psycho-Analysis* 3:43–47.

14

"Am I My Mother's Keeper?": Certain Vicissitudes Concerning Envy in the Mother–Daughter Dyad

Marilyn B. Meyers

"I can't have children, I would be too envious of a baby and it would be dangerous."

Thus, Ms. K succinctly describes a dynamic she is loath to repeat that she experienced as a baby with her mother. This dynamic is one that exists in the early mother–daughter relationship in many women. The danger that Ms. K perceives, and knows all too well, lies in the aftermath of an early mother–infant relationship that is tinged with a particular type of envy: envy that the mother feels toward the child whose dependency needs she is meeting. Such envy occurs within a dyad where one individual envies the other for some possession or quality and wants to spoil or destroy what the other has (Klein 1957). The mother envies the baby's dependency needs, which she both wants to meet and resents, thus clouding the "gleam in the mother's eye." Mother is faced with both wanting to spoil the dependency relationship and wanting to fulfill the baby's needs. At its worst, attacks of envy exceed the mother's capacity to love and the result is thwarted development of the daughter's capacity to love.

The mother, herself a daughter, views the child ambivalently. On the one hand she sees the potential for a break in an old pattern that she herself had with her mother while on the other she views the child as offering the possibility of filling the void that exists in her as a result of her early relationship with mother. At the core of this early object relation is a reversal around giving and receiving between mother and child wherein the child is called upon to fulfill the unmet dependency needs in the mother. McDougall (1982) has described the "chasmic mother and the cork-child" (p. 78): a relationship in which the degree of fusion between mother and child is such that neither can take full possession of the body or the self. As a result both are subject to psychological and psychosomatic symptoms.

Another central feature of this dyad is the mother's inability to tolerate aggression from the baby; this coexists with the mother's envy of the infant's ability to be aggressive. The mother's narcissistic vulnerability is such that aggression on the part of the baby is experienced by the mother as an attack on herself. Within this dyad the mother requires that the child mirror her, that is, be in empathic attunement with the mother rather than the other way around. As an adaptive response, the infant learns very quickly that she must be affectively responsive to the caregiver in order to get her needs met and that any signs of aggression may threaten the availability of nurturing supplies. Thus the child may establish patterns of relating based on this early mother–infant dyad wherein openly expressed aggressive feelings are experienced as dangerous, potentially leading to withdrawal of nurturance and love.

Within this dynamic it is also disturbing for a mother to acknowledge aggressive or hostile feelings toward her baby (Spillius 1993). Mothers are supposed to love their babies "with all their heart." In particular, the mother who was herself deprived in having her own dependency needs adequately met is faced with a dilemma with her baby. She wants to nurture the baby freely and fully as she longed to be nurtured in her infancy, and bears resentment toward the very object of that nurturance. I want to emphasize that envy, per se, is not necessarily destructive; however, when envy arises in a situation in which what is envied is beyond one's acquisition, there is a problematic scenario (Boris 1994). In the most extreme cases of the type that I am describing, what the baby has is beyond the mother's grasp. Thus provision of nurturance by mother is both gratifying and depleting, fulfilling and enraging; this oscillation between gratification and frustation may be experienced by both mother and baby, either simultaneously or independently. The extent to which this impairs the development of the child is centered on the perceived relation between the giver (mother) and the receiver (baby) (Spillius 1993). The mother experiences conscious and unconscious feelings about giving, and these feelings are perceived and misperceived both consciously and unconsciously by the baby. This relationship can lay the groundwork for a character structure in which caregiving to others and exquisite sensitivity to the affective state of others is core.

Consequently, a template is established for the compliant, good girls for whom everyone else's needs come first, with a split-off, rageful, and envious aspect of the self. This split-off, envious, and aggressive aspect of the self had to be dissociated in order to gain the nurturance of the mother who was unable to tolerate and metabolize the infantile aggression. This baby grows into an adult who believes her "true" self to be toxic, shameful, and greedy. Thus what is adaptive within the context of the early dyad becomes maladaptive and problematic in later life. This personality structure has been referred to as the "False Self" (Winnicott 1960), "normopathic" (McDougall 1989), and "normotic" (Bollas 1987).

A self-perpetuating cycle of deprivation and envy ensues, an intergenerational pattern of mothers and daughters fraught with projective identificatory processes and defenses that can be daunting to unravel (Spillius 1993). To psychically enter this early primitive dyad challenges both the therapist and the patient. However, the therapeutic relationship may provide a "background presence of safety" (Grotstein 1980, p. 479) wherein the longings and terrors can be verbally symbolized and understood. Since the earliest aspects of this dyad occurred within the bodily based relationship and are thus encoded nonverbally, access to this material is frequently obtained through listening to the patient's bodily symptoms and attending to bodily based transference and countertransference manifestations. Even so, both therapist and patient may sometimes feel themselves in a "hall of mirrors" in which self and object boundaries are lost and then recovered—sometimes fleetingly within a session.

Clinically there appears to be a common constellation of features in many of the adult relationships of these women, which has also permeated the mother–daughter relationships across generations. Relationships are often characterized by rigid idealization, oscillating back and forth with mutual devaluing. A high degree of psychic merger is evidenced, which has origins in the early idealization, a form of love and a defense against envy. Within these relationships self-object boundaries are often subject to confusion. This is a consequence of self-object merger within the primary object relationship wherein the baby is experienced by mother as a narcissistic self-object. The baby is thus a need-satisfying object for the mother rather than a separate being with a distinct destiny of its own (the "cork child"). The child grows into an adult whose relationships are often narcissistically based in a similar way. An ongoing theme in the psychotherapeutic work with one woman patient was the complex task of untangling her own goals for herself from those of her mother. She stated: "Sometimes I don't know whose life I'm living, hers or my own. Sometimes I think that I won't be able to know until she dies."

This psychically merged relationship with mother also plays out in a complex pattern of yearning for and fearing intimacy in adulthood. Split-off aspects of the self that carry aggressive and hostile feelings are projected into others; the individual then experiences herself as under attack, threatened, controlled, and frustrated by others. Another form this dynamic takes is a life scenario that has as an undercurrent a renunciation of womanhood and various pleasures of the body. This can be viewed as a statement of separation from mother and mother's body. This renunciation often takes the form of a variety of eating disorders (bulimia, anorexia, binge eating) that signify a kind of battle with natural appetites. Self-hatred in which the body and its needs are viewed as "too much," greedy, and loathsome are prevalent. These women view their bodies as something to conquer, mold, reduce, and change as a representation of hated needs. This is a painful introjection of mother's envy of the dependent and needy baby. The mother experienced the baby as greedy and attacking the breast, potentially depleting her limited resources. The baby, unconsciously knowing the mother's disavowed resentment and fear of the baby, seeks to deny her appetites and to assume a "False Self" identification as contented, self-contained, and self-sufficient. She erects a bastion of psychic strength that can scarcely be penetrated, although she longs to rid herself of this armor as well.

Some of these women develop an overcathexis toward work or other pursuits outside the realm of intimate relationships; they may assume a kind of "masculine" identification—a kind of tough, hard shell along with a devaluing of all that is traditionally thought of as "feminine." The goal, both unconscious and conscious, may be to craft a thoroughly self-sufficient persona and thus eliminate the envy/deprivation cycle. This is an extension of the adaptation to the early relationship, an adaptation that often carries with it a price of loneliness and deadness. The woman both longs for and is terrified of a relationship that is free of this burden, in which both giving and receiving can flow freely back and forth, but she does not believe it to be possible.

I particularly want to emphasize the role of bodily manifestations of these difficulties because I believe that they may provide a window on these very early patterns. Since what I am proposing occurs in the preverbal phase of development, the experiences of the baby cannot be verbalized and symbolically represented and thus are encoded somatically. These somatically represented experiences are then played out in the form of later object relations as well as in the woman's relation to herself as object (Bollas 1987). It is in the psychotherapeutic encounter, particularly in paying close heed to the bodily based experiences within the transference–countertransference matrix that this early object relation can be elucidated experientially. These women routinely convert signals from the psyche to "action messages" that become somatic symptoms that it is incumbent upon the therapist to decode (McDougall 1989).

Ms. S, a successful businesswoman, reports that her mother recently made a remark to her to the effect that as long as Ms. S pursued her career she would ruin her chances of ever being happily married and having a family. She felt the sting of this remark, but also internalized it to some extent as evidenced by thoughts such as, "I must have to give up my own aspirations and dreams if I want to have a family." One could imagine the nonverbal, primitive form that such projections might have taken in the infancy of this woman. The mother may have unconsciously communicated to the baby that if she was too needy she would be deprived by mother. In the treatment relationship this woman presents herself as thoroughly self-sufficient, denying that I am important to her. She views me as a consultant or a "coach." She thus defensively avoids re-creating with me the fantasied relationship in which I would deprive her if her needs were openly expressed.

Bollas (1987) has written that the "structure of the ego is a form of constitutive memory . . . and . . . in some respects it informs us of how [the mother] mothered this particular baby" (p. 59). Thus, within the transference–countertransference matrix, the therapist can get a sense of this early object relationship and can utilize this to inform the treatment. For example, in the consulting room one gets a "feel" of the person that provides data regarding not only how this person relates to people in her life, but something about the infant–mother dyad; a "feel" as it were about that early relationship.

My sense in the work with Ms. S is that I have more to offer her than she can allow herself to take in. I think of this as a kind of reenactment of the ambivalently giving mother wherein I experience the baby as difficult to feed. Our work together has an element of difficulty around giving and receiving. This is a very complex projective identificatory process in which Ms. S is keeping me at bay, as she does with others in her life, with her self-sufficient persona as a preemptive defense against being deprived. The deprivation is her fantasied view of the price of revealing her needy self. The price that she pays for this defense, of course, is that she feels deprived in her relationships.

A variety of sensorially based countertransference manifestations can provide clues to the therapist about this dynamic. These include, but are not limited to, interactions that feel stilted and rigid, the therapist feeling closely scrutinized, the therapist feeling self-conscious about "messes" in the office, the therapist being particularly concerned with his/her dress on days when seeing this particular patient. Other manifestations include getting sleepy, excited, or fidgety in sessions. If the therapist is attuned to a broad array of bodily based material, and his/her own bodily based experiences within the treatment dyad, it can prove useful in elucidating patterns of relating that have their origins in the early object relationship, since access to this material may be as yet inaccessible through words.

How the patient uses words can also provide access to what is not verbally encoded. The patient who speaks of "needing to do cart-wheels" to get her needs met and the patient who says that she always has to "walk a tightrope" are both creating images with words that are primarily physical in nature. Working with these word images and the feelings and fantasies connected with them can bring both patient and therapist into the early psychic world of the mother–infant dyad.

CLINICAL MANIFESTATIONS

The patient in the consulting room, if invited to do so, will talk about her body, both directly and indirectly, and in the process will be informing us about her own mother's treatment of the baby's body.

Ms. M spoke about her niece: "She has snot pouring out of her nose and Mary just reaches over with her bare hands and catches it; that's so disgusting; that's one reason why I'm not ready to have children and I don't know if I ever will be. I could never do that. They have stuff, messy stuff, coming out of all their openings. I couldn't deal with that."

This same patient talks about her experience of using a public bathroom: "I have to wait until no one is in there. I can't stand the idea that anyone would hear the noises when I go. Especially with bowel movements, but even when I pee. It's so disgusting."

She talks about feelings, particularly angry feelings, as if they too are disgusting fecal matter or pee. This young woman's mother relates to her adult daughter along lines of maintaining propriety, keeping relations "clean and neat." As a young mother she was overwhelmed by poor health and the premature death of her own mother. Ms. M's mother's response to any expression of negative affect is: "Let's talk some other time." It is my hypothesis that my patient identified with mother's projections and thus came to believe that her insides contain toxic elements that will poison those who are near her. She must hide her shameful, dirty, needy, greedy self. In actuality, she frequently does have explosive episodes of rage when her capacity to contain all that she seeks to disavow is exceeded. When people react negatively to these outbursts it serves to confirm her fear that expressing negative affect is dangerous to relationships and that she herself is toxic.

Ms. R is a woman who places great emphasis on "niceness." She oscillates between being in control of everything in her internal life and trying to control those around her as well as episodes of sheer panic, terror, and fragmentation. She intermittently suffers from multiple psychosomatic difficulties—tightness in her throat, dizzy spells, ear infections, and gastric problems. I often have difficulty making emotional contact with her, yet she reports how helpful and meaningful our work is for her. I have no doubt that this is her experience of the relationship, despite my feelings that I am not really "getting through." Well into our work together Ms. L reports that she has just learned something disturbing about her infancy. Her story is that she was not picked up and held for the first three months of life and that all feeding was done with a propped-up bottle. A family friend reacted with shock and consternation when witnessing this treatment of the baby and prevailed on Ms. R's mother to handle her baby differently. The friend emphasized that a baby needs more than a clean diaper and a full tummy to thrive. Up to this point the mother had reportedly been "obeying doctor's orders." There is much to consider in this scenario, but within the scope of this discussion this piece of history helped me to understand an aspect of the counter-transference. I frequently felt frustrated in my capacity to connect meaningfully with her and thus frustrated in my capacity to nurture. Thus I felt more like a propped bottle than a breast: a distant yet nurturing connection. I was able to see the frustration that I experienced less as a resistance and more as a reenactment of the early object relation both with the propped bottle and the mother who created that feeding environment.

A patient who has just broken up with her boyfriend had cancelled our prior session due to a bad case of "stomach flu." At the outset of the next session she speaks of her gastric distress: "It was coming out of both ends, it was really disgusting. It was all over the place. I couldn't tell what was happening, whether I had gas or had to go. I got into bed and messed my bed. I just couldn't tell. The doctor only gave me the Pepto-Bismol. I needed something stronger, but you know I really didn't tell her how bad it was, so she gave me something mild when I really needed more. My stomach was bloated. If you looked at me you'd think I was pregnant, sticking out to here."

I inquire whether she thinks that her stomach upset had anything to do with feelings about the breakup.

"Oh, of course," she says. "I had the flu but this was about Stuart. This is just like what happened when I broke up with David, I was terribly ill. I told myself this time to try to move the feelings out of my body and into my heart and head, but I couldn't. I tried to move it from the brain in my stomach to the brain in my head but it just wouldn't make that move. It would be too much. And besides this way it was real, I could see it, smell it, touch it. When I feel it I'm not sure it's real. . . . After I messed the bed I washed the sheets and made the bed up nice and clean. You know how it is when you make the bed up with freshly washed linens and it smells so good and it looks and feels so crisp. I opened the windows, it was great, but then I didn't want to get in the bed. I didn't want to mess it."

These word images were richly elaborated such that my bodily countertransference response mirrored her experience of the various affective and somatic states she described. I was able to identify with the experience of humiliation associated with the messed bed, the feeling of bodily explosions and relief at the release of the pressure accompanied by shame at making a mess. I believe that a communication occurred between us without words in which she felt that I understood her painful experience and was helped by my entering her psychic world. A toxic and frightening archaic experience was metabolized within the analytic space, thus enhancing Ms. R's capacity to symbolically represent her primitive anxieties and therefore contain them psychically.

This patient's somatic expression of her psychic pain and rage illustrates a primitive process in which the feelings are converted to bodily symptoms. McDougall (1989) considers this type of somatic explosion to be an archaic form of hysteria. In this view the symptoms are "intended to take the place of or act as a punishment for libidinal wishes" (p. 54). The psychosomatic phenomena are concerned with protecting one's very right to exist and are thus more than a somatization of forbidden libidinal strivings. When the mother's envy of the baby is of such magnitude that the baby unconsciously feels her right to exist as threatened by the very figure on whom she is utterly dependent, the terror is "unspeakable." McDougall states: "A body organ or somatic function might . . . act as though it were called upon to take psychological action in a biologically threatening situation" (p. 55).

In my patient's fantasy, she would psychically explode if she were to allow herself to feel the pain "in the brain in her head," whereas the somatic explosion was experienced as manageable, safer, and "real." Feeling the pain in the form of a bodily function (diarrhea) was a version of this archaic hysteria. The patient's fantasy is supported by a family context in which physical distress is attended to with concern, while emotional distress is dismissed as "babyish." In fact, a family member, when hearing of her severe gastric distress, expressed great sympathy and concern and was very solicitous of her distress. This same family member will respond, "Stop being such a baby," if psychic distress is expressed. Thus the early adaptation within her particular relational matrix was to keep painful affect, most specifically dependency needs and aggression, suppressed and carried somatically.

This young woman and others like her often seek to establish and maintain a therapeutic relationship devoid of conflict. They are the overly compliant patients, the ones who are never late, never fail to be current on their bills, never do anything that might annoy the therapist. It can be very comfortable and "easy" and rather dead. In this scenario the patient may be re-creating an aspect of her early relationship in which the baby couldn't be a rageful baby, that to be the rageful baby would lead to withdrawal of supplies. So the baby learns to take care of mommy by being a "good" baby. This "good" baby grows up into a woman who sees aggression as dangerous to relationships. The therapy can feel comfortable, but too "nice." For the patient to see the therapist as not vulnerable to being destroyed by aggression may be both reassuring and threatening. The therapist offers the promise of a new kind of relationship, a new object, and the threat of releasing the long-suppressed rage at a mother who required compliance and thus a false self development.

These patients are also unconsciously envious of the therapist's absence of a need to be made whole by the patient. Within this relationship the therapist is not the "chasmic mother" seeking the "cork child." In fact, the scenario may be reversed whereby the patient longs for the therapist to fill the void that mother did not fill, thus wishing to maintain the cycle of deprivations and envy that occurred intergenerationally in her family. At some level, however, the patient longs for a mature, whole object relationship in which two distinct individuals can engage each other. The potential for a relationship in which there is no requirement for caretaking of the caregiver is both a relief and threatening. A freely flowing giving and receiving, without resentment at giving and without envy of the receiver, can seem at first a merely longed-for fantasy rather than a true possibility.

Thus the patient may exert subtle or overt pressures to re-create the early dyad. To be separate within the relationship may be experienced as a frightening isolation. A patient objected to my referring to our relationship using the pronoun "we." In her view, if I am separate and autonomous in my own right, there is no "we." Thus she would exert pressures of all types to enviously attack my autonomy, usually through efforts to make me feel guilty during absences with the hope that she could disrupt my time off and thus not lose her sense of "we-ness." My autonomy, my lack of requirement that she take care of me, was experienced as a rupture in the affective bond, causing our entire relationship to feel tenuous. Repeated interpretations of the multitude of ways that she exerted pressure for merger and the accompanying painful feelings of rejection that my autonomy evoked helped her to mourn the loss of the at-oneness with the symbiotically bound omnipotent mother.

SUMMARY

A dynamic exists in the early mother–daughter relationship that involves the mother's envy of the baby's dependency needs. The mother relates to her baby ambivalently, both wanting to nurture the baby and wanting the baby to fill her own unmet needs (the "chasmic mother" and the "cork child"). This envy may be expressed via lack of tolerance of the baby's aggression and an unconscious requirement within the relationship that the baby mirror the mother rather than the mother mirror the child. This dynamic results in the child's developing a particular character structure and a mode of relating in which there is a precocious and long-standing attunement to the needs of others and a fantasy that one must please others in order to have one's nurturance needs met. Women who have this history are often thwarted in their adult development, particularly in the sphere of establishing and maintaining adult intimate relationships. Clinical material that is strongly bodily based offers a particular opportunity to explore these issues as they are primarily preverbal and therefore not verbally symbolized. In particular, attending to somatic manifestations of the transference and countertransference can assist in elucidating and thereby verbally representing these early phenomena. Treatment can then lead to a break in an intergenerational cycle of deprivation and envy. Thus the woman may no longer be bound to be her "mother's keeper."

REFERENCES

Bollas, C. (1987). *The Shadow of the Object*. New York: Columbia University Press.

Boris, H. N. (1994). *Envy*. Northvale, NJ: Jason Aronson.

Grotstein, J. (1980). Primitive mental states. *Contemporary Psychoanalysis* 16:479–546.

Klein, M. (1957). *Envy and Gratitude*. London: Tavistock; New York: Basic Books.

McDougall, J. (1982). *Theaters of the Mind: Illusion and Truth on the Psychoanalytic Stage*. New York: Basic Books.

——— (1989). *Theater of the Body*. New York: Norton.

Spillius, E. B. (1993). Varieties of envious experience. *International Journal of Psycho-Analysis* 74:1199–1212.

Winnicott, D. W. (1960). Ego distortions in terms of true and false self. In *The Maturational Process and the Facilitating Environment*, pp. 140–152. New York: International Universities Press, 1965.

15

Unconscious Conflicts in the Preoedipal Mother–Daughter Relationship as Revealed through Dreams

Jill C. Morris

During the course of therapy a dream may appear that will shed light on unresolved issues, giving direction, intensity, and hope to the therapy. Dreams have a way of clarifying the conflict and even offering a solution to the problem, write Ullman and Zimmerman (1979). The dream expresses in symbols what the patient is feeling on an unconscious level. And the knowledgeable therapist can guide the patient to the repressed feelings beneath the surface.

There has been much speculation as to why this occurs, and why dreams offer such uncanny wisdom. Most practitioners agree that all experiences are stored in the brain and can be retrieved once repression is lifted. According to C. G. Jung (1954), dreams speak the language of the unconscious, and they speak almost exclusively in visual images. These images are akin to the preverbal experience of infants who do not know how to put their feelings into words.

Dream symbols are always unconscious representations. When one fully feels an event in his or her life, there is no need to dream it.

But when the feelings are not completely felt, they go underground and may reappear in dream form. Dreams provide an outlet for the emotional expression necessary to preserve a person's psychic equilibrium.

Patients, or anyone else for that matter, usually do not remember their dreams unless they are able to handle the messages contained within them. Somewhere the dreamer knows this, although not on a conscious level. The dream may go undecoded, and will keep returning if it contains a vital message. How many times has a patient told a therapist that he has a recurring dream! If the patient is willing to explore the dream, the chances are he or she will gain an invaluable insight.

Intellectual understanding, though, in my experience, while important, is not enough for real transformation to occur in the dreamer. Intellectual understanding may be the first step in putting the patient on the right track, but only the reexperiencing of the feelings can create change, as I stated in *Transformational Dreaming* (Morris 1996). In the three examples that follow, I will show how dreams uncovered unconscious conflict in the mother–daughter preoedipal relationship. I will also discuss how I worked with the patient to access the feelings that could resolve the conflict.

MARGARET

The first patient, whom I call Margaret, entered therapy because of marital problems. She was married to a man who initially swept her off her feet. He was handsome, personable, and very funny. It was primarily his sense of humor that endeared him to her. He was humorous in a way that often made fun of other people, and after the initial romance wore off, this humor turned into criticism of her. The patient recognized in him the same kind of humor and criticism lavished upon her by her mother all through her childhood, and even adulthood.

Margaret came to therapy when her husband's criticism became unbearable; his humor was only a thin veil to cover his hostility toward her. He was critical of her management of the home, the meals she served, and even her sexual performance. She felt her self-confidence, which was precarious to begin with, dwindle away. In addition, she wanted to have a child, and she perceived his resistance as a lack of commitment to their marriage. As he became more critical, she became more insecure and dependent on him for approval. This in turn made him reject her more and he openly stated his desire to be free. It was during a period of extreme anxiety that she had the following dream:

> I'm living on a horse ranch. I see a very tall, terrifying murderous-looking female horse. Everybody is frightened of this maniac horse. I quickly get inside a building and close my shutters, thinking I am safe now. I find myself in a small enclosed space. There is a kitchen and a counter on the other side of the windows, which are triangular in shape. Suddenly the frightening horse bursts through the glass windows and is in my space. Nobody but me knows that this has happened. I am sitting on the floor with the horse. The soles of our feet meet.

The dreamer said she was frightened when she awakened from this dream. Upon reflection she realized she was placating the horse at the end of the dream because at any minute it could become violent and kill her. The sexual symbolism in this dream seems obvious: an intruder (in this case, a horse) breaks through a locked door or window. Often this kind of dream is interpreted as a forbidden desire for sex on the part of the dreamer. However, the danger in making an interpretation like this is that it does not take the dreamer into account. Since the dreamer created the dream, she is the only true authority on the dream's meaning. And it is to her whom we have to defer.

Margaret acknowledged the sexual implication of her dream but questioned why the horse was female. I asked her if there was any female currently in her life who was threatening her, since the dream symbolism suggested not only sexuality but aggression. She responded that her mother was calling her daily as usual and subtly undermining her. Her mother questioned practically everything Margaret said, implying that Margaret was incompetent and would be better off doing things her mother's way. "How does that make you feel?" I asked Margaret. "As if I'd like to kill her," Margaret admitted. "And how do you respond when your mother treats you that way?" I asked. Margaret said she ignored it, but it was apparent to me that her wish to kill her critical mother went underground. This rage more than likely had something to do with the rage in her dream and fear that the horse was going to kill her. But instead of directly expressing the anger, Margaret ended up playing tootsies with the horse as a way of placating it.

As we explored Margaret's angry feelings toward her mother, she recalled a very early memory. She was a toddler and her mother had put her in a swimming tube in the family pool. Margaret was terrified and screamed to be taken out. Her mother merely watched her and let her scream. In those moments Margaret recalls feeling hopeless and defeated. Throughout her childhood and adult life Margaret could never protest or show anger to her mother; she just did not feel safe with her. Bit by bit as the therapy progressed I helped Margaret realize that nothing would happen to her if she let herself be angry at her mother during the session. Her mother would never know about it. This brought up guilt feelings that somehow her mother would find out because she could read Margaret's mind and consequently Margaret would be punished for this. But Margaret gradually worked through her guilt, which often took the form of coming to her mother's defense instead of her feeling her own feelings. As Margaret began to experience how much her mother intimidated her, she became justifiably enraged, and also less afraid of her husband's criticism. He noticed the change in her and his sadistic urges lessened toward her. When she finally told him in an assertive way that she would no longer put up with his criticism, he backed off and displayed a new respect for her.

To the dream again. The female horse represented a combination of the two critical people in Margaret's life—her husband and her mother. The sexual aspect of the dream reflected her feelings toward her husband. But dreaming of the horse as female revealed the source of the criticism, and Margaret's submission. It was this dream that brought to light Margaret's self-defeating behavior—her intimidation and fear of standing up to the powerful, sadistic mother.

JANET

The second dreamer, Janet, came to therapy still suffering from depression and withdrawal three years after her lover left her. Janet, now in her early fifties, had gone through a series of men (or rather they had gone through her). She had experienced lengthy depressions on two previous occasions when relationships ended. But this was the worst, she claimed. She felt little hope of ever meeting anyone again, which was partly because of her age. She also felt it was her fault that the relationship had failed. The therapy so far had not helped significantly, although talking and having someone listen did allow her some relief during the sessions. But her morbid feelings reappeared soon after our meetings and she often spoke of killing herself if life were to continue this way. One morning she brought in a dream:

> I am all by myself in a rented shack in the country. In the doorway I see a birdlike creature. It is bewildered and hurt, and it is screeching. I save the bird from being squashed in the door. I put it outside, close the door, and feel pride in having saved it and in being kind. But I also realized that I did not want to deal with the injured bird. One of its legs is mangled and dangling by a small amount of flesh and fur. It occurred to me to cut off the leg, causing the creature unbearable pain for the moment, but freeing it ultimately from the mess that is hanging from it.

Often we are the dream characters of our dreams, and the suffering, injured creature in this dream is Janet. How powerfully and accurately her dream depicts the quality of her inner world. It illustrates too how the dreamer abandons herself when she is in pain. Janet does not want to deal with the injury, and puts the bird outside the house (out of sight, out of mind), separating the creature from herself. By doing this she is unwittingly making her pain so much worse in her present life. The dream clearly shows what must be done in order for Janet to heal. She must come to terms with her pain and not abandon herself.

It was also apparent to me that this pattern of abandoning herself when she was in pain was a learned behavior on Janet's part. And there was no doubt in my mind that the person who had abandoned her early on was her mother. She often described her mother during the course of therapy as distant and uninvolved. When Janet had her tonsils taken out at age 5, her mother agreed to stay in the operating room. The child, strapped down on the table, awakened from the ether to hear her mother tiptoe out of the room. The child was unable to utter a cry or to move. She tried to thrash around, only to be immediately subdued by the doctors and their assistants, and then they gave her an additional dose of anesthetic. The experience highlighted the child's sense of helplessness, her distrust of her mother, and her terror of being abandoned.

I asked her to recreate this early event in the present. As she lay on the couch she said the following, which I wrote down immediately after the session so I would not forget:

> I am on the operating table. A nurse is smiling at me, and telling me there is nothing to be afraid of. Soon it will be over and I will be eating my favorite ice cream—pistachio. I keep looking over for my mother. She is standing off to the side, in the room but not looking at me. Her stance is familiar. How many times did I sit on trains, separated from her; she would sit behind me somewhere nearby, and I'd have to keep turning around and checking to see if she were still there. Right now I feel frightened that she is not within reach. I want to draw her closer. She seems so far away from me. My mother says nothing. Someone in a green mask puts a cuplike object over my nose and mouth and I begin to feel like I'm dying. This is the ether I heard about. It's the worst sensation of my life. I can do nothing. The next thing I remember is that someone is shoving a spoon down my throat. I want to say, "Get that spoon out of my throat," but instead I just gurgle. I can't speak because it is there. I start to struggle, and someone holds me down. I want to scream to my mother, but she begins tiptoeing out of the room, leaving me alone with my terror.

After Janet recounted this, I asked her what she wanted to scream to her mother. "Don't leave me," she said. Janet began to cry. And as she cried, she got more in touch with her feelings of abandonment. More memories of her mother's indifference and unavailability came forth, and Janet began to *feel*, not just know intellectually, the pain that this caused her. She began to see now the connection between her depression and the feelings induced in her by her mother. She blamed herself for her mother's distance, believing that if she had been a better child her mother would love her. As she felt her old pain, I asked her what she thought about a parent who's supposed to love and cherish a baby but who instead is distant and disinterested. The question helped her to realize that it wasn't because she was a not-good-enough baby, unworthy of love, but that her mother was inadequate as a mother. Nevertheless, she still felt the need to protect her mother. This was the same early defense she used to bury her rage rather than risk losing her mother's love. But as I encouraged her to focus on her own feelings, rather than those of her mother's, she started to feel the early rage. By mourning what she didn't have and raging over what should have been hers, Janet was able to work through her depression.

HELEN

The last patient, Helen, was unable to sustain a relationship with a man. She'd go from man to man, always finding something wrong with each one of them. This behavior was leading to increasing frustration, failure, and fear that she would end up alone. She knew she was frigid, but that was only part of the story. Helen described her mother as a highly sensitive, anxious woman who had very low self-esteem. She had always been protective of her mother and took her side in the many fights between her parents. Her mother used her as a confidante against the father, and the patient kept him at a distance, seeing him as the perpetrator of her mother's distress. The father usually was a good-natured man who occasionally had violent temper tantrums. This frightened both Helen and her mother.

Therapy proceeded uneventfully, and it wasn't until Helen had this dream that significant changes began to occur. This was her dream:

> I hear a woman screaming. I look outside and a handsome, blond man, about six foot four, is threatening a woman. Although he's handsome, he's very mean-looking and dangerous, and I'm afraid he's going to rape and kill the woman. I rush outside and begin yelling things at the man to divert his attention from the woman. He leaves the woman and begins chasing me. I am terrified. I awaken from this nightmare with my heart pounding, relieved that it was only a dream. However, later that night I have another dream. I look outside my childhood home and see a dead animal on the road. I keep thinking it is a muskrat as I observe it from the den. A wispy-like thing appears. It is long and looks like a

fox. It's the baby. It strokes the mother, nuzzles up to her, and makes her head move as if she is alive. Someone comes over and examines the mother's head. The baby goes off alone. I wake up and start sobbing.

After each of the above dreams, Helen awakened with a deep feeling. After the first dream it was terror; after the second, it was grief. In the first dream Helen feared being raped and killed; in the second she grieved over the dead mother and the orphaned baby. The messages of both the dreams seemed quite apparent to Helen. However, what she hadn't understood before was that in protecting her mother, she constantly put herself in danger from her father. Her father's violence had left her frozen (frigid), but she suppressed her fear in her effort to rescue what she assumed to be her endangered mother. The mother, in reality, was probably not in danger, but the child's fear of losing her mother heightened her anxiety. If the mother herself had not appeared so anxious and helpless, Helen might not have felt she needed to protect her. One could easily hypothesize that Helen's mother was frightened of men before she married, and had transferred some of these fears to her husband.

Helen not only feared her father but feared she would be left without a mother. Nobody comforted Helen after her father's rages. On the contrary, Helen swallowed her own feelings and tried to reassure her mother.

Hers was an untenable conflict. She was put in the role of being her mother's own mother, to the detriment of her own childhood and maturation.

After the dream, Helen remembered the innumerable times she could not enjoy herself while she was playing with other children; she invariably thought about her mother and worried if she were all right.

I told Helen that she had sacrificed her childhood because of her mother. It was her mother who should have been looking out for her. Helen was in truth her mother's mother. Eventually Helen began to recognize all that she had lost. This mother, whom she adored, had also cheated her out of a relationship with her father. The most important person in a healthy person's life should be oneself; in Helen's case it was her mother.

This was a great conflict for Helen, because she truly cared about her mother. How was she ever to free herself from her mother's dependency on her, and her codependency, as protector, on her mother? It was as if she had a monkey on her back and there was no escape. She knew she was entitled to be angry at her mother for stealing her life from her, but how could she be angry at this inept, well-meaning, childlike, fragile mother!

It was time for her to think about her own life, I told her. Her mother had lived hers in the way she knew how. Helen now had to focus on herself and fight for the happiness she was entitled to. She said she felt like the baby fox in the dream, leaving the dying mother. She believed that if she left her mother her mother would surely die. "What will happen to you," I asked her, "if you don't begin taking care of your own needs?" It was important for Helen to replay the scenes from her dream in order to accept her feelings. I asked her to envision the baby fox trying to revive its dead mother. Helen let herself feel deep grief for the dead mother, and also for the orphaned child, which she would be one day. She recognized that the baby fox was her and the fox's mother was her own mother. After feeling sadness and grief, she asked her mother, within the therapy session itself, to forgive her. She wanted her mother to understand that she still loved her even if she needed to have her own life. Helen also needed to know it wasn't an either/or situation and that she was not abandoning her mother. She felt she needed to talk to her mother in real life and tell her that she still loved her, even though Helen now needed to grow up and become an adult.

It's noteworthy that Helen's inability to sustain relationships with men was partly predicated on her belief that her mother had to be number one in her life. Working on her independence helped Helen form new loyalties.

This was not the only work of the therapy. Helen had to face her terror of her father, which the dream was clearly pointing out. In working on her terror of her father, I again returned to the dream as a starting place. I asked her to reexperience her fear in the dream when the man chased her. She realized her terror was too much for her to feel. In the dream she had woken up, while in waking life she dealt with the fear by suppressing it. She recalled all the times in her life that she had felt frightened by her father's rages. Gradually, by allowing herself to experience the fear as it came up, Helen was able to tap some of the deeper terror that kept her at arm's length both from her father and the other men in her life. The more she could feel the fear, the more she was able to let the love for her father (which was also there, buried) surface. She began enjoying sex with men and feeling more attached to them. She also realized that her father was not as much of a monster as her mother had made him out to be. She began to be her own person rather than a duplicate of her mother. Instead of continuing to repeat the past and transfer her own unresolved conflicts on to the next generation, she was giving herself and her possibly yet unborn children the chance to have happier and more fulfilling lives.

Dreams are not only accurate indicators of the unconscious problems at hand, they are tools for exploring repressed feelings. By encouraging my patients to replay the crucial dream scenes with all the accompanying emotions, I am able to help them experience firsthand the early damage that was done to them. In this way they can repair that damage and release the burden of unfelt traumas—in the form of psychological symptoms and barriers to happiness.

REFERENCES

Jung, C. G. (1954). The aims of psychotherapy. *The Practice of Psychotherapy* Bollingen series 20:47.

Morris, J. (1996). *Transformational Dreaming*. New York: Fawcett Crest.

Ullman, M., and Zimmerman, N. (1979). *Working with Dreams*. New York: Dell.

16

Transference-Cure in the Positive-Oedipal, Mother–Daughter Dimensions of Countertransference and Therapeutic Repair

Roberta Ann Shechter

INTRODUCTION

Our recent clinical world seems enamored with the nurturing power of the preoedipal mother and the dyadic transference. Often lost from view and out of range of therapeutic sensitivity is a field of ideation of equal nurturing power, the oedipal mother. This is the triadic transference figure of female competition and identification. This transference promotes the conflict resolution that leads to object choice and the benign superego introjects of guilt-free sexuality. This chapter explores the complexity of transference and countertransference that can unfold when both patient and analyst are female, and the patient's developmental level is predominantly oedipal. It is proposed that mother–daughter countertransference ideation can foster a new understanding of transference and what is required of the analyst in therapy. When the analyst's behavior and interpretations run counter to the patient's negative transference expectations, a transference-cure can unfold. Rooted in the ideas of classical ego psychology, this chapter explores the clinical theory that underpins transference-cure. This theory is applied to observations of a psychotherapy case in which transference-cure led to intrapsychic structural change. Mother–daughter self and object configurations were altered and oedipal conflict resolved.

THEORETICAL FRAMEWORK

Transference-cure is defined as the resolution of a patient's core conflict that has come about through two basic functions of treatment. The first is the patient's identification with a therapist's analytical skills. The second is the patient's corrective emotional experience in treatment (Alexander and French 1946). This is an experience, in the transference, that alters negative self-representations (Blanck and Blanck 1974) and increases socially adaptive behaviors (Hartmann 1958).

Transference-cure is a much maligned concept. Many psychoanalysts believe that transference-cure is little more than a therapeutic Band-Aid—it binds pain, but chiefly results in superficial behaviors that have no relation to structural change. They insist that these behaviors are transitory and have no connection to a more healthful alignment of id, ego, and superego. Such clinicians often put transference-cure into the same category as "flight into health," a patient's effort to avoid continued treatment by repressing painful internal reality (Greenson 1991). I believe that these dismissive opinions overlook the psychodynamic value of transference-cure in once-weekly treatment. These negative opinions may be more reflective of the different use made of transference in psychoanalysis and psychotherapy than arising from any serious consideration of the concept of transference-cure. In this chapter I discuss the psychodynamic nature of transference-cure and illustrate these ideas with the description of a treatment in which transference-cure resulted in structural change. The dominant transference in the case was oedipal. Both therapist and patient were female. Repair in the ego—of mother–daughter intrapsychic configurations—led to conflict resolution.

Transference-cure in once-a-week individual psychotherapy is based on a reparative relationship. Transference—feelings and thoughts about significant figures of childhood that are projected onto the person of the therapist (Moore and Fine 1990)—is central to this relationship. Clinical concepts that explain the healing power of transference in more intensive treatment situations are useful to our understanding of the dynamics of transference-cure in once-weekly therapy (Fenichel 1954). All psychoanalytically informed treatments tend to encourage a deep engagement with a patient's unconscious. The emotional intensity of this engagement and its purpose in the therapeutic situation varies. In psychoanalysis, transference is intensely felt. Old memory traces are given new life in the treatment room. Therapeutic time is spent reenacting the pathological encounters of childhood. Reenactment is done through the screen of new language and current life situations, but the affects remain the same. These regressive experiences are triggered by the analyst's silence and neutrality (Menninger 1958). In the safe haven of a three- to five-day-a-week therapy, defenses loosen and history moves into the present. The patient's unrequited childhood longings surface and go in search of satisfaction. The quiet and ungratifying analyst becomes the focus of these longings. A struggle for satisfaction ensues. The analyst's neutral responses to these demands frustrate the patient and infantile neurosis is reexperienced. Infantile neurosis, the pain of childhood that is the basis of adult pathology (Nagera 1966), is given voice in the fantasies of transference neurosis. Transference neurosis evolves when the therapist becomes a personification of the patient's most depriving early object relation. This is, of course, a fantasy in the mind of a patient, but the capacity for reality testing may be momentarily lost, lending transference neurosis a psychoticlike reality.

Since transference neurosis arises from the reliving of very early deprivation, a time in life when psychic structure was being built, it is a powerful change agent. Under the sway of transference neurosis, analyst and patient are on a joint voyage through an unconscious terrain that bleeds into the present. The seeds of adult pathology that interfere with current adaptation are dramatized. Present-day dysfunctional fantasies and defenses are traced to their early roots, interpreted, and worked through in interchanges within the transference neurosis. Over time, in a six- to fifteen-year psychoanalysis, transference neurosis dissipates as core conflicts in the patient's psychic structure resolve.

Transference in a once- or twice-a-week psychotherapy is less intrusive to the patient's psychic structure. Defenses are usually maintained, regression discouraged. While transference may be emotionally intense and meaningful, links to reality are seldom lost and full-blown transference neurosis rarely surfaces. Engagement with the unconscious is gently done. This is the arena of transference-cure. Transference-cure is based on a struggle to change that is close to conscious thought. It is, nevertheless, an intrapsychic process. Working in the here-and-now experience of transference, transference-cure unfolds as the therapist interprets, normalizes, and partially gratifies wish-fulfilling fantasies (Garcia 1990). The therapist's treatment technique is based on four assumptions: (1) the unrequited longings of a patient's infantile neurosis are brought into every therapeutic situation; (2) transference neurosis, with its expectation of deprivation, is in the deepest ideation levels of every transference; (3) a therapist supplies a patient with a new, reparative object relation that challenges, supports, and helps to expand that patient's ego functions; and (4) there is a close connection between interpersonal and intrapsychic phenomena. As interpersonal behavior changes and adaptation improves, a patient's intrapsychic self and object representations alter, and structural change occurs. This change is a transference-cure.

Transference-cure requires the presence of a positive transference. This positive transference is built on positive aspects of the patient's remembered past. When weekly therapy is long enough for an abiding trust to be established, between three and six years' duration, the patient introjects the therapist's analytical skills. This identification forces the patient to question his or her own maladaptive character styles—dysfunctional defenses. The patient is not alone in this effort. The therapist is an active presence. He or she overtly displays an empathic analytic attitude and uses educative genetic interpretations. These therapeutic activities help the patient contain anxieties that are stirred by the exploration of feelings and thoughts. Interpretations often address dysfunctional preconscious fantasies that prevent satisfying interpersonal contacts. In treatment exchanges, the patient experienced the therapist as an alive parental object, an ego enabler. The patient identifies with this object. The patient internalizes the object and the self that are experienced in the therapeutic hour. When negative transference emerges, it is quickly interpreted in ways that do not allow it to escalate and interfere with the rational therapeutic alliance between patient and therapist, or derail the reparative process that is unfolding.

Transference-cure is a new level of ego integration. Reparative treatment interactions and more positive interpersonal experiences in daily life have a direct influence on the patient's psychic structure. Change is reciprocal. The interpersonal has an impact on the intrapsychic. As this change occurs, positive self- and object representations in the patient's internal world move into ascendancy. Id longings are more easily satisfied. The superego is more benign. Sources of guilt become less powerful, and self-esteem grows. The world is then faced with new vigor, and the stimulus for change continues. The case illustration that follows is a four-year treatment. It was an insight-oriented therapy in which transference-cure occurred. Experiential transference and genetic interpretations were ego directed. Improved object relations promoted intrapsychic change. Countertransference, the therapist's recall of personal mother–daughter experiences, stimulated in the clinical session, influenced her understanding of the patient's oedipal transference. Fantasies and longings were underscored. This countertransference was used as a guide for selective gratification, gratification aimed at growth.

CASE STUDY:
ALICE IN SEARCH OF A HUSBAND

Alice sought treatment at the encouragement of a colleague in her law firm, a former patient of mine. Alice had told Jack, her colleague, that she would "rather be married unhappily than lead a single life." Jack was alarmed by what he considered to be Alice's irrational investment in an unhappy relationship. He confronted Alice with his conclusion that she "deserves better," and she agreed with him but shared her fear that "I will never find anyone better than Michael."

When I met Alice my first impression of her was one of flowing vitality. A big woman, close to six feet tall and stocky in body build, she sat snugly in my waiting-room bentwood chair. Strands of thick, shoulder-length black hair hid her face from view as she leaned forward, reading *People* magazine in single-minded concentration. She was so engrossed in the pages of *People* that she looked up startled when I quietly introduced myself. Regaining her composure, she rose and extended her hand in greeting. I accepted her hand. Her fingers were long and thin, her grasp firm, her palm cool. Anxiety showed in her need to avert her eyes from mine as she said, "Hi, I'm Alice," and followed me into my office.

We sat in silence as she scanned the bookshelf near her right shoulder. She took a deep breath, blew air dramatically through her lips, smiled, and said, "Well, I'm here!" I responded with a smiling, "Yes, tell me, what brings you here today?" and Alice began our first treatment session with complaints about her boyfriend, Michael. "He is a good catch," she said cynically. "He has a thriving business and explosive bank account. Unfortunately, his temperament matches his ability to accumulate money." Alice was unhappy about her countless verbal battles with Michael. The couple bickered about everything and nothing. Their encounters were seldom over important issues. Sparring seemed unavoidable and unsettling. Coming close to winning her point could be exhilarating for Alice, but even that, when it occurred, was exhausting. "I've never had a boyfriend like Michael. He's a first. I've always liked sweet, kindly men," she reflected. Alice then readily admitted that her fear of being alone kept her in their relationship. "Having Michael is better than having no one," she said, and continued in a bitter tone, "I'll kill myself if I'm not married by the age of 40. I know that is a crazy idea, but that is how I feel, and I have only six more years to go."

Alice denied having a definitive suicide plan, and seemed amazed to be asked this question. She dismissed my concern with a strident, "I'm only talking about how I feel, not what I will actually do." Focusing back on her dissention with Michael, she said, "I can never satisfy him. He wants a thinner woman, one with blond hair. My full figure and dark tresses turn him off. Maybe I look too much like his mother." She laughed, then paused, reflecting, "The thing that bothers me most about Michael is that he lectures me and seldom listens. He has ideas about everything, and is always right. He even has ideas about my own profession. He lectures me on points of law and discounts my opinions. He talks about marriage, but how can I live with such an egotistical man? He would drive me crazy." Ambivalence forcefully surfaced as Alice wailed, "I should get rid of the bastard, but somehow I just can't!" She took a deep breath and continued in a calmer voice, "I try constantly to please Michael. We spend our free time doing the things that he enjoys. I like the outdoors and active sports, he doesn't."

She was silent for a moment, then continued. "Maybe I shouldn't complain so much. We attend wonderful concerts and go on fancy vacations at luxury hotels. Michael spends his money freely. He can be very generous. It is probably unreasonable of me, but just once I'd like to go hiking in the Berkshires, or run with him around the reservoir early one morning. I want someone who is more down to earth, someone who will share my interests and appreciate me," she sighed. "I admit that Michael has his good points. He can hold his own at my family gatherings. He fits better around the dinner table than I do. My sister, brother, and mother like him very much. They would be devastated if I broke off our relationship."

Addressing the preoedipal differentiation struggle (Mahler et al. 1975) that appeared to be at the heart of Alice's pain, I said softly, "Pleasing your family seems to be an important factor in your relationship with Michael. What do you mean when you say that he fits in better with them than you do?"

My comment was meant as an empathic developmental interpretation. Alice heard my words as a challenge to her defenses. Her response was a decisive and angry flow of oedipal derivations. Alice gave voice to intense competition and castration anxiety. "My family are a bunch of intellectual snobs, and so is Michael." Alice was the daughter of two university professors. Her parents divorced when she was 19. Father had been a historian. Her mother, more recently retired, taught biochemistry. The mind was king in the household of childhood, and Alice was the family dunce. The youngest of three, and the only child who did not earn either a merit or Rhodes scholarship, Alice felt intellectually inferior. She said, "At the dinner table, when I was a teenager, I could never keep up with conversations. Everyone read *The New Republic* and had their ideas about its editorials. Their interests bored me. I was the social daughter."

Alice was, in reality, less intellectually accomplished than her siblings. She claimed that her parents were careful not to ridicule her. Nevertheless, she experienced the feeling of being somewhat different from other family members. This difference was a basic element in her self-image. When she finished high school and entered college, Alice was surprised to find herself considered a campus intellectual. She said, "I went to a good state school. People there were smart, and I actually fit in. I guess the I.Q. points that one needs to have a high standing in my family are different than in the rest of the world." When Alice graduated from a prestigious law school, she earned status in her family. She was now, in her words, the only one who had a "down-to-earth profession. I don't have a Ph.D., but I'm earning good money," she said. "My brother, John, occasionally asks me for legal advice. That is a real turn-on."

Making a historical comparison with her siblings, Alice said, "My only claim to fame as a child was a good sense of humor and the ability to make friends." While her brother and sister studied, Alice partied. Moving her thoughts to the present, she continued, "My mother is surprised that I'm not married. At age 34, she considers me an old maid. Growing up I was the daughter with the most dates. Maybe mother had expected me to marry right out of college. Now she tells me that I should make sure that my stock portfolio is steady. She reminds me that a woman alone can't be too careful about money. I think my mother now believes that I will never marry," Alice mourned.

To kindle hope and expand her observing ego by interpreting the defense of projection, I said, "Perhaps your perception of mother's worry about your unmarried state is a reflection of your own worst fears. Preoccupation with these fears brings you to treatment. Perhaps once we understand the reason for your fears, you will have freedom from them." Alice listened and smiled.

By the end of our first session I was impressed with the adolescent quality of Alice's story and the strength of her ego. These were conflicting personality factors. She was, at one moment in time, both mature and immature. The illogical nature of this inconsistency seemed to make sense when I thought about it as a product of oedipal conflict. Intelligent, well related, and psychologically minded, Alice functioned well in the work world and had satisfying platonic friendships. Her intimate life, with family and boyfriends, was filled with conflict. In this interpersonal world she suffered from intense castration anxiety. Her preoccupation with intellectual differences from family functioned as a defense. It pushed castration anxiety deep within her unconscious. In her unconscious Alice equated intelligence with genital powers. She displaced power and anxiety downward from her brain to her genitals, and felt inadequate. Her mother and sister were blessed with the power that she lacked. Both were, in Alice's view, more intelligent and womanly than she. Both had gained recognition for their mental power, and had married. Having less adequate intellectual endowment than the other women in her family and being unable to please a man seemed equated in Alice's mind.

I wondered how this family history would affect the nature of Alice's fantasies about me, her therapist, and how transference would emerge between us. She described her mother as a domineering critic, yet she seemed ready to trust me. This was initially perplexing. Following sessions clarified the transference fantasy that underpinned our early relationship. Alice was in search of a woman who would teach her how to deal with the emotional world of men, not the mind. Expressing her libidinal wish in a reversal, she would calmly claim, "You're a therapist. I don't expect you to tell me what to do." I didn't give Alice advice. But I did explore her anxieties about men, and in that action I indirectly gratified her longings. Thus a transference-cure began to unfold.

The first year of treatment centered on an intense hunt for a husband. Three weeks after beginning therapy, influenced by our work together, Alice accepted the reality of her incompatibility with Michael. She broke off with him and put a personal ad in *New York Magazine*. Through this effort she met several men. Each was interested in Alice, and she in them. But after six or seven dates the relationships grew cold. Each one of these men, by objective economic and educational criteria, were socially beneath Alice. She was enamored of a Russian taxi driver. The superintendent of an apartment building was another boyfriend. She claimed that her egalitarian attitude about men was a conscious reaction to her family. "Anyone who would be accepted by them has no sex appeal for me," she said. Slowly we explored Alice's history of unacceptable men. All her boyfriends were unmarried and available for relationships, but lacked "the right credentials." In time, Alice admitted that academic achievement was as important to her as to her intellectually striving family. This admission was crucial. It gave Alice greater freedom in her choice of men. Before Alice could acknowledge that she shared the high value that her family placed on education, she needed to confront the oedipal conflicts that kept her in a single state; namely, her belief that she could not measure up to the companionship expectations of an intellectual man, and her fear of maternal retribution if she outdid her divorced mother by capturing and keeping a man like Father. My supportive analytic attitude contained Alice's anxiety while I actively interpreted her wishes and fears. The content of our sessions fluctuated between the pain of the past and daily-life struggles.

The following clinical example of this repetitive therapeutic process occurred in the eighteenth month of treatment. In this session I had a countertransference response that helped me understand the unique form of oedipal drama that imprisoned Alice. After this session my interpretations and therapeutic technique became better attuned. And I was more aware of transference-cure aspects of her therapy.

It was a bleak winter morning. Alice was lamenting her loneliness. I knew that she was dating Bob, an insurance salesman. I also knew that he bored her. She claimed that "being with Bob was like being alone." Suddenly I found myself thinking about my adult daughter and her need, as a teenager, to keep dating details from my curious eyes. I knew that my daughter had successfully negotiated the oedipal when this behavior changed. She began to openly share, in her senior college year, the trials and tribulations of dealing with men, and valued my opinions. I respectfully acknowledged her sexual needs and her stated wish to find a man who was as smart and emotionally available as her father. Moving my thoughts back to Alice, I pondered her need for active feminine acknowledgement from a woman. With this countertransference in mind I praised Alice's ability to "attract men" by pointing out that her "difficulty was not being alone, but whether or not [she] want[ed] the men who want[ed] [her]." In the associations that followed, Alice focused on her mother's choice of remaining alone following divorce from father.

"Perhaps I'm like my mother," she said, "never satisfied. Daddy's a hard act to follow. Mother could have remarried. She is a good-looking woman, an independent spirit, and smart. Mother dates occasionally, but it has been fifteen years since father left, and no man seems good enough for her. Maybe she is looking for a replica of Father like I am," Alice mused.

"You're looking for Father?" I said.

Alice responded, "I would like a man like my father—smart, warm, appreciative of me. No matter how much I look for such a man, I don't find him."

I said simply, "Wanting a man like your father is a normal, womanly longing. I wonder if you screen out dating possibilities by avoiding social situations where you might meet such a man, someone with the same educational background as your family. Of course, you would have to deal with the discomfort that you once had at the dinner table and anxiety stirred by doing better in the dating world than mother does." I paused, then continued, "If you find a man who is like your father, and begin to date him, bring the anxieties that surface into our sessions."

Alice smiled broadly. She was elated by my ego-directed interpretations and treatment plan. She seemed to hear everything as advice and was pleased. Her associations were quick and intense. Referring to the nurturing aspect of the positive-oedipal transference and her deprivation, she said, "Talking about the details of a date would be helpful, I think." What Alice wanted from a maternal experiential transference was implied in her description of mother's behavior. She said, "My mother never asks about my boyfriends. We talk on the phone at least once a week. She asks me about work and my investments, but never about men. I volunteer information. I tell her that I am going on a date, and she gives a supportive grunt, but never follows up with questions after the date. She could ask, 'How did it go?' but never does. She means to be respectful of my privacy. I know that. Still, I feel hurt. My boyfriend could have two heads and she would never know it."

As the session closed, I said, "You feel that your mother is indifferent to your dating struggles, and you feel sad." Alice agreed.

Positive-oedipal transference seemed to contain Alice's anxiety, and in the weeks that followed she continued dating with renewed energy. Alice let it be known among her many friends that she was looking for a new man, one who might make an appropriate marriage partner. She went on a number of blind dates, and she met Fred. Fred, like Alice, was an attorney. His specialty, finance, was close to hers.

They had much to talk about. They both enjoyed the outdoors. Their first date was a bike trip through the New Jersey countryside. In a matter of weeks Alice was smitten. Fred, in Alice's eyes, far exceeded her own intellectual capabilities. He, in fact, could hold his own at her family gatherings. The only difficulty between the two was a finely felt level of competition. In the bedroom both were happy and sexually compatible. But in the outside world Fred challenged Alice constantly. Would she hold her own on a biking trip? Could she cook as well as he? Was her spaghetti sauce as flavorful as the one that he produced in the kitchen?

Following each contact with Fred, Alice shared the details of her feelings, thoughts, and anxieties. Fred, at age 42, had never considered marriage to be an option. He admitted this to Alice in their third month together, and she was devastated. She said, "If only I can persuade him." Persuasion, for Alice, meant performing. She would meet Fred on his own turf. She would try never to disappoint him in anything they did together. In the end, she believed, he would relent, give up his precious independence and marry her.

As therapy proceeded, it became apparent, to me, that Alice withheld from Fred on the most intimate level of verbal communication. After six months of dating, Alice wanted an engagement ring, while Fred hardly knew about her aspirations for marriage. She had stated them, but vaguely. When I challenged this directly, asking her why, if she loves Fred and knows that he loves her, isn't she more emotionally honest with him, Alice said, "If I confront him, he'll run."

In the associations that followed, Alice shared childhood memories of being "tongue-tied at the dinner table." She could never say the right thing to express her ideas in a language that was clearly heard by family members. When her parents argued, she would try to intercede and felt helpless when no result was achieved. "I thought that I should be able to bring peace between them," she said. "I know now that was ridiculous." Alice claimed that the final breakup of her parents came as no surprise and was not devastating for her. She said, "I knew that each of my parents loved me in their own way, no matter what they felt about each other."

When I interpreted that her worries about being "direct with Fred in what you feel and think might be connected to fear of abandonment, based on the loss of your parents' marriage," Alice was startled, then agreed. "I keep thinking that my mother is right. Maybe marriage is not in the cards for me," she said. "Mother never found a man who would stick with her, so why should I do better and find someone of my own?"

I said, simply, "Why not?" and Alice's eyes filled with tears. I continued in a more interpretive mode by implying that she need not follow in her mother's footsteps out of guilt for wanting something more, a permanent relationship that would not end in divorce. "Alice," I said, "you are so worried about doing better than your mother that it's hard for you to begin life." She agreed, saying, "My mother—and her intent professional life—scares me. She wants me to have the same. She thinks that my work should be the pivot of my existence. She thinks I can't have anything else. Why is she so convinced of that? Her tenaciousness in this frightens me."

In the weeks that followed, Alice mourned anew the loss, as a teenager, of stability in her family household. She said, "If my father could leave, anyone could." She tearfully forgave her father for wanting a different life. "He is like me," she said, "a social being. He was simply unhappy with my mother."

Slowly Alice seemed to muster courage and confronted Fred with her desire for a committed relationship. He balked anew, and sadly she began dating again. Within weeks she met William. William was an old friend. The two had been high school classmates. Reintroduced by mutual friends while on vacation in the Berkshires, it was love at first sight. Alice and William were totally compatible. Within a week William took Alice home to meet mother. She stayed the weekend in his family house, an accepted girlfriend. While Fred was still in the emotional background, Alice realized that her relationship with William had a natural intensity that she had never experienced with Fred. And then, unaccountably, Alice became pregnant. William was attentive. The couple discussed keeping the child and recognized that a month into their relationship was too early for such a decision. Both Alice and William were upset at the idea of an abortion, Alice because she was worried about the dictates of her biological clock, William because he would have loved to have had a little Alice "to bounce on his knee." The total acceptance and joy of William's ideation pleased Alice to the core. She had never been so appreciated by any man. Yet she had doubts about William as a marital choice. William was a college graduate, but not a high achiever. He was a businessman. He did not have an advanced degree and claimed to have had little interest in academic studies. His attitude confused Alice. Did this mean that he was not smart enough for her? Or had she at last found a man with whom she could excel? As they got to know each other, Alice realized that William was a natural intellectual. Like her, he enjoyed a social existence, went to theater, and explored the out-of-doors. The more she knew him, the more they seemed to have in common. And there was nothing she could not "tell him." Their relationship seemed blissful. This positive feeling state was marred by family pressure.

William was not readily accepted by Alice's family. Mother had her reservations. She liked William, his social manners, and the fact that he came from a family in "their old neighborhood." But mother wondered if William made enough money and would be able to keep up with Alice both professionally and in her intellectual interests. Here Alice, for the first time, rebelled openly. She made it clear to her mother that she did not intend to let professional achievement dictate her life. Nor did she believe that William was of a lesser breed intellectually. In therapy sessions Alice cried bitter tears over her need to confront her mother and demand William's acceptance. She said, "When he's at the dinner table, I feel that the room is filled with joy. My siblings like him. My mother will never be satisfied with any man that I bring home. I can never please her. I think I'm going to stop trying. I'll be my own person, and choose a man that I appreciate and one who appreciates me."

In these words we hear the oedipal struggle with its undercurrent of anal-phase differentiation difficulty. For Alice, confronting these issues was essential to moving on in life. Alice can now readily take on mother as a competitor. She can hold her own in the world of adult women. She doesn't need mother to confirm her choice of a man, and she can demand an acceptance of her own values, however different they may be from those of her family. These behaviors are an indication that intrapsychic structural change has occurred, and Alice is on her way to the resolution of oedipal conflict.

At the end of the third year of treatment William proposed to Alice, and she was ecstatic. They made wedding plans. All went well until it occurred to Alice that, although she was open with William in every aspect, soon they would share a bank account and he would learn of the money that she had managed to "sock away over the years." She said, "I know I should be proud of my ability to invest. Business interests me. I think William will appreciate my natural common sense where money is concerned. He is, after all, a successful businessman. He understands money. But he puts his money into his business and doesn't have liquid assets. That is what bothers me. I have so much money in the bank, and he has so little, I feel that he will be intimidated by my hoard." In her following associations, Alice connected money and intelligence. She said, "I used to worry that William was not smart enough. Now I'm concerned that his lack of a nest egg will intrude into the beauty of our relationship. He may envy me. I guess I'm also worried that eventually he will envy my investment talent, just as I used to envy my siblings' capacities."

I listened to Alice explore her anxiety over hiding from William the amount of money she had accumulated in her bank account. The connection between intellect and money and the threat of loss was in her conscious thoughts. I confirmed these insights and actively supported her ability to tolerate anxiety when I said, "You're worried that William will be envious of your bank account, just as you were envious as a child of your siblings' intellectual capacities. You have learned to appreciate your own capacities. You don't seem to trust that William can do the same, or trust that he will be overjoyed at your dowry." Alice laughed, "It is a dowry. But I'm not sure if it is a laughing matter. We'll see."

Alice terminated treatment planfully four months after she and William were married. In the final weeks she referred Fred, her former boyfriend, to me. When I explored the reason for this referral, labeling Fred as a replacement for her in my professional life, Alice disagreed. The persistence of a positive-oedipal transference in which I was her nurturing mother underpinned her pensive retort. Alice voiced her oedipal fantasy. She spoke from the heart of her transference longing, saying, "I think I would really like you to tell me where I went wrong with Fred. I know, in reality, you won't tell me anything. But I wish that you would. Once you get to know Fred, you'll know how I could've handled him better. I'm happy with William. He is the man for me. Fred lacked something. I know that I'm being irrational, but I think I should have been able to make up for that lack. I don't love

Fred. I doubt if I ever really did. But still, I feel I should've been the one to push Fred out of my life rather than be rejected by him. I should have been able to handle him and persuade him to marry me." In a final interpretation on the matter, I said, "I guess it's like trying to persuade your father not to leave. Losing Fred was difficult. It had to be. The loss of Father from your childhood home had to be accepted. But one is never comfortable with loss."

CONCLUDING COMMENT

The case of Alice and the story of her treatment is not unique. The good outcome of many once-weekly therapies may be the result of transference-cure. The treatment of Alice was not a rigorous defense analysis, yet much change occurred. Alice used the therapeutic relationship as a reparative ego experience. Transference served a curative function. It countered existing negative internalization by supplying a corrective relationship, one that fostered new definitions of self- and object representations. The therapist, based on a counter-transference response to her patient's longings for feminine nurturing and affirmation, gratified these transference fantasies. Gratification was consistently given in the context of insight-oriented interpretations that were aimed at improved social and emotional adaptation. The patient identified with the therapist's concept of how one achieves heterosexual intimacy. She felt supported in her strivings and oedipal conflict was confronted and resolved. As a consequence of transference-cure, the patient's perception of herself as an adult woman had a positive valence. She faced life with new vigor and improved capacities for relationship.

REFERENCES

Alexander, F., and French, T. (1946). *Psychoanalytic Therapy*. New York: Ronald.

Blanck, G., and Blanck, R. (1974). The contributions of Edith Jacobson. In *Ego Psychology: Theory and Practice*. New York/London: Columbia University Press.

Fenichel, O. (1954). Brief psychotherapy. In *The Collected Papers of Otto Fenichel, Second Series*, pp. 243–259. New York: Norton.

Garcia, E. (1990). Somatic interpretation in a transference cure. *International Review of Psycho-Analysis* 17(1):83–88.

Greenson, R. (1991). Beginnings, the preliminary contacts with the patient. In *The Technique and Practice of Psychoanalysis, Volume 2: A Memorial Volume to Ralph R. Greenson*, ed. A. Sugarman, R. Nemiroff, and D. Greenson, pp. 1–41. Madison, CT: International Universities Press.

Hartmann, H. (1958). *Ego Psychology and the Problem of Adaptation*. New York: International Universities Press.

Mahler, M., Pine, F., and Bergman, A. (1975). *The Psychological Birth of the Human Infant*. New York: Basic Books.

Menninger, K. (1958). *Theory of Psychoanalytic Technique*. New York: Harper Torchbooks.

Moore, B., and Fine, B. (1990). *Psychoanalytic Terms and Concepts*. New Haven, CT/London: American Psychoanalytic Association and Yale University Press.

Nagera, H. (1966). *Early Childhood Disturbances: The Infantile Neurosis and Adult Disturbances*. New York: International Universities Press.

PART V

AGING
PARENTS

From the beginning of life we are on a path toward old age and dying. Contemplating the end, loss of powers, and loss of loved ones evokes grief and mourning. Difficulties with mourning were illustrated by Freud in his paper on melancholia (1917). Grieving for a loved one is energy consuming and represents a final separation. Along similar lines, we can also mourn our parents' becoming older, which also reflects our own aging. The more narcissism is invested in such a relationship, the more difficult the grieving and the possible involvement with melancholic processes.

Women have a harder time during menopause and aging than men. Cultural emphasis on appearance, youth, and beauty offers no solution to this problem. Since the gradual loss of one's faculties and physical competence necessitates the availability of persons who are "ministering," the process recapitulates early bonding. Bodily comfort, touch and sensitivity, and soothing are called for. When confronted with such issues daughters have another opportunity to bond with their mothers, albeit with role reversal. Helen Adler examines the problem of aging and/or infirm parents with sensitivity and compassion. The end of our lives represents another opportunity to accept the limits of our narcissism, relive the good parts of our history in remembrance, and prepare ourselves for departure. We should not forget that the minute we are born death becomes our companion. Freud had wisely accepted this melodrama by providing for a death instinct.

Aging and infirmity frequently lessen inhibitions. There may be a reawakening of oedipal conflicts and bisexual solutions may be more easily permitted. According to Pines (1993), sexual foreplay and touching revives earliest pleasures of the mother–infant relationship. The frequency with which doctors may be consulted for hypochondriacal reasons would confirm that such visits serve to reconfirm life, love, and being cared for.

REFERENCES

Freud, S. (1917). On mourning and melancholia. *Standard Edition* 14:239–258.

Pines, D. (1993). *A Woman's Unconscious Use of Her Body*. New Haven, CT/London: Yale University Press.

17

Ministering to the Dying Mother: Reparative and Psychodynamic Opportunities for the Female Patient

Helen O. Adler

Since Freud's classic study (1917), "Mourning and Melancholia," one of the major themes of psychoanalytic thinking about object relations has centered around the impact of grief and mourning. Despite this emphasis, there has been very little interest in exploring the dynamic impact of the *process* of terminal illness on the loved one. This is rather surprising since the process of losing a primary love object is one of life's most difficult and poignant experiences, one that often *begins* long before death. Many of the most influential psychoanalytic theorists have devoted careful attention to the evolution and vicissitudes of the infant–mother relationship and the effects of separation on the child's psychological development (Bowlby 1969, Mahler et al. 1975, and others). More recently, Oldham (1989) has extended Mahler and colleagues' ideas to the experience of parental loss in middle age, viewing it broadly as a final opportunity to resolve separation-individuation struggles that compromise internalized object relations. However, the impact of the *interaction* between the terminally ill or aging mother and her adult child, with its necessary undoing of previously renounced bodily intimacies, has drawn almost no attention in the clinical or theoretical literature.

This surprising neglect was brought home to me by my work with female patients whose mothers suffered prolonged debilitating illnesses leading to death during the course of their analytic treatment. In this chapter I will present extensive clinical material from these treatments in order to develop the thesis that the adult child's devotion to the dying mother can result in the reworking and resolution of lifelong conflicts. I will also quote throughout from Simone de Beauvoir's (1965) autobiographical account of her own mother's death. The psychological dynamics of this author's relationship with a domineering mother was in many ways parallel to my patients' experiences. I avail myself of the richness of her literary gifts to illustrate my points. I also speculate about the broader social implications of this thesis, especially as it pertains to contemporary patterns of caring for aging and dying parents in our society.

The earliest mode of relationship with the mother is *bodily*. The infant is ministered to by her mother, fed, cleaned, diapered, bathed, and held, from the beginning of life. This provides the fundamental hub from which a more mature relationship branches out to include its myriad complex dimensions. This primary bodily connection is unconsciously yearned for throughout life. However, the vicissitudes of psychological evolution and development make this problematic when it threatens the achievement of psychological differentiation. Margaret Mahler and colleagues (1975), in elucidating the difficulties inherent in personality development, observed that

> smooth and consistently progressive personality development, even under ordinary favorable circumstances, is difficult if not impossible. This, we found was due precisely to the fact that separation and individuation derive from and are dependent upon the symbiotic origin of the human condition, upon that very symbiosis with another human being, the mother. This creates an everlasting longing for the actual coenesthetically fantasized wish-fulfillment and absolutely protected state of primary identification. [p. 227]

Ordinarily these longings are held in check through reaction formations, symbolic compensations, and other adaptive mechanisms that create barriers to the full awareness of their lasting depth and significance. In her autobiographical account of her mother's death, Beauvoir (1965) poetically captures the power of this virtually universal conflict.

> The sight of my mother's nakedness had jarred me. No body existed less for me: none existed more. As a child I had loved it dearly; as an adolescent it filled me with an uneasy repulsion: all this was perfectly in the ordinary course of things and it seemed reasonable to me that her body should retain its dual nature, that it should be both repugnant and holy—a taboo. [pp. 19–20]

Satisfaction of suppressed wishes for reunion with the mother's body in adulthood are achieved to some degree through their integration in adult sexual relationships. Martin Bergmann (1987), in comparing Plato's and Freud's theories of love, emphasizes how both thinkers understood the passionate yearning for reunion as the animating force of romantic love. Whereas Plato saw the reunion as taking place with a lost half of an original, unitary, androgenous self, Freud revealed the unconscious genetic link to the nursing mother of infancy. The persistent force of this longing was dramatically illuminated by a 70-year-old female patient whose mother died when she was only 16. For more than fifty years she harbored unremitting remorse that she had not visited her mother's grave before leaving her birthplace to emigrate to the United States. In analysis, this guilty preoccupation was revealed to cover a deep unconscious wish to be reunited with her mother's body, as symbolized by the grave, and an angry accusation against her mother for abandoning her at such an early age.

In treating two adult women whose mothers suffered terminal illness during the course of therapy, it became clear that ministering to their mother's physical needs represented a second chance for a close bodily connection without the attendant threat of an engulfing or devouring union that could compromise their separateness. For both of these patients, whom I will discuss in some detail, this extended period of intimacy provided an opportunity to renew and finally master previously unresolved struggles around attachment and separation. Ministering to their mothers included actual physical caregiving, bathing, and feeding as well as intimate conversation about bodily functions and related physical and emotional experiences. Although these patients often experienced frightening and painful emotions in the process of caring for their mothers, powerful feelings and fantasies of maternal union were evoked and tolerated.

ANNA MARIA

Anna Maria, a 38-year-old woman, lost her mother to cancer after a prolonged period of gradual deterioration and incapacitation. Prior to this illness Anna Maria had found her mother's presence generally intolerable. Inevitably her mother would grate on her nerves, and more often than not provoke a fury that she contained only at great cost. To control her anger and refrain from arguing, she would emotionally disconnect to the point where she would not even hear what her mother was saying. This was graphically depicted during phone conversations, when Anna Maria would hold the receiver away from her ear, waiting until the mother's chatter subsided. The latter, oblivious of her daughter's disconnection, was apparently content with having her say in the absence of any responsive dialogue. This detachment characterized the overall quality of her relatedness. In raising them, she rarely responded to her children as individuals who had differentiated needs, but functioned like an army sergeant. She had rules for everything and everything had to be done according to the book. The "platoon" all ate the same food; there was no choice about what or even in what order the food could be taken. Her mother, a woman of limited resources, had received little emotional support from Anna Maria's father. She was also phobic. Her fearfulness centered around germs, dirt, and diseases, and she cared for her children in a compulsively dedicated style that was intended to protect them from contamination. In her fears she went so far as to prohibit her children from lying on the sofa, a surface that had been exposed to the potentially contaminating "bottoms" of other people. They were forbidden to get too close to their father, a laborer, whose soiled clothing presumably carried germs into the household. The boundaries of her mother's fearfulness extended to the world beyond her immediate neighborhood. She often became disorganized and/or immobilized at the prospect of venturing outside the narrow confines of a highly constricted environment.

Anna Maria's relationship with her father offered little solace. During her early years she recalled accompanying him on fun-filled outings. However, as his drinking escalated and his relationship with her mother deteriorated, he became more withdrawn. Their happy times dwindled and he was not sufficiently involved with Anna Maria to offer any emotional comfort. She and the other children were often enlisted by her mother—who coerced the children to side with her against their father—to check the local bars and spy on his whereabouts.

Despite the mother's concerns with physical protection and bodily sustenance, her child rearing was marked by considerable emotional and spiritual deprivation. During the first few years of treatment, Anna Maria was incapable of referring to herself in the first person. She would say "you" instead of "I," as in the sentence, "When *you're* lonely *you* want someone to keep *you* company." Winnicott (1958) emphasizes that the use of the word "I" represents an important developmental milestone: "The individual is established as a unit. Integration is a fact. The external world is repudiated and the internal world has become possible" (p. 33). As an adult, Anna Maria was prone to becoming periodically absorbed in frightening fantasies about bodily deterioration and debilitating disease. Alternatively, she would seem oblivious to her bodily self, longing to be only "a head without a body." This was manifested in a marked indifference to her physical appearance, dress, and grooming.

As an adult, Anna Maria lived in fear of her mother's anger, which was expressed through hostile, obliterating withdrawals. In her eyes her mother was "a witch on a broomstick" who would tolerate no challenge or criticism. The silent treatment was as frightening a weapon as the broomstick. Anna Maria resorted to a strategy of pacification, compliance, and withdrawal, which took its toll as she began to suffer from periods of overwhelming depression and functional collapse. At these times she was so withdrawn that she neglected her own young child's cries of pain. When her isolation and terror reached unbearable levels she would telephone her nurturing husband, begging him to come home from work immediately to "keep me company." In Winnicott's terms, the capacity to be alone always implies the internalized presence of the other. Anna Maria's panic arose in the presence of an internalized maternal imago infused by hate and menace. Anna Maria consciously viewed her therapy as her chance at being "reparented."

In the transference I was experienced exclusively as a good object, one who didn't impose rules and controls, while allowing her to explore and discover her individuality. She was able to use this internalized "new parent" to struggle to emerge from fragmenting experiences of inner chaos that frequently overwhelmed her ego functioning. These experiences were vividly depicted in metaphors and dream images of chaotic, dilapidated, and crumbling houses occupied by strange or dead animals. As she developed more inner resources and structure, her dream houses became correspondingly beautiful and orderly. Increasingly, Anna Maria showed signs of being able to structure her inner life reliably. The meaning of her internal disorganization was overdetermined. In addition to representing her fragile psychic stability, chaos expressed an unconscious rebellion against her mother's obsession with rules and regulations. For example, in raising her own family, Anna Maria avoided planned meals and encouraged her children to eat what they wanted whenever they wanted. She found it difficult to discipline herself regarding her own food intake. To eat out of a can was an act of liberation after years of her mother's "kitchen patrol." As these issues were worked over, she began to provide the needed structure for herself and her family, as distinguished from her mother's pathological methods of control.

By the time her mother became seriously ill, Anna Maria had made many advances in all areas of her life. She had embarked upon a promising professional career and made many positive strides in her roles as wife and mother. Her stance vis-à-vis her own mother continued to be distant, however. Although she was dutifully available when her mother called upon her, she was mechanical and emotionally withdrawn in her presence. When she couldn't "tune her out" she would literally go off to sleep to protect her sense of autonomy from the mother's intrusive voice and to avoid ugly confrontations that might trigger overwhelming rage. This fortified stance gave way during her mother's illness. As her mother became more incapacitated, feelings of tenderness began to emerge. Although her mother continued to be angry and controlling and often refused to follow medical advice, Anna Maria visited her at the hospital daily lest her mother feel alone and abandoned. She could not tolerate the possibility that her mother would not be cared for properly by nurses who provide "assembly line, impersonal care." It was difficult for her to control the rage she felt toward these incompetent and uncompassionate caregivers. She bathed her mother's body, washed her hair, and seemed on the whole remarkably comfortable with this level of physical intimacy. In therapy sessions Anna Maria was moved to tears when she talked about her mother's excruciating and paralyzing pain. Significantly, her devotion extended to tending to her mother's flower garden. She gave voice to the fantasy that she could keep these precious flowers alive by replanting them in a garden of her own, identifying symbolically with her mother as a "tender nurturer of beloved children."

There had been two other times in her life that Anna Maria *now* remembered having experienced similar closeness and calm in her mother's company. Both occasions had involved intimate bodily contact and nurturing. The first memory went back to Anna Maria's early adolescence when her mother had suffered a "nervous breakdown" and was confined to bed for weeks. As the oldest child, she was the one to stay home from school to care for her. These she recalled as "happy days" spent in her mother's exclusive company, sitting by her bed and serving her meals. A more recent memory emerged from a time when Anna Maria herself had to have surgery that required a postoperative period of complete bed rest. Her mother came and took care of Anna Maria's household. She described this brief period nostalgically as one in which she was freed of all responsibility: she stayed in bed, reading and being fed. Her illness entitled her to withdraw from family responsibilities, absolved her of all adult burdens, and sanctioned a return to a dependent state of helplessness. It should be noted that these relatively brief and circumscribed interludes of intimacy with her mother were tolerated only when one party was in the role of a nearly helpless dependent.

NAOMI

Naomi, a 40-year-old woman, struggled throughout life in a conflict-ridden relationship with her mother. Anxious themes of her mother's insensitive impingement and intrusiveness reverberated throughout the analysis. Although she functioned autonomously—she had married, raised a family, achieved professional success—her inner world was plagued by the ever-present threat of being engulfed, even devoured, by a "needy, greedy mother." Throughout her life, her mother was somatically preoccupied. Indeed, she reveled in recounting, almost flaunting, detailed accounts of all aspects of her bodily experience. This ranged from endless discussions of her wardrobe, her weight, and her makeup to more worrisome aches and pains and signs of physical decline. For Naomi, these narcissistic preoccupations threatened to reawaken childhood longings associated with overstimulating physical acts of bodily exhibitionism to which she had been regularly exposed.

It was psychologically imperative for Naomi to keep her mother at arm's length. She cautiously guarded her mother's access to her person, hiding facts about her life through secretiveness and dissembling. She anticipated her mother's intrusion into her private life and fantasized vivid scenes of her mother "barging in" and demanding inclusion in private situations. She lived in fear that her mother would discover her "secret life" and imagined that she would feel betrayed and bereft at having been excluded. This need to create a veil of secrecy around her activities became an organizing theme of her object relations. Simone de Beauvoir, who also vigilantly guarded her privacy and separateness, gives voice to sentiments that could have been Naomi's: "I wanted my ramparts to be impregnable. I was particularly diligent in giving away nothing to Maman, out of fear of my distress and horror of having her peer into me. Soon she no longer ventured to ask me questions" (1965, p. 67). This scenario was lived out in Naomi's marriage and in the transference, where she felt compelled to withhold details and plans that inevitably involved intimacy with a third party. For instance, she hid from her husband the intensity of her involvement in treatment, symbolized by the frequency of our sessions. In the transference she was afraid to tell me of her plans to miss sessions for fear that I would be angered at her placing something or someone else before me. On the other hand, intense reactions were provoked when she noticed that I wore a new item of clothing or piece of jewelry, or even when she sensed a note of enthusiasm in my interpretative voice. These were taken as evidence of my self-involvement, as if any pleasure in my person or in my functioning precluded a genuine interest in her. As might be expected, vacations and unexpected absences were met with anger and jealousy.

In her accounts of childhood, her mother was depicted exclusively as an exhibitionistic narcissist whose intimacy lacked appropriate boundaries. Naomi recounted many hours spent in the mother's bathroom, talking to her while she bathed, defecated, and changed her sanitary napkins. Her mother's toilet activities were accompanied by a running commentary elaborating nuances of these daily functions. During summer vacations at the beach, Naomi recalled what seemed like countless hours spent with her mother in their cabana, watching while she oiled her skin, changed her clothes, and posed admiringly in front of the mirror. These occasions afforded her many opportunities to intimately observe her mother's body, which, in the beginning of treatment, was recalled with feelings of repugnance and distaste. She complained that her mother had no shame and that it was destructive to expose her to such upsetting scenes. She also resented the intensity of the mother's self-preoccupation. Naomi recalled the mother sitting at her vanity table totally absorbed in beauty rituals, virtually unaware of her child's presence. This self-preoccupation also took acutely depressive forms. Periods of not getting out of bed, sleeping for much of the day, and becoming enraged when Naomi intruded on her solitude were not uncommon.

Themes of exclusion were central in Naomi's account of childhood experience, and extended beyond feeling ignored by her mother's bodily obsessions. They permeated her relationship with both of her parents in complex interactions frequently commemorated in memories of being left out and humiliated. Her mother's absorption in her appearance not only symbolized her self-involvement, but also her sexual intimacy with Naomi's father. Her tendency to wear low-cut dresses and sexy lingerie were a constant reminder of this exclusion. Although the door to her mother's bathroom was never locked, access to the bedroom *could* be closed to her. The image of the closed door signified her shameful betrayal. She recalled acute jealousy when her parents prepared for an evening out, or took a trip together. Her jealousy could be incited by seemingly small events. For instance, she recalled going shopping with her parents one afternoon and witnessing their mutual absorption and excitement in contemplating a prospective purchase. She felt enraged and humiliated at her insignificance in the moment, reduced to an irrelevant bystander. Although her reactions were not always clearly differentiated, the primary focus of her jealousy seemed directed at replacing her mother as her father's partner. When they rode in the car together, she coveted her mother's place in the front seat.

With regard to her mother, however, any wishes to be the chosen one, or to be her intimate, were defended against by projecting these yearnings onto her mother and then fending off her advances. On occasion these defenses crumbled when she felt rejected by her mother. During a more recent trip they took together, her mother chose to go off by herself to pursue her pleasures, lunching at a special restaurant and shopping at an elegant store. Naomi reacted with hurt and outrage, "How could she go off and *not* invite me to join her!" Except for such rare moments, these feelings were repressed and found expression only indirectly, in her mother's relationship with Naomi's own children. This grandmotherly attention gave Naomi intense pleasure. Through her own parenting she actively tried to undue this lasting sense of humiliation at being excluded, creating a world in which her children were never left out or made to feel like second fiddle.

Surprisingly, from the moment her mother was diagnosed as suffering from stomach cancer, Naomi insisted on being involved in all decisions regarding her care. She did not experience her mother's preoccupation with *these* physical symptoms as at all burdensome. On the contrary, they became for her the focal point of many special, shared moments. She vividly described having lunch with her mother at a hospital coffee shop after a medical procedure. She savored every detail of the experience, what they ate, what they talked about, as if it had been an exquisitely memorable event. The intimacy of their chatter, to her surprise, reminded her of the bathroom talks she had had with her mother in childhood. *We* now began to realize that those occasions, which in memory had always been colored by intense feelings of repugnance and disgust about her mother's body, had in fact been very special times. Naomi recognized that she had shared a special bond with her mother, and that she was *chosen* to be her confidante and partner. The intense shame and humiliation that she had remembered in the face of undeniable evidence of her parents' erotic intimacy was now understood as a reaction of betrayal at her mother's faithlessness. She realized that she must have been feeling *possessive* of her intimacy with her mother's body. In this context the locked bedroom door was an upsetting reminder of her inexplicable exclusion. Whereas for most of her adulthood the prospect of traveling with her mother would have filled her with dread, she now fantasized about taking a trip with her mother, and longingly imagined the pleasures of sharing a hotel room together. At the same time, her relationship with her husband changed as well. Her anger at what she had described as his intrusiveness abated.

During her mother's hospitalizations, Naomi was aware of paying exquisite attention to the surround and to the details of her mother's physicality. It was as if she were trying to imprint every detail into her memory. She was somewhat surprised at the intensity of her curiosity. She even wished to examine the surgical scars on her mother's body. On one occasion her mother suggested that perhaps Naomi would be more comfortable waiting outside while she changed. Naomi was stunned to realize that her mother did not wish to hold her hostage or force her to stay in the room. It was *she* who wanted to stay and look at her mother's naked body. On another occasion, when her mother needed to be diapered, Naomi considered not calling the nurse, thinking that if she were the one in need, her mother would have cleaned her. In analysis, she was now capable of remembering, without reactive disgust, how much she had enjoyed the opportunities to look at her mother's nakedness in the bathroom of childhood. At the end of her mother's life, Naomi openly longed to be alone with her at her bedside. Other family members were experienced as unwelcome intruders threatening to undermine her feeling that she was indeed her mother's most beloved. Despite the sadness and pain she felt about her mother's terrible deterioration and suffering, she basked in the intimacy she felt they now shared once again. She was able to express her love, gratitude, and admiration for her beautiful mother. Uncannily, Simone de Beauvoir's feelings about her own mother echo my patient's experience: "I had grown very fond of this dying woman. As we talked in the half-darkness I assuaged an old unhappiness; I was renewing the dialogue that had been broken off during my adolescence and that our differences and our likenesses had never allowed us to take up again. And the early tenderness that I had thought dead forever came to life again, since it had become possible for it to slip into simple words and actions" (1965, p. 76).

DISCUSSION

Both patients, Naomi and Anna Maria, struggled vainly throughout their lives to find an "optimal distance" (Mahler et al. 1975) between themselves and their mothers. Prior to their mothers' illnesses, their primary solutions to their conflict-ridden relationships were, for the most part, to erect barriers and emotional fortifications. In Anna Maria's case she had to fortify herself against what she experienced as controlling, rageful, maternal intrusions that threatened to overwhelm her with retaliatory rage and loss of autonomy. For Naomi, angry distance was a means of safeguarding her separateness in the face of engulfment by her narcissistic and overstimulating mother. Each was eternally vigilant, as if ready to repel the "enemy" at the first threat of invasion. It was not until their mothers' illnesses that they were able to move closer without dread and to achieve a more comfortable and comforting distance. Defenses of disavowed love and projected images of maternal destructiveness were ameliorated. They were consistently able to experience their mothers as separate from themselves, differentiated people possessing both positive and negative characteristics. With this increased tolerance for their own ambivalence, they were able to express tender and loving feelings while still consciously acknowledging their resentments.

How do we account for these dramatic changes? Reflecting on the crucial psychodynamic role that internalized images of mother-as-invader, engulfer, and omnipotent enemy played in their previous adaptation, the most obvious hypothesis is that these derivative imagoes of the all-powerful mother of infancy had been neutralized by the mothers' *actual* helpless dependence. Tables had been turned, roles reversed, as they now "mothered" their own mothers. Although Anna Maria's mother still gave orders and tried to control the world from her deathbed, Anna Maria's own sense of autonomy was no longer threatened by this behavior. Presumably, maternal helplessness had been a necessary precondition for this shift to take place. As their mothers deteriorated, both of these daughters assumed greater roles as decision makers and caregivers, unimpeded by the fear that the mother would swoop down and take over. However, metaphors of slain enemies and a changing of the guard take us only so far in our understanding; as we know, internal object representations of childhood are not necessarily tempered by corresponding changes in external reality.

Pursuing this theme further, the specific impact of the mother's *impending* death must be taken into consideration. The knowledge that their mother's days were numbered was a painful but important realization for both of these patients. For Naomi, this resulted in an urgency to spend as much time alone with her mother as possible. Anna Maria, on the other hand, had more difficulty in fully accepting the terminal nature of her mother's illness and was continually shocked by the signs of weakening that were in daily evidence. However, awareness of their mothers' impending deaths was also an unconscious source of reassurance, allowing for a time-limited, reparative reunion without the fear of eternal entrapment. For patients in whom fears of fusion are too great, such a reunion will be precluded by the anticipation of suffering an identical fate as the dying mother. Unconscious identifications with one's mother—fantasies of oneness—are universal, and at this terminal juncture often arouse overwhelming anxiety. The fear of suffering a similar death leads many women to remain distant and disengaged. On the other hand, this unconscious identification can be a pathway for intensifying the compassionate bond with the suffering mother. This is evident in the following passage, as Simone de Beauvoir describes how she compulsively mimicked her mother's mouth movements during her pain-wracked final days: ". . . my own mouth was not obeying me any more: I had put Mama's mouth on my face and in spite of myself, I copied its movements. Her whole person, her whole being, was concentrated there, and compassion wrung my heart" (1965, p. 31). Similarly, a middle-aged analysand of mine whose mother had recently died observed herself unconsciously imitating the agonized grimaces characteristic of her dying mother as a means of expressing her own moods of distress and unhappiness.

In the two cases under consideration, however, these identifications did not appear to be connected primarily to the current realities of their mothers' suffering as an omen of their own ultimate fates. The core identifications that were stimulated were with the mother of infancy who ministered to their bodily needs. This enabled these adult children to symbolically care for their mother's body as they themselves had once been cared for. In this nurturing role the daughter became centrally important to the ailing mother and commanded a sustained focus of attention that had not been reliably present for most of their lives. Their mothers, who had been self-preoccupied and relatively oblivious of their children except as extensions of themselves, could no longer afford to ignore them.

The ability to involve oneself in a mother's physical care is determined by factors that extend beyond the fate of unconscious identifications. One of the most emotionally laden experiences during this time relates to the intimate involvement the daughter may have with her mother's body in visual, and tactile, contact with her nakedness. A variety of anxieties may be evoked, not only by the painful exposure to a body ravaged by old age and disease, but by the inevitable awakening of repressed childhood erotic feelings. Loving feelings in their relational and erotic manifestations have their origins in early bodily interactions between mother and child whose impact continues to reverberate throughout life. The evocative intensity of such early experience is commemorated in Simone de Beauvoir's (1958) tender and sensual memory: "My mother, more distant and more capricious, inspired the tenderest feelings in me; I would sit upon her knees, enclosed by the perfumed softness of her arms and cover with kisses her fresh youthful skin. Sometimes, beautiful as a picture, she would appear at night beside my bed in her dress of green tulle decorated with a single mauve flower, or the scintillating dress of black velvet covered with jet" (p. 6).

During the time of a mother's illness these feelings are reawakened. If they are too intense and cannot be sublimated through acts of devotion, defenses of disengagement and avoidance are not uncommon. I am reminded in this regard of a patient who would cringe at the touch of her mother's hand. Others, like de Beauvoir (1965), attempt to dissociate the body from the actual mother. The following recollection captures her struggle: "I was not worried by her nakedness anymore: it was no longer my mother, but a poor tormented body. Yet, I was frightened by the horrible mystery that I sensed without in any way visualizing anything, under the dressings, and I was afraid of hurting her" (p. 53). Surprisingly, for Naomi and Anna Maria, their anxieties about actual physical contact were minimal. In fact, they welcomed the chance to be helpful.

A reading of Freud's (1915) paper, "Our Attitude towards Death," suggests that reaction formations against death wishes is another important dimension in our understanding of the loving devotion that these daughters extended to their mothers. Freud said, "In our unconscious impulses we daily and hourly get rid of anyone who stands in our way, of anyone who has offended or injured us" (p. 297). For the patients discussed, the defense of reaction formation, with its accompanying intensification of available libidinal wishes, became possible during this period *for the first time*, allowing for the suppression of previously manifest murderous impulses. In other cases the reverse proves true. For instance, a patient who was intensely devoted to her mother throughout her life immediately took her mother to live with her when she learned of her illness. She remained her constant nurse and companion until her mother finally had to be hospitalized. This woman encouraged heroic measures to prolong her mother's life, but eventually was forced to make the tormenting decision to remove her mother from life support. Unexpectedly, when her mother died, this self-sacrificing, almost saintly daughter felt "elated, jubilant, and triumphant" rather than grief stricken. This is reminiscent of a manic statement of a 12-year-old boy who wrote concerning his feelings upon his mother's death: "If I felt the death of my mother at all, it was as the lightening of a burden and as a stimulating excitement" (Storr 1988, p. 139). Intensities of aggression, mobilized by the prolonged burden of care and worry, proved too powerful to be repressed.

The issue of repressed sadism inherent in the defense of reaction formation requires further consideration in regard to Naomi and Anna Maria's capacity to sustain loving feelings for their terminally ill mothers. Rage and unconscious wishes to retaliate against the destructive maternal imago find gratification in the ravages of the mother's suffering body as well as vicariously through the frequently observed insensitive or negligent care administered by doctors and nurses. This freed the daughters to be *exclusively* loving caregivers. In conjunction with experiencing themselves as loving daughters identified with loving mothers, I observed a concomitant decrease in the harshness of their superegos. This was manifested not only by a decrease in self-criticism, but by a lessening of generalized anxiety. They seemed to experience a greater sense of safety in the world, despite the obvious difficulties of their present circumstances. This recalls Melanie Klein's (1957) insight into the dynamic connection between a positive maternal introject and one's sense of personal security: "We find in the analysis of our patients that the breast in its good aspect is the prototype of maternal goodness, inexhaustible patience and generosity, as well as creativeness. It is these phantasies and instinctual needs that so enrich the primal object that it remains the foundation for hope, trust and a belief in goodness" (p. 180).

The amelioration of the severity of the superego, with the resultant decrease of guilt and internal persecutory attacks, allowed room for Naomi to consolidate a new vision of herself as a giving, loving daughter. The dynamics underlying this significant change were overdetermined. In addition to the meanings already addressed, her lifelong guilt over her greedy and envious wishes toward her mother were key factors. Her envy of her mother was intense and deeply moved. Her mother's ample, full-bosomed, glamorously adorned body overshadowed her own, both before and after puberty. Her mother's beauty was widely admired, and it caused her particular anguish that her father seemed oblivious to her own appearance. She had coped with these oedipally based feelings of mortification by defensively devaluing the mother's musical talent and creativity. In this final victory of the mother's decline, she began to rediscover a suppressed vision of her mother as both talented and beautiful. This shift was accompanied by a reawakening of early childhood idealizations of her mother's physical being. Several days before her death, as her mother lay emaciated in a hospital bed, Naomi was deeply moved by a vision of her mother's beauty, which she poignantly shared with her.

While Naomi's aggression was contained within a predominantly neurotic personality structure, Anna Maria's aggression had a more diffuse and unbounded aspect. Unconscious superego attacks had a profoundly fragmenting and disorganizing effect upon her, resulting in episodes of crippling depression. These depressions often threatened her functioning and required, at times, therapeutic parameters to manage the severity of her symptoms. During the period of her mother's illness, much of her rage was displaced from her self and her mother onto other caregivers and medical personnel. This permitted Anna Maria to experience manageable levels of rage toward her mother that could be neutralized by compassion and empathy for her suffering. Although her mother continued to be controlling for as long as she had the energy to speak, Anna Maria's sense of autonomy was no longer at risk. In fact, after her mother died, she was able to tolerate painful feelings of loss and anger at her mother's suffering without becoming overwhelmed by depression. She did, however, experience some residual feelings of guilt at not having talked to her mother about her impending death. Her mother never acknowledged the criticalness of her condition, and other family members were opposed to broaching the topic. Anna Maria's guilt related to her feeling that, in the end, her mother was left to die alone. For Naomi, the situation was different, as her mother became increasingly willing to talk about her impending death. This enabled Naomi and her mother to share feelings and say goodbye. Her self-reproaches related to rivalry with other family members and her wish—now fully acknowledged—to be her mother's chosen beloved. It is rare for a daughter not to feel some remorse at her mother's death. In the words of Simone de Beauvoir, "But since you never do all you might for anyone—not even within the arguable limits that you have set yourself—you have plenty of room for self-reproach" (1965, p. 94).

Naomi and Anna Maria were able to cope with the deaths of their mothers as a result of having worked through significant dimensions of their conflictual relationships. Mourning was characterized by intensely felt grief without signs of pathological guilt or depression. During their mothers' terminal phase of life, maternal attachment, previously hidden by an angry, distant stance, flowered. By the time of their mothers' deaths they were able to integrate the experience of themselves as a loving daughter burying a loving mother.

CONCLUSION

This chapter emphasizes the significance of a mother's terminal phase of life for her adult daughter. The case material presented demonstrates the reparative and psychodynamic opportunities in this last chance to resolve attachment and separation issues by ministering to one's dying mother. The crucial impact and evocative power of the daughter's close *physical* involvement with her mother's body, in either actual physical caregiving or in intimate conversations, is strongly suggested. This form of intimacy was shown to rekindle a complex array of early childhood feelings that offered the possibility of a reparative reunion with the caregiving mother of infancy and early childhood. Early experiences of emotional and physical closeness that have been disavowed and defended against in the service of separation could be reawakened and tolerated. The patients presented were able to experience love as well as physical and emotional closeness in the process of solidifying repressed identifications with their mothers as nurturing persons. The daughters no longer saw themselves exclusively as "takers" but as "caretakers," giving back some of the nurturant attention that they had received in childhood. This intensification and enrichment of the mother–daughter bond in the mother's terminal phase represents a natural completion of the life cycle, stabilizing and neutralizing the inherent tensions of the lifelong separation process. My clinical material confirms that a key component in the psychodynamic tensions that regulate this process is the degree of aggression mobilized in the service of separation-individuation (Jacobson 1964). Guilty feelings over real and imagined injuries to the mother and her body are assuaged as the daughter mothers her own mother.

The question that inevitably arises with regard to these cases in whether the remarkable changes observed in both patients should be viewed primarily as a result of psychoanalytic therapy or whether this life-cycle phase has inherent healing and reparative potential. Without making detailed observations outside a clinical context it is impossible to answer with certainty. My strong impression, however, is that in this instance both factors operated synergistically. The events and experiences summarized in the case material presented had been the subject of a good deal of analytic exploration and interpretive discussion. Certainly the analytic setting afforded the possibility of working through the reactions evoked by their mothers' terminal illnesses. On the other hand, very little of the most intense emotional work was *centered* on the transference at that time. The analyst remained a relatively neutral presence in regard to the reawakened love and idealizing impulses that had emerged. I would propose that the analytic process propelled and gave sustained momentum to a process that would have taken a similar course of its own accord in the absence of an ongoing analytic relationship.

I am not addressing the more complex question of whether, and in what ways, the analytic work that had been accomplished prior to the period of the mothers' terminal illnesses made it possible for these *particular* patients to use the experience as they did to further their emotional development. I strongly believe that this was the case, particularly for Anna Maria. Obviously, similar issues are involved in assessing the therapeutic impact of psychoanalysis or psychoanalytic psychotherapy in the life of every patient.

It is in the nature of things that the aging and decline of elderly mothers offers a chance for a child to become increasingly involved in all aspects of their mother's lives, revitalizing intimacies and identifications that may have grown less central. That the physicality and infirmity of aging repositions the body as the focal point of mother–daughter interactions serves to evoke very specific and powerful connections with the earliest and most intimate period of mother–daughter bonding. Intensified conflicts around dependency are to be expected in both the mother and the daughter in the face of this regressive pull. Although the roles are reversed, a daughter may fear becoming reenmeshed with the mother of infancy and early childhood. Fears of fusion and threats to autonomous functioning are unconsciously aroused at the prospect of an intimate physical relationship. As a result, the daughter may defensively embrace prevailing social norms that sanction arranging for strangers to care for one's mother. The mother herself may resist the dependency on her daughter as well, for this threatens to undermine a long-standing identity as a maternal being. Reliance on professional health care workers, which is an extension of engaging doctors and nurses, does not pose the same psychic risk, or opportunity, for either party.

The avoidance of intimacy between mother and daughter in the terminal phase of the mother's life is widely reinforced by current socioeconomic conditions, especially in middle and upper classes, where cultural values and employment patterns discourage intergenerational intimacy and interdependence. Emotional independence as well as executive self-sufficiency are highly prized values and frequently symbolized by a willingness to live at great distance from parents. This physical and emotional distance is widely extolled as a pivotal achievement of mature adulthood in our culture. In the complexity of modern life a daughter typically finds much encouragement for resorting to pragmatic solutions and arrangements that, if my thesis is correct, ultimately deprives her of an important developmental opportunity. Without the support of the social group and in the absence of strong supportive family ties, the motivation for mastering the anxieties of renewed bodily intimacy will most likely be buried by "real" considerations of time and expedience. Certainly, there are many factors that might preclude a patient's assuming extensive responsibility for a mother's care. However, our awareness as analysts of their possible defensive functions, in conjunction with a greater appreciation of the potential developmental benefits of such commitments, will add a significant dimension to our understanding and handling of these dilemmas. We may be helpful in transforming the terminal period of a mother's life from simply a time of emotional pain and loss for her daughter into the final and profoundly enriching phase of a lifelong struggle for healthy individuation.

REFERENCES

Beauvoir, S. de (1958). *Memoirs of a Dutiful Daughter*. New York: Harper & Row.

———— (1965). *A Very Easy Death*. New York: Pantheon.

Bergmann, M. S. (1987). *The Anatomy of Loving*. New York: Columbia University Press.

Bowlby, J. (1969). *Attachment and Loss*. Vol. 1. New York: Basic Books.

Freud, S. (1915). Thoughts for the times on war and death, Pt. II: Our attitude towards death. *Standard Edition* 4:289–300.

———— (1917). Mourning and melancholia. *Standard Edition* 14:237–258.

Jacobson, E. (1964). *The Self and the Object World*. New York: International Universities Press.

Klein, M. (1957). Envy and gratitude. In *Envy and Gratitude*, pp. 176–235. London: Hogarth, 1975.

Mahler, M., Pine, F., and Bergman, A. (1975). *The Psychological Birth of the Human Infant*. New York: Basic Books.

Oldham, J. (1989). The third individuation: middle-aged children and their parents. In *New Psychoanalytic Perspectives, The Middle Years*, ed. J. M. Oldham and R. S. Liebert, pp. 89–104. New Haven, CT: Yale University Press.

Storr, A. (1988). *Solitude: A Return to the Self*. New York: Free Press.

Winnicott, D. W. (1958). The capacity to be alone. In *The Maturational Processes and the Facilitating Environment*, pp. 29–36. New York: International Universities Press, 1965.

Index

ABOUT THE EDITOR

Gerd H. Fenchel, Ph.D., is a psychologist and psychoanalyst. He received his clinical training at the City University of New York and at the Graduate School of Arts and Sciences, New York University. He became enthused about the concept of establishing a psychoanalytic clinic in the Greenwich Village area of New York City, and since 1960 has been a founder and later Dean/Director of the Washington Square Institute for Psychotherapy and Mental Health. At present, the Institute affiliates 150 professional clinicians and maintains a psychoanalytic training component, specializing in understanding characterological conditions.

Dr. Fenchel has taught and supervised at diverse institutes, and is widely published in clinical journals. Editor of a quarterly newsletter *Notes and Comments* and a member of the editorial board of the Institute journal *Issues in Psychoanalytic Psychology*, he is co-author of the Aronson book *The Developing Ego and the Emerging Self* and editor of the book *Psychoanalysis at 100*. Dr. Fenchel maintains a private practice in New York City and Pennsylvania.